THE RECONQUEST OF THE NEW WORLD

A mis padres, Carmina y Luís,
y a mis hermanas, Azucena y Yolanda

The Reconquest of the New World

Multinational enterprises and Spain's direct investment in Latin America

PABLO TORAL
Florida International University

Routledge
Taylor & Francis Group

LONDON AND NEW YORK

First published 2001 by Ashgate Publishing

Reissued 2018 by Routledge
2 Park Square, Milton Park, Abingdon, Oxon OX14 4RN
711 Third Avenue, New York, NY 10017, USA

Routledge is an imprint of the Taylor & Francis Group, an informa business

Copyright © Pablo Toral 2001

Notice:
Product or corporate names may be trademarks or registered trademarks, and are used only for identification and explanation without intent to infringe.

Publisher's Note
The publisher has gone to great lengths to ensure the quality of this reprint but points out that some imperfections in the original copies may be apparent.

Disclaimer
The publisher has made every effort to trace copyright holders and welcomes correspondence from those they have been unable to contact.

A Library of Congress record exists under LC control number: 2001088795

ISBN 13: 978-1-138-72522-5 (hbk)
ISBN 13: 978-1-138-72519-5 (pbk)
ISBN 13: 978-1-315-19200-0 (ebk)

Contents

List of Tables

List of Figures

Acknowledgements

This book would not have been possible without the help of Mira Wilkins, Eduardo Gamarra and Bruce Kelley, who read every line of my manuscript and made valuable recommendations. To them, my dearest appreciation and intellectual admiration. I thank David Callejo, Thomas Castillo, John Clasca and Paul Vicary for editing my final work. I am also indebted to the following people, who read parts or all of the manuscript and guided me through my research with their suggestions, comments and help: Arghyris Argyrhou, Mayra Beers, Ziulyn Chan, Noble David Cook, Alexander Easdale, Jerome Egger, Damián Fernández, César Francis, Horacio Godoy, Saeed Hashemi, Jesse Hingson, Aart Holtslag, Manuel Moreno Fraginals, Diego Méndez, Rod Neumann, Nicholas Onuf, Roberto Pacheco, Teresita Pedraza, Nicolás Sánchez-Albornoz, Mark Szuchman, Joseph Ward, and Laura Zanotti.

I extend my gratitude to my friends and colleagues in the Departments of International Relations, Economics, and History, in the Latin American and Caribbean Center, and in the library of Florida International University in Miami, Universidad de Oviedo (Spain), Universidad Complutense de Madrid, the Spanish Ministries of Trade, Industry, and Infrastructure in Madrid, Universidad Católica and Universidad San Carlos in Lima, and Centro Bartolomé de las Casas in Cusco (Peru). All of them helped me do research and invited me to present my finished work. I am also thankful to Dolores García and José Montserrat for encouraging me all the time, to my family, for their permanent support, and to René Fernández, who will not be able to read the book he encouraged me to write. This book is also dedicated to him.

List of Abbreviations

AA	American Airlines
ACP	Africa-Caribbean-Pacific
AEC	Agreements of Economic Cooperation
Aerolíneas Argentinas	Argentinean Airlines
AIRTEL	Spanish company providing cellular telephony
ARGENTARIA	Spanish bank, partly owned by the state until 1998
AT&T	American Telegraph and Telephone
AVANTEL	Mexican telephone company owned partly by Banamex and MCI
BA	British Airways
BANAMEX	National Bank of Mexico
BANESTO	Banco Español de Crédito
BARPPIs	Bilateral agreements for reciprocal promotion and protection of investments
BBV	Banco Bilbao Vizcaya
BCH	Banco Central Hispanoamericano
BEX	Banco Exterior de España (Spanish bank)
BP	British Petroleum
BS	Banco de Santander
BSCH	Banco Santander Central Hispano
BT	British Telecom
CACM	Central American Common Market
CANTV	Compañía Nacional de Teléfonos de Venezuela
CAP	Compañía de Acero del Pacífico (Chilean steel company)
CARICOM	Caribbean Free Trade Area
CEPSA	Spanish oil producer and distributer
CERJ	Companhia de Electricidade do Rio do Janeiro (Brazilian electricity company)

CESCE	Compañía Española de Seguro de Crédito a la Exportación (Spanish Insurance Company of Credit for Export)
CHADE	Compañía Hispanoamericana de Electricidad
CODELCO	Colombian telephone company
CODENSA	Companñía Comercializadora y Distribuidora de Energía S.A. (Colombian electricity company)
COELBA	Companhia de Electricidade do Estado da Bahia (Brazilian electricity company)
COELCE	Companhia Energética do Ceará (Brazilian electricity company)
COFIDES	Compañía Española de Financiación del Desarrollo (Spanish Company of Finance for Development)
COFIVACASA	Investment company (Iberia's partner in Aerolíneas Argentinas)
CONPES	Consejo Nacional de Políticas Económicas y Sociales (Colombian National Council on Economic and Social Policies)
CONTACTEL	Portuguese telecommunication operator
COSERN	Companhia Energética de Rio Grande do Norte (Brazilian electricity company)
CPT	Compañía Peruana de Teléfonos
CRT	Companhia Riograndense de Telecomunicações
CTC	Compañía Telefónica de Chile (Chilean Telephone Company)
DBT	Deutsche Bundespost Telekom
DGEITE	Dirección General de Economía Internacional y Transacciones Exteriores de España (General Directorate for International Economy and External Transactions)
DNP	Departamento Nacional de Planeación (Colombian National Planning Department)
DyC	Dragados y Construcciones (Spanish firm specialized in construction and public works)
ECIP	European Community Investment Partners

ECLAC	UN Economic Commission for Latin America and the Caribbean
ECOPETROL	Empresa Colombiana de Petróleos (Colombian Petroleum Company)
ECU	European Currency Unit
EDELNOR	Empresa de Distribución Eléctrica de Lima Norte S.A. (Peruvian electricity company)
EDF	European Development Fund
EEP	Empresa Eléctrica de Piura (Peruvian electricity company)
EG3	Argentinean gasoline distributor and asphalt producer
EIB	European Investment Bank
EMBRATEL	Empresa Brasileira de Telefone (Brazilian telephone company)
EMU	European Monetary Union
ENDESA	Empresa Nacional de Electricidad Sociedad Anónima (Spanish electricity company)
ENERSIS	Endesa's partner in Chile
ENI	Italian hydrocarbon company
ENTEL	Empresa Nacional de Teléfonos (Peruvian telephone company)
EU	European Union
FCC	Fomento de Construcciones y Contratas (firm in the construction and public works sector)
FDI	Foreign direct investment
FNA	Association of the world's leading international telephone companies
FT	France Télécom
Gas Natural	Spanish producer and distributor of natural gas.
GATT	General Agreement on Trade and Tariffs
GDP	Gross domestic product
GTE	U.S. telecommunications company
HC	Hidroeléctrica del Cantábrico (Spanish hydroelectric company)
Iberdrola	Spanish regional electricity company
Iberia	Spain's flag airline carrier

ICE	Información Comercial Española (Journal of Spanish Trade Information)
ICEX	Instituto de Comercio Exterior (Spanish Institute of External Trade)
ICO	Instituto de Crédito Oficial (Spanish Institute of Official Credit)
ICSID	International Center for Settlement of Investment Disputes
IDB	Inter-American Development Bank
IFC	International Finance Corporation (World Bank Group)
IIC	Interamerican Investment Corporation
IMF	International Monetary Fund
INI	Instituto Nacional de Hidrocarburos (Spanish National Institute of Hydrocarbons)
INTEL	Internacional de Telecomunicaciones (Salvadoran telecommunications company providing cellular telephony)
IRELA	Instituto de Relaciones Europeo-Latinoamericanas (Institute of European-Latin American Relations)
IRHE	Instituto de Recursos Hidráulicos y de Electrificación (Panamanian Institute of Hydraulic Resources and Electrification)
ISI	Import substitution industrialization
ITT	International Telephone and Telegraph Corp.
KDD	Kokusai Denshin Denwa (Japanese company that provides international telecommunications services)
KLM	Koninklijke Luchtvaart Maatschappij (Royal Dutch Airlines)
KPN	Dutch telecommunication operator
La Caixa	Largest savings institution in Catalonia (Spain)
LADECO	Chilean Airline
LAFTA	Latin American Free Trade Area
LAPSA	Líneas Aéreas Paraguayas SA (Paraguayan Airlines)
LDCs	Less developed countries

MERCOSUR	Mercado Común del Sur (Common Market of the South)
MIBOR	Mumbai Inter-bank Offer Rate
MIFLA	Multilateral Investment Fund for Latin America
MIGA	Multilateral Investment Guarantee Agency
MNEs	Multinational enterprises
NAFTA	North American Free Trade Agreement
NGOs	Non-governmental organizations
NTT	Nippon Telephone and Telegraph
OECD	Organization of Economic Co-Operation and Development
PND II	Brazil's Second National Development Plan.
PT	Portugal Telecom
PTT	Post, Telephone & Telegraph
RBS	Brazilian television channel
REPSOL	Largest oil producer and distributor in Spain
RETEVISIÓN	Spanish telephone company
RTT	Results Through Technology, Inc. U.S. consulting firm that specializes in computer technology
SAS	Scandinavian Airline System
SEPI	Sociedad Española de Promociones Industriales
Sintelar	Telefonica's subsidiary in Argentina that specializes in engineering services, installation of telephone lines and in telecommunications equipment
Southern Bell Corporation	Formerly, Bell South
Statoil	Norwegian oil producer
SUMOC	Superintendência da Moneda e do Crédito (Brazilian monetary authority)
TAM	Táxi Aéreo Marília (Brazilian Airline)
Tele Leste Celular	Brazilian cellular telephone company operating in Bahia and Segirpe
Tele Sudeste Celular	Brazilian cellular telephone company operating in Rio do Janeiro and Espíritu Santo
TELEBRAS	Brazil's national telephone company
TELESP	Telefone São Paulo

TELESP Celular	Brazilian cellular telephone company operating in São Paulo
TELIA	Swedish telephone company
TELMEX	Teléfonos de México
TISA	Telefónica Internacional Sociedad Anónima (subsidiary of Telefónica de España encompassing all of its subsidiaries outside of Spain)
TLD	Puerto Rican telephone company
TPAM	Telefónica Panamericana MCI (proposed name for Telefónica's subsidiary encompassing all of its Latin American subsidiaries)
UN	United Nations
UNCITRAL	United Nations Commission of International Trade Law
UNIDO	United Nations Industrial Development Organization
Unión Fenosa	Spanish electricity company
Unisource	international telecommunications group led by AT&T
VIASA	Venezuelan air carrier
WB	World Bank
W.W.I	World War I
W.W.II	World War II
YPF	Yacimientos Petrolíferos Fiscales (Argentinean oil company)

1 Introduction

Spanish firms had a notable presence in the process of liberalization experienced by many Latin American countries since the late 1980s. By participating in the privatization of many state-owned enterprises, by buying controlling interest in local private companies, by creating joint-ventures, or through greenfield investments, Spanish firms moved quickly to position themselves in an advantageous situation in the newly liberalized and fast-growing markets of Latin America.

For the period 1990-1994 Spain was the second largest investor in Latin America and the Caribbean, after the United States. Flows of Spanish direct investment amounted to $2.654 billion.[1] Spanish companies became very notable, both in the eyes of locals and in those of investors from other western countries. Before the 1990s Spanish companies had never invested abroad significant sums of money and, overall, Spanish investment had never represented an important share of foreign direct investment (FDI) for Latin American countries. By investing large amounts in Latin America and the Caribbean, Spanish firms became major players in the local economies.

The importance of Spanish FDI in this region, however, transcends its size. Spanish multinational enterprises (MNEs) bought domestic companies in key sectors, such as telecommunications, energy, and banking. These sectors constitute the economic infrastructure of a country. Companies in these industries provide goods and services that are needed by local companies in other sectors. Their performance thus determines, to a large extent, the overall productivity of the local economy. Efficient telecommunications, sufficient energy, and availability of credit are necessary for firms to operate. Productivity and efficiency increases in these areas translates automatically to other activities in the form of better and cheaper inputs or infrastructure.

To many analysts, Spanish firms assumed a very high degree of risk by investing in Latin America in the late 1980s and early 1990s, when the economic panorama was unclear. The debt crisis of the 1980s triggered a process of divestment during which many North American and European companies decided to withdraw from the Latin American markets. Lack of macroeconomic stability, little economic growth, and the lack of a sizeable domestic demand, generated very low returns for foreign investors. The debt crisis affected the subsidiaries of many foreign MNEs and investors saw their revenue decrease.

Restrictions on FDI limited the freedom of foreign investors to operate within a country, making Latin America less appealing overall. Besides, western investors perceived that the crisis was structural, rather than temporary, and believed that unless profound structural reforms took place, economic conditions would not improve in the long term. Protectionism and restrictions on FDI had increased in Latin America after World War II. Import-substitution strategies put a lot of emphasis on the role of the state and limited FDI to those areas in which domestic capital was not sufficient. The governments of Latin America created state companies, which lost efficiency overtime and accumulated large deficits.

Within this framework, the promises of liberalization that followed the debt crisis in the late 1980s did not have much credibility. Some foreign investors feared that liberalization would be either too limited or reversed by future governments, as had been the case previously in many occasions. Investment in Latin America in the late 1980s was thus deemed too risky. Most countries did not have legal frameworks that would offer foreign investors guarantees to operate freely in the market, without government intervention. Since most Latin American governments had had a tradition of heavy borrowing, there was no certainty about the extent to which they were willing to reduce their fiscal deficits.

This book examines the factors that triggered the large amounts of Spanish direct investment in Latin America in the 1990s. Some Spanish companies took the lead and began investing considerable amounts of money in Latin America. What seemed to be a risky business in 1990, proved to be very profitable in most cases. This chapter deals with a series of methodological and statistical clarifications. Chapter two provides a historical approach to Spanish direct investment from colonial times. It reveals the lack of sizeable Spanish direct investment in Latin America prior to the 1990s (even during the colonial period), making the emergence of Spanish MNEs after 1990 a new economic and social phenomenon that has not yet been studied.

Chapter three reviews the most important theories of foreign direct investment. This chapter serves two purposes. On the one hand, it provides theoretical support to the analysis and helps determine to what extent Spanish investment in Latin America was predictable. On the other, the application of the theories to this empirical case tests which one of them is more useful in predicting a multinational firm's behavior.

Chapter four reveals the developments in the 1990s within Latin American countries that made their economies appealing to foreign investors, especially to Spanish investors. The first independent variable is "economic liberalization in Latin America". Economic liberalization is measured in terms of the degree of openness of the economy to trade and foreign competition, regional integration, and the size and role of the state (degree of involvement in the economy). These factors are measured descriptively. Chapter four also examines the role that FDI played in the development strategies of these nations in the post-World War II period. It reviews changes in FDI legislation in the late 1980s and 1990s in some of the largest countries. It also assesses the efforts of governments to achieve macroeconomic stability: reduction of fiscal deficits, more restrictive monetary policies, and inflation management. Overall, these policies are observed in a broader framework, namely, structural economic reform.

At this point, it is necessary to tell the other part of the story: what developments took place within the Spanish economy in the 1990s that encouraged Spanish firms to invest abroad. The objective of Chapter five is to assess the degree of maturity reached by the Spanish economy and Spanish firms, in terms of economic and technological development. This is the second independent variable. A conjunction of factors are analyzed: (1) the recent economic history of Spain, (2) its inclusion in the European Union, and (3) its transition from a protected economy to an open one. From this analysis emerges a third independent variable, the "degree of openness and competition within the Spanish economy," as determined by Spanish regulation. This analysis shows the active role of the Spanish government in fostering Spanish direct investments abroad.

The conjunction of the appropriate factors on the Latin American as well as on the Spanish side took place in the late 1980s and early 1990s. Chapters four and five thus explain why Spanish firms decided to invest large amounts of money in Latin America in the 1990s. Chapter six analyzes Spanish investment in Latin America in detail. Some sectors stand out for their significance. Special scrutiny of the participation of Spanish firms in the privatization process is provided, as well as a sectoral analysis of the banking, telecommunications, air transportation and energy sectors. This chapter also analyzes the alliances created by Spanish multinationals from various areas of economic activity to cooperate in their Latin American ventures. The material from Chapter four illuminates this discussion, and helps compare Spanish FDI in Latin America with FDI in Latin America from other countries. Finally, Chapter seven provides some conclusions from the previous analysis and pinpoints the competitive advantage of Spanish firms *vis-à-vis* Latin American and Western multinational corporations.

Prior to this discussion, a few conceptual clarifications have to be made, as well as some explanations about the nature and origin of the figures used in this book. All Spanish firms (those with headquarters in Spain) making investments in Latin America are labeled as "multinational enterprises" (MNEs). Sometimes, the literature is confined to manufacturing MNEs. This book does not follow that pattern. In the literature referring to MNEs there are also terms such as "transnational enterprise," "multinational corporation," "international business," and "global firm". These nouns and adjectives are perfectly interchangeable. However, the book uses the term "multinational enterprise" because it is the one that has come to be most widely used among scholars.

The book deals with Spanish "direct investment" only, that is to say, "portfolio investment" is excluded from the figures and from the analysis. Interest rates and high returns to equity are the driving force behind portfolio investment. Investors seek to maximize profits by investing where returns are highest. "Direct investment" is prompted by other factors, such as the ability of a firm to exploit its comparative advantage in foreign markets, its decision to internalize transaction costs across borders, the will to eliminate competition in a foreign market, different growth expectations within an industry between the investor country and the recipient country, and overall worldwide strategy of the firm making the investment.

The adjective "multinational" refers to the expansion of companies abroad through direct investment. Direct investment is the investment made by a firm (the parent), which is directly connected with the business operations of its subsidiary. The U.S. Department of Commerce first, and the International Monetary Fund (IMF) after, consider direct investment those investments made by a company to acquire over 10 percent of a firm's equity. This share grants an investor a certain degree of "control" over the firm's operations, or at least implies potential for control. The IMF recommends that governments use the 10 percent criterion, because that share is large enough to involve a long-term business relationship with a significant degree of control or influence of the investor over the recipient.

Spanish authorities, however, did not begin using the 10 percent criterion until 1992 (they had previously used a 20 percent cut off). Important methodological modifications were introduced that year and were applied to the statistics referring to 1993 for the first time. On 1 February 1992, the Spanish government eliminated all restrictions on capital movements. This was the culmination of a process of liberalization initiated in 1977 and accelerated after 1986, when Spain joined the European Union. In 1992, the minimum percent of capital owned by an investor in order to qualify an investment as "direct" was established at 10 percent (applied in the statistics of the year 1993 for the first time).

Beginning in 1993, all subsequent flows of capital following the original direct investment, between the Spanish investor and its firm abroad, are considered "direct investment". After 1993, these include intra-firm loans and reinvested earnings. This change implies that figures on investment prior to the year 1993 are lower than they might have been if the 10 percent criteria had been applied.

Spanish investment abroad was regulated in the 1990s by Royal Decree 672 of 2 July 1992. Most of the figures used in this book are taken from the *Dirección General de Economía Internacional y Transacciones Exteriores* (General Directorate for International Economy and External Transactions - DGEITE). DGEITE compiled these data from the applications for authorization or verification of investment abroad made by Spanish firms at the Spanish Registry of Investments. These figures measure annual flows of investment, not stock. "Flow" refers to the amount of investment within a period of time (in this case one year), as opposed to "stock" (also called "position"), which measures the value of investment at a particular point in time. The latest census of the "stock" value of Spanish investment abroad was made in 1991. Since investment flows were significantly high thereafter, the 1991 figures are not very relevant because the "stock" value of Spanish firms abroad increased considerably.

Even though Spanish firms willing to invest abroad were required to present an application for authorization or verification of investment at the Registry of Investments, this procedure served statistical purposes only. After liberalization in 1992, only investments over 250 million pesetas (around $2 million) were subject to this requirement, as well as investments in countries or territories considered fiscal havens (as established by Royal Decree 1080 of 5 July 1991) and investments in societies constituted for holding securities. With these new requirements, which provide for investment activities in different categories, the figures of Spanish investment abroad for the years beginning in 1993 are not uniform with prior years.

Three more observations have to be made about the figures compiled by the DGEITE. Its data refer to investment "projects", which might not have materialized. That is to say, the same investment operation might show up several times in the statistics, as many as the company requested authorization for investment (i.e., a company might request authorization for an investment in 1992 that does not take place, but the amount of the request will be reflected in the statistics for that year). Secondly, there is an inconsistency between the definitions of the Spanish law and that of the DGEITE. Whereas the DGEITE only deemed as direct investment those loans with a maturity period longer than five years, Spanish law, following recommendations by the IMF, considered all types of loans direct investment once the FDI criterion was met. Finally, DGEITE statistics do not reflect divestment. In other words, they show direct investments made but cannot be used to understand the level of FDI since they do not cover bankruptcies, sales, or other forms of assets disposal.[2]

Another reason for caution when studying the Spanish statistics is that in 1992 the government changed the classification of economic activities. Prior to that year there were ten different categories, divided as follows:[3]

0. Agriculture, cattle raising, hunting, forestry and fishing.
1. Energy and water.
2. Extraction and transformation of non-energy minerals and products derived from the chemical industry.
3. Industries for transformation of metals, precision mechanics.
4. Other manufacturing industries.
5. Construction.
6. Commerce, restaurants and hotels.
7. Transport and communications.
8. Financial institutions, insurance, services provided to enterprises and rents.
9. Other services.

The classification adopted in 1993 established fourteen categories:[4]

1. Agriculture, cattle raising, hunting, forestry and fishing.
2. Production / distribution of electric energy, gas and water.
3. Extractive industries, oil refining and fuel treatment.
4. Food / beverages and tobacco.
5. Textile industry and confection.
6. Paper industry, edition and graphic arts.
7. Chemical industry.
8. Other manufactures.
9. Construction.
10. Commerce.
11. Hotels.
12. Transport and communications.
13. Financial intermediaries, banking and insurance.
14. Holding and others.

The firm based in Spain making the investment is called "parent", as opposed to the Latin American firm receiving the investment, known as "subsidiary", "affiliate," or "branch". Spain is thus the "home" country for Spanish MNEs, the one in which the investment originates, and the Latin American or Caribbean country where the subsidiary is based is called the "host" country. Thus, a "Spanish MNE" is an enterprise whose headquarters is in Spain and makes direct investments in other countries.

In this case study, host countries are Latin American and Caribbean countries. The definition of Latin America and the Caribbean used in this book is the one adopted by the IMF: all the countries situated to the south of the United States. In other words, all the countries in the Western Hemisphere with the exception of Canada and the United States. A few comments have to be made about Puerto Rico. For cultural and historical reasons, Spanish authorities include Puerto Rico in their statistics as an independent political entity, separate from the United States, under the category of "non-European OECD countries".

Puerto Rico alone was one of the major recipients of Spanish FDI. Some years the flows of FDI from Spain to Puerto Rico were larger than those to the continental United States as a whole. In fact, in the late 1970s and in the 1980s Puerto Rico received more Spanish FDI than most Latin American and Caribbean countries, with rates similar to those of Mexico, Argentina, and Chile. The book, however, excludes Puerto Rico from the analysis because it is politically part of the United States and because the motivations driving Spanish investment to that island differ significantly from the ones driving investment to Latin America and the Caribbean as a whole. Notwithstanding this, the book provides figures referring to Puerto Rico when Spanish firms include their subsidiaries in this island as part of their Latin American organization.

Finally, a distinction has to be made between a "state-owned" and a "private" enterprise that is investing abroad. The former is a company in which the state is the only owner. A private enterprise is that in which stockholders are private parties. There are many cases of "mixed" enterprises (in both Spain and the host countries), those in which the government owns only part of the equity, with the remaining shares being distributed among private parties. That is the case, for instance, with respect to all enterprises with foreign participation in Cuba.

Notes

[1]   IRELA, *European Union-Latin American Economic Relations. Statistical Profile*, 15 November 1996, Madrid, p. 10.

2   Maitena Duce Hernando, "La Estimación de las Inversiones Directas en la Balanza de Pagos", *ICE*, No. 752, April 1996, p. 67.

3   *ICE*, "Las Inversiones Españolas Directas e Inmobiliarias en el Exterior Durante 1989", No. 1002, March 1989, pp.12-15.

4   Ana de la Cueva, "Las Inversiones Españolas en el Exterior Durante 1993", *ICE*, No. 2415, 6-12 June 1994, p. 1408.

2 Spanish Direct Investment in Latin America and the Caribbean: A Historical Approach

Introduction

The abdication of Cuba and Puerto Rico in 1898 triggered one of the richest political debates ever in Spain. Spanish intellectuals interpreted Spain's loss of its last American colonies as the culmination of three centuries of decline. A very fertile generation of Spanish writers emerged called *Generación del 98* (Generation of 98). The writers of *Generación del 98* made Spain the main subject of their writings and called for a redefinition of the fundamentals of Spanish life: society, culture, religion, the political system, and the economy.

What Spain's role would be in the international arena, dwarfed by the powerful colonial powers of Europe and the emerging United States of America, centered the intellectual arguments. This debate spread from the intellectual circles to all spheres of Spanish society, dominating discussion for decades. The intellectual community, and society as a whole, became polarized between those who thought Spain belonged among the modern societies of western and central Europe, and should therefore strive to increase its involvement in European affairs, and those who looked back to the colonial period with nostalgia and asserted that Spain had strong cultural ties with Latin America and should strengthen its bonds with its "American brother nations".

Nevertheless, in the early twentieth century Spain retreated from world affairs even further. Economic conditions kept worsening and deteriorated significantly after the Civil War (1936-1939). Until the 1960s, Franco's regime was isolated politically and economically and forced to pursue autarkic economic policies. Surprisingly, social ties with Latin America and Europe increased. Latin America in the first decades of the century and

9

central and Western Europe in the 1950s and 1960s received considerable waves of Spanish migrants seeking to improve their economic conditions. The Civil War also caused a flow of "forced" migrants who had to seek asylum abroad (mainly in Europe and Latin America) for political reasons.

The debate initiated by *Generación del 98* was exacerbated by these social factors, as well as by many unsuccessful attempts by Francisco Franco's regime to gain international recognition, especially from the European Community. Spain reentered the world community after Franco's death in 1975. Some historians, economists, and political scientists regarded the access of Spain to the European Union in 1986 as Spain's most important achievement in the twentieth century. It was the fulfillment of one of Spain's obsessive objectives. By 2000 Spain was an active participant in European affairs, and the Union provided a great boost for the Spanish economy.

Once the European goal was achieved, Spanish intellectuals insisted that Spain still had an important debt to history: it had to define its relation with Latin America. The European associations provided new ideas, namely, Spain could now finally act as a "bridge" between Europe and the Americas. Far from the paternalistic fashion in which Spain approached Latin America up until well into the twentieth century, Spanish-American relations became fraternal in nature. In the 1990s Spain approached Latin American countries like a brother nation that could contribute with its own experience to ease the way to democracy. Iberian-American political summits became regular and cultural exchanges increased.

The relation between Spain and Latin America in the 1990s, however, was shaped by Spain's contribution to economic liberalization. Spanish direct investment in Latin America increased significantly in absolute terms, especially after the privatization programs instituted by many Latin American governments. Spain's successful transition to democracy and its economic success were viewed by the Latin American intellectual elites (politicians, economists, political scientists and writers) as an example from which some valuable lessons could be learned.[1]

The Colonial Period

Spanish direct investment in Latin America throughout the sixteenth, seventeenth and eighteenth centuries geared toward the political administration of the American empire. The government's trade policy between the metropole and the colonies, driven by the economic philosophy of mercantilism, shaped investment. The chief economic objectives of the Spanish state (acquisition of precious metals, revenue for the Crown and trading profits)[2] directed the colonization of the vast, unexplored, and sparsely populated "Iberian-America". With the exception of Mexico, Central America and Peru, neither the Spanish Crown nor the Spanish business class realized the importance this area could have as a market for Spanish products and the immense investment opportunities it would offer for Spanish-based firms as colonization proceeded.

The Spaniards and the Portuguese clashed in South America in the sixteenth century in their expansion to the interior, the Spaniards from the west eastwards, and the Portuguese from the east, westward. Both powers had attempted to settle these matters through the Treaty of Tordesillas, signed in 1494, which separated the Portuguese and the Spanish South American territories with an imaginary line that extended southwards from the mouth of the Amazon. 'The juridical bases for this settlement rested upon papal bulls that embodied the medieval canonistic tradition of universal papal jurisdiction over the world. This gave the Pope legitimate authority to assign monopoly rights over newly discovered lands and seas to rulers who would undertake to evangelize them'.[3] Only Castile recognized the bulls and the Treaty of Tordesillas. Portugal, however, during the last decades of the sixteenth century and first half of the seventeenth century, expanded to the interior of Brazil far beyond the lines demarcated by the treaty. In 1750, Spain recognized Portugal's sovereignty over all the territories occupied by Lisbon to the west of the line demarcated in Tordesillas.

Jurisdiction over the Spanish "Indies" resided with the kingdom of Castile through Pope Alexander VI's mandate. The Spanish monarchy grouped a series of realms, acquired either by conquest or by inheritance, which owed allegiance to a single ruler (the Crown of Aragon enjoyed more autonomy). Although most of these realms were legally and politically equal, Castile enjoyed an effective political predominance thanks to its control over the Indies, which were regarded as a possession of Castile and thus governed by the laws and institutions of Castile like all other Iberian realms.[4]

The responsibilities of the Council of the Indies, created in 1524 and composed mainly of jurists, included the power to draft decisions concerning the Indies, to consult the king, and to confirm ordinances and statutes promulgated by the authorities established in the colonies.[5] The *Casa de Contratación*, established in Seville in 1503, exercised official supervision over ships and passengers, customs and the receipt and recording of precious metals dispatched to private individuals by the king, and it levied taxes for military defense.[6]

The first administrative unit and basic political entity in the Indies was the local governorship, which exercised judicial functions of first instance and certain governmental prerogatives, including the power to legislate by means of ordinances.[7] As new territories were conquered, more complex entities were designed. The *Audiencias* specialized in the dispensing of justice. They functioned as a court of appeals and sometimes as an ordinary law court of first instance, especially in litigation between natives and Spaniards, which were considered privileged "court cases".[8] The viceroyalties took upon the task of government, war, supervision of the Royal Treasury and ordinary justice. Finally, the *Cabildo* worked as an organ of municipal government. Viceroys, *Audiencias*, governors and *Cabildos* had legislative powers, even though their ordinances had to be ratified by the Crown.[9]

By the year 1700 the essential elements of the Spanish colonial economy were established: a series of mining cores in Mexico and Peru and smaller mines in New Granada (Colombia) and Chile; agricultural and ranching areas peripheral to the mining core developed for the supply of foodstuffs and raw materials; a commercial system designed to funnel silver and gold as specie or bullion to Spain to pay for goods produced by Western Europe and funneled through the Spanish ports of Seville and Cádiz for distribution to the American colonies.[10]

Mining represented the most profitable economic activity throughout the colonial period. In fact, the capital paid to the Crown covered all the administrative costs of the empire. The royal authority kept a nominal fifth (*quinto*) of silver mined and minted (evasion was high and Irving Stone calculates that only one forth of Potosi's output paid the dues between 1545 and 1802).[11]

Mercury became another important source of revenue for the state. It was needed for the process of amalgamation of silver developed by the Spaniards and the Crown established a royal monopoly for its distribution.[12] Mercury production in Latin America took place in the mine of Huancavelica in Peru, which supplied the mines of that area and sent some to Mexico via coastal Pacific shipping. Mexico's needs were not fulfilled with Peruvian mercury and extra supplies were provided from the mines of Almadén, in western Andalusia. When Peruvian mines went into decay in the seventeenth century, the state used mercury as a subsidy to increase production. It lowered its price in the 1730s, but this incentive was not enough to stimulate production and output did not increase significantly. Production in Huancavelica declined after 1780. Restrictions on the import of European mercury were higher in Peru than in Mexico, which placed severe limits on the quantity of mercury available for silver production.[13]

Overall, mining was a very profitable activity. The mine of Potosí alone (located in the viceroyalty of Peru, presently Bolivia) yielded over 1 billion ounces of silver by 1803 and in 1611 Potosí was already the largest city in the new world, with a population of 160,000 people.[14] Latin America's mineral resources were located deep in the continental heartland. Nevertheless, mineral exploitation was not confined to the discoverers. Spanish law stated that underground wealth belonged to the public domain. Consequently, political authorities distributed mines to those individuals with political or economic power in the Latin American Spanish community.

Mining required significant amounts of capital forcing mine owners to get credit for their enterprise. They borrowed from the many Church endowments (*obras pías*) and especially from the *encomenderos*, who also contributed with their own slave native labor. The *encomienda* was a 'contractual arrangement whereby Indians were entrusted to the temporal and to some extent the spiritual care of a Spaniard in return for their labor and some of their surplus goods'.[15] It worked as a restricted and well-defined institution in which the holder performed certain governmental duties in the colonies and in return received tribute, which residually belonged to the Crown. As mining became a profitable business, a mining entrepreneurial class, without direct ties with the *encomenderos*, emerged in the colonies.[16]

Spanish entrepreneurs did not engage in colonial mining. The local representatives of the big Spanish trading companies were sometimes tempted to invest in the growing local economies (in mining as well as in agriculture and manufacturing) but their Seville partners were increasingly inclined to sell to or buy from local traders rather than assume the expense of American facilities and the worry about grasping distant junior partners. Merchants wanted liquidity. Had they invested in mining, they would have lost liquidity. Consequently, local companies in America led by professional merchants soon developed, but they lacked direct connection with the Seville networks. However, they did have senior partners in the main colonial cities, like Mexico City and Lima. First serving as suppliers to miners, these merchants soon became mining financiers, and eventually mining entrepreneurs.[17]

Spaniards only became engaged directly in the mining business in the seventeenth century. Many natives of Spain had set up commercial businesses in Latin America and worked as intermediaries, buying goods from the Seville-based companies and distributing them in the local markets. These merchants provided goods on credit and they even lent miners money. In the seventeenth century the state stopped selling mercury on credit. Mining entrepreneurs had to borrow from these local merchants, who soon became the main financiers of the mining industry. In addition, they profited most from it, buying unlimited amounts of silver at a discount.[18]

In many occasions, these so-called "silver merchants" (*mercaderes de plata*) were drawn into actual mine ownership, although this was an option they would rather have avoided.[19] Although many of them had been born in Spain, they never returned to their mother country nor reinvested their profits in Europe. Their operations cannot be categorized as direct Spanish investment. The only non-precious metal that businessmen based in Spain exploited was copper. Small copper mines were established in Chile, Santiago de Cuba, and Hispaniola in the sixteenth century.

Spanish trade monopoly consisted of three institutions: the Board of Trade (*Casa de Contratación*), a merchant guild (*Consulado*), both located in Seville, and convoys of escorted vessels (*flotas* and *galeones*) that belonged to the state. The Crown also obtained fiscal gains from these institutions, while registered Spanish merchants earned income as expediters, not owners of cargoes, and sometimes shippers. A wealthy minority supervising the entry of new members dominated the guild. This sanctioned corporate oligopoly excluded non-Castilians. The Consulado collected commission fees from merchants and maintained official contact with designated ports in the Caribbean, like Cartagena, Portobello, Panama and Veracruz. It had representatives in the capitals of the viceroyalties of New Spain (Mexico City) and Peru (in Lima). It fixed prices according to the available purchasing power represented by the silver and gold supply in the hands of the colonial merchant intermediaries gathered for the arrival of the convoys.[20]

In spite of the restrictions set by the Consulado, non-Spaniards residents in Seville dominated colonial trade. These non-Spanish merchants advanced goods and credit, and employed Spanish merchants willing to lend their names to merchandise wholly owned by foreigners and shipped in foreign ships under foreign supervision. Hence, the returns on colonial trade to Spanish guild members were low compared to those that flowed to Italian and Bavarian suppliers in the sixteenth century, to Dutch ones in the seventeenth century, and to French and English ones thereafter.[21] Besides, Spain's lack of industrial development disabled it from meeting the growing needs of the colonists. Britain was the main supplier of goods re-exported from Spain to Spanish America in the seventeenth and eighteenth centuries. It provided steel and iron goods, woolen goods, salt cod from the Newfoundland fisheries, lead and tin. When Britain ended the Spanish trade monopoly in the eighteenth century and began smuggling these goods directly from England to New Spain (Mexico), Spanish authorities permitted it because Britain was the main customer for Spanish exports.[22]

Spanish direct investment appeared only in those sectors deemed strategic by the authorities, even if there was not a strong domestic demand. Some crops such as bananas (brought by the Spaniards from the Canary

Islands in the early years of colonization) and sugar, flourished. The colonization of the Atlantic islands (Azores, Madeira, the Canaries and São Tomé), by Spain and Portugal was accompanied and stimulated by the expansion of sugar in the last quarter of the fifteenth century. The Portuguese introduced sugar in Brazil in the first quarter of the sixteenth century. The mills (called *ingenios* by the Spaniards and *engenhos* by the Portuguese) were owned and managed by colonists from Portugal and Spain. Although European demand for sugar was low and production in the Atlantic islands was sufficient, in the mid-sixteenth century Castilian merchants brought technicians from the Canarian *ingenios* to the Caribbean, hoping to build sugar mills patterned after those on the islands off Africa.[23] Sugar production in Brazil grew faster, because the Portuguese had more penetration in European markets.[24]

Dyestuffs became very important commodities. Royal corregidores and encomenderos pressured the Indian communities of New Spain into gathering and processing the insects that produced cochineal, a red dye. In the second half of the sixteenth century dyestuffs became the main export after silver. On the Pacific coast of present-day Nicaragua and El Salvador a blue dye was also produced.[25]

Spanish America during the sixteenth century underwent hispanization as a result of constant immigration from Spain. Immigrants transferred their cultural traditions to the Americas. As the urban indigenous population became hispanicized, their income increased. At this point, a local homogeneous market emerged.[26] The Spaniards introduced crops from Spain to satisfy an increasing demand in this new market and, at the same time, colonists discovered the possibilities of several native crops. Vines and olives were introduced in Peru.[27] Cultivation of maize, cocoa and pulque on a large scale began, not only for the domestic market, but also for Europe. Over time, many of the owners of these businesses lost ties with Spain. They concentrated on local production and sold their produce to the Spanish merchants, who commercialized them in America and Europe, thus reinforcing the pattern of Spanish colonial trade.

The Spaniards took cocoa from New Spain and introduced it in the tropical shorelands of Ecuador and Venezuela. At first their produce was exported to Mexico. When cacao became salable in Europe in the seventeenth century, the state gave a monopoly concession on Venezuelan trade to an association of Basques: *Real Compañía Guipuzcoana* or The Caracas Company, based in San Sebastián. Many local landowners profited from this business until Spanish authorities abolished the monopoly in the late eighteenth century. Tobacco was introduced in Venezuela in the seventeenth century, when Spanish firms established tobacco plantations in the coastal areas of Venezuela.[28]

The textile industry also emerged in the late sixteenth century. There was a growing demand for Spanish garments that the metropole could no longer meet. Besides, the sheep population had grown big enough to provide sufficient raw material for local production. The Spanish colonialists demanded the same type of woolen clothes that people in Spain wore. However, the textile business had a marginal character. There was not a significant proliferation of *obrajes* or small mills or shops, which produced textiles for local consumption, using Spanish or Spanish-affected technology. The main concentration was 200 in Quito. Their owners were people who had acquired enough wealth for the investment but were neither a large estate owner, miner, nor import-export merchant, and their market was made up by low-income locally born Spaniards and urban Indians who could not afford Castilian clothes (*ropa de Castilla*), and had to buy cheaper local garments (*ropa de la tierra*). Profitability was very low. Thus, those entrepreneurs based in Spain chose to invest in activities connected to the export sector, rather than in the textile sector, which was geared toward local consumption.[29]

Shipbuilding flourished in the late sixteenth and in the seventeenth century. Spanish vessels had a long and dangerous journey to transport goods around the Horn to the Pacific coast. The abundance of timber led the Spaniards to set up local yards, first in Central America and then in the Guayaquil area (New Granada, present-day Ecuador), to build ships for the run from Peru to Panama and Mexico. Technological improvements in shipbuilding in the eighteenth century made vessels strong enough to get around the Horn safely. Consequently, local shipbuilding went into decline.[30]

The economic relations between Spain and its American colonies changed considerably in the eighteenth century, after the Spanish War of Succession. The Bourbon Dynasty attained power early in the eighteenth century, when Spain was still losing ground in her colonial trade to the main European countries. The first Bourbon king, Philip V, led a period of economic "nationalization", during which he revoked some trade concessions made to Britain. This policy was the result of the "family pacts" between the Spanish and the French Bourbons, which pushed Spain to the French orbit. Growing European demand for certain tropical foodstuffs, bullion, and raw materials, led Spain to increase its investment in the production of those items. The creation of chartered companies also stimulated production for export. The government granted regional companies in Barcelona, Zaragoza and Guipúzcoa special sectors of the colonial market to guarantee profitability. Spanish manufactures were not as competitive as those of other European nations, especially Britain, and producers could only make a profit in highly protected markets.[31]

When Charles III came to power in 1759, little had changed. He believed that economic autonomy would only occur by maximizing the colonial compact. Thus, he encouraged development of neglected colonial lands and economic activities, such as sugar, cocoa, tobacco and hide production. The Spaniards realized the potential of the Argentinean prairies for ranching, and merchants and firms (the majority of them from northern Spain) settled in Buenos Aires to participate in the export and import of leather, cattle, salted beef and animal hides. Most of these firms were subsidiaries of Spanish companies and they kept strong ties with Spain.[32] Herbert S. Klein argues, however, that the Spanish Crown "overspent" overwhelmingly in the Intendency of Buenos Aires because the city was unable to generate local income to pay for the maintenance of Royal civil, religious, and military bureaucracy.[33]

The economic importance of Cuba also grew considerably in the late eighteenth century. As in the case of Argentina, ranching became very important. Nevertheless, agriculture continued as the most viable economic activity on the island. Tropical exports grew greatly. Tobacco represented the main crop throughout the century. Investment in the sugar industry also increased significantly in the last decades of the century, especially in Cuba and Venezuela. By the 1790s, the fast growing coffee industry became the lead crop export.

The liberalization of trade made the late eighteenth century economic boom possible. In 1774 Charles III permitted the colonies to trade with each other and in 1778 all Spaniards were allowed to trade from nine designated Spanish ports with any American port (except Veracruz in Mexico and La Guaira, in Venezuela). In twenty years, Spanish exports to the colonies quintupled and imports increased nine-fold. Profits and surpluses grew, contraband decreased and Cádiz still channeled eighty-five percent of colonial trade. Many new companies settled in this city to take advantage of its commercial facilities.[34]

This honeymoon period for Spanish colonial trade was short. In 1796 hostilities erupted between Spain and Britain. Liberal economic and political ideas from Europe, especially from Britain, helped develop a self-conscious, moderately wealthy and moderately well educated Creole bourgeoisie that began calling for independence. The restoration of an old-fashioned type of absolutism in Spain in 1814 by Ferdinand VII triggered liberation wars in most American colonies.[35] In 1821 only Cuba and Puerto Rico pledged allegiance to the Spanish Crown. After independence, British investors and merchants took over. Surprisingly, French companies did not invest in Latin America immediately after independence, though strong ideological and dynastic affinities between the French and the Spanish Bourbons suggested otherwise. France waited for a Spanish attempt at reconquest (France was willing to support Spain in this enterprise) to open up Latin America for French trade and capital. The reconquest never took place. French firms, however, finally began to operate in Latin America in the 1830s. U.S. and Swiss companies also began to operate in Latin America in the 1830s.[36]

Britain never obtained absolute hegemony. Trade and economic specialization also allowed Spaniards to share foreign trade with the newcomers. Spaniards were reduced to traditional products, wines and food specialties. '...Urban and retail trade remained in Spanish or Portuguese hands because of linguistic advantage, superior knowledge of domestic patterns of distribution and greater readiness to accept the rigors of life in the interior'.[37]

The Nineteenth Century

Around twenty million people lived in Latin America and the Caribbean in 1825. Although most of the goods produced in this region were geared to the domestic market, the silver of Peru and Mexico, the coffee and sugar of Brazil and Cuba and the dyes of Central America succeeded in world markets. Nevertheless, only a small fraction of the Spanish Latin American economy was involved in production for export, except in Cuba. When the Spanish American territories became independent, they adopted a free trade liberal economic model. Latin American and Caribbean states suppressed the Spanish monopolistic export-import guilds (*consulados*) and resident Spanish merchants were thrown out or deemed unwelcome. Non-Iberian merchants, mostly British, replaced the Spanish and Portuguese in the ports and major cities.[38] Britain's trade strategy in Latin America responded to Napoleon's Continental System in Europe. When Britain was deprived of its European markets, it tried to develop new commercial networks. Britain tried to turn Brazil into a British dependency and helped the Portuguese prince, John, move to Brazil. Once there, the Prince avoided British pressure and declared '...the ports of Brazil open to the commerce of all friendly nations'.[39] The other Latin American nations followed Brazil's example.

Until 1850, only Cuba was a main recipient of FDI (not only Spanish). Local demand dried up quickly and many North American and European financiers had to return to their countries penniless. Locals financed domestic production. Political stability and improvement in shipping technologies increased demand for some Latin American perishable commodities, such as Argentinean cattle and hides, sugar and coffee, and Chilean minerals. British and French capital financed the development of the textile industry, as well as infrastructure. Latin American liberals encouraged capital and migration from northern and central Europe, in the belief that investment and immigrants would bring new ideas and attitudes beneficial for economic and social progress.[40]

Spanish capital in the Western Hemisphere retreated to Cuba and Puerto Rico, which still remained under Spanish rule. Spanish migration to these islands was considerable, especially to Cuba, where phenomenal economic prosperity attracted immigrants. Spanish companies, however, did not invest significant amounts of capital in Cuba. Direct investment from the metropole came mostly from the Spanish government. Sugar and coffee production increased after the 1790s. The Spanish government eliminated restrictions on the importation of technology to Cuba. The sugar industry benefited from this. In 1819 steampower was applied to drive the sugar mills, increasing the productivity of Cuban *ingenios* tremendously. In 1817 the Spanish government permitted Cubans to trade freely with non-Spaniards. The first railroad in Latin America, built in Western Cuba in 1837 and even before the construction of the railroad in metropolitan Spain, provided quicker transportation of sugar from the interior to the port of Havana. This was an important development, considering that sugar begins to spoil twenty-four hours after being cut. A commission consisting of the Spanish Consulate, the Havana City Hall, the Sociedad Económica and the General Chaptaincy and the Capitanía e Intendencia General developed this project, which was financed by a London company.[41] All these technological developments made the Cuban sugar industry the most efficient in Latin America. The result was phenomenal rates of economic growth. By 1860 Cuba accounted for one quarter of the world's sugar production, with the United States buying around 50 percent of it.[42]

After the enactment of the liberalization laws in 1818, Spanish merchants without roots in Cuba increased their investment in sugar. These were merchants that amassed fortunes with the slave trade. When they invested in the sugar industry, they introduced much of the new technology. By 1860 Spanish direct investment displaced the control of the Cuban sugar market held by the traditional oligarchy.[43] Spanish preeminence came to an end around 1880, when U.S. companies introduced newer technology that increased the productivity of their mills.

Spanish direct investment in other sectors in Cuba was mainly public, confined to the development of infrastructure. The state led the construction of the first twenty-seven kilometers of railroads, but it encouraged private companies to take the lead thereafter, by giving land to private contractors, tax exemptions, privileged access to public natural resources and concession to manage the train service for a period of ninety-nine years. Sugar growers provided the funding. The railroad between 1837 and 1860 covered 1,029 kilometers. In 1898 the total Cuban railroad network encompassed 1,561 km.[44]

To promote even development on the island, the government tried to integrate Cuba into a sole economic entity. Its efforts were thus devoted to development of communication systems. The state built the first telegraphic lines in 1853 and demanded railway companies to develop their own telegraphic infrastructure. By 1866 the state had 2,561 lines and the railway companies 1,021.[45] The state withdrew the postal service from a private Spanish company, nationalizing the system. Reorganization on the basis of the new available infrastructure made the new postal system more efficient. The Dirección de Obras Públicas completed this developmental effort with the construction of roads. The idea of an integrated Cuban economy became a reality in 1878.

The sugar boom increased the need for financing. In 1854 the Spanish authorities created the first Cuban bank, Real Caja de Descuentos, renamed as Banco Español de La Habana and finally as Banco Español de la Isla de Cuba.[46] Many private banks appeared between 1854 and 1858, but after the crisis of 1866 the Banco Español, as it was known, was the only one left. Its purpose was to finance the war against the independentists. When the uprising was suffocated, it provided funds for trade and construction.[47]

The other Spanish-American dependency in the nineteenth century, Puerto Rico, lacked a financial infrastructure. Even though several banks were created since the 1850s, their operations were very limited. Pressures by local merchants and especially by Spanish merchant houses, who worked as actual financial institutions, opposed the creation of banks. The first bank to provide loans, Sociedad Anónima de Crédito Mercantil, did not appear until the late 1870s.[48]

Spanish authorities restricted credit to prevent the appearance of manufacturing industries that competed with metropolitan goods. In the first half of the nineteenth century, Puerto Rico, like Cuba, produced mainly agricultural goods and manufactures that could not be provided by Spain or by other industrialized nations. Sugar, cattle-raising, hides and rum and cigar production were the main industries.[49] The liberalization measures implemented by Spain in the late 1810s increased economic growth: lower taxes, the allotment of free land to immigrants, trade liberalization, and imported Spanish machinery increased local economic activity.[50] Nevertheless, the key for Puerto Rico's economic development was external. In the second half of the century, beet-sugar production rose in Europe, harming Puerto Rican exports. At the same time, the United States opened its markets to Brazilian coffee, causing a shortage in the supply of coffee in Europe. This worked as a stimulus for Puerto Rico's coffee industry, which became the main industry on the island.[51]

Spanish direct investment in Puerto Rico was small. Only 159 miles of railroad were built in the century, its construction being financed by the sugar producers.[52] Spanish authorities funded the improvement of port facilities to serve the export sector. Spaniards, however, came to dominate the coffee industry, either directly through production or as creditors. Especially important was the role of Catalonian and Majorcan immigrants, who developed prosperous businesses as immigrants that later were inherited or sold to relatives or run directly from Spain. It was common for them to sell the whole business at a certain age and return to their home regions in Spain.[53]

Spanish merchants also played a crucial role in the development of the coffee industry as creditors. They established a credit system that revolved around land mortgages and coffee deliveries. If obligations could not be met, foreclosures and land alienation resulted.[54] When coffee and land prices rose in the 1880s and 1890s, many Spanish coffee growers sold their businesses and returned to Spain (a large number went back to Majorca). Merchants mainly dominated the coffee industry since the 1840s to the end of the century. Profit repatriation to Spain was a fundamental feature of this business.[55]

Spanish direct investment in the nineteenth century in Cuba and Puerto Rico followed the same pattern observed throughout the colonial period. It was basically limited to the provision of basic infrastructure and to those industries crucial for the interests of the Spanish authorities. European immigrants (mostly Spaniards) and locals pursued the production of goods and provision of services. Spanish merchants played a key role as financiers, providing capital to local entrepreneurs.

The Twentieth Century

The first half of the twentieth century was a very turbulent period in Spain. After the loss of Cuba and Puerto Rico in 1898, Spanish authorities tried to keep the Spanish colonial dream alive in northern Africa. Revolt in Morocco against Spanish colonial rule hurt that goal. Poor economic conditions led to social unrest. In 1923, king Alfonso XIII accepted the dictatorship of General José Antonio Primo de Rivera, in the belief that a strong hand was needed to pacify internal affairs. Spaniards withdrew legitimacy from the king in 1931, when the Republican Party won broad support from the electorate in the municipal elections. The king left for exile and the Second Republic was proclaimed. The republican political panorama became very polarized and led to a Civil War in the years 1936-1939.

Political instability prevented economic growth throughout this period. Spain lagged behind other western European countries in terms of economic, political and social development. Spanish companies were small and could not compete with foreign rivals. Spanish foreign direct investment declined to an insignificant level. One of the few exceptions was CHADE, a Spain-based electrical corporation with investments in Latin America, largely in Argentina. The Government of Juan Domingo Perón nationalized CHADE without any complaint from the Franco Government.[56] Spain initiated its economic takeoff in the 1960s and Spanish FDI began to grow in the late 1970s, although it did not reach significant levels until the late 1980s.

In the late 1970s, Spanish firms invested in Latin America 55.5 percent of their FDI. Venezuela and Mexico alone received 45.24 percent of the total. The sectors receiving more investment were industrial machinery, bus and truck manufacturing, and shipyards. Fishing also got a big share of investment, as well as commerce (distribution), tourism and extraction of non-energy related minerals. The oil price increase of the late 1970s hurt Spanish industrial firms seriously. They invested in oil-rich countries in the late 1970s as a strategy to have easier access to cheap fuel. For this reason, Mexico and Venezuela got the largest shares of Spanish FDI.[57] Investment in the fishing industry was also considerable. Spanish vessels lost access to some of their traditional fisheries and many fishing companies decided to operate from South America, especially from Argentina, in order to gain access to alternative fisheries.

The 1980s

Spanish FDI in Latin America and the Caribbean in the 1970s and 1980s included investment in distribution networks, which served Spanish exports into the region. Before investing to initiate local production, Spanish firms decided to strengthen the distribution networks to channel their exports from Spain into the local markets. Investment in the tourist sector was also important. Tourism played a key role as engine of the Spanish economy since the 1960s. Spanish tourist firms were also pioneers of Spanish FDI, especially in Latin America and the Caribbean.

Spanish banks expanded abroad in the early 1980s, especially in Latin America. As banks from other western countries divested, Spanish banks saw in Latin America's desolate banking panorama an opportunity for business, and decided to take the lead. Rather than concentrating on wholesale banking, Spanish banks began opening offices in an effort to develop a strong network to operate as retail banking.

The weakness of the Spanish domestic demand encouraged firms to expand abroad in the early 1980s. Many Spanish companies sought extra markets for their products in Latin America. They invested more in Chile and Argentina, pulled by the schemes designed by the governments of these countries to re-negotiate their commercial and financial debts. Nevertheless, investment in Latin America and the Caribbean as a share of total Spanish FDI decreased considerably after Spain joined the European Union in 1986.

Figure 2.1 Spain's FDI in Latin America and the Caribbean, 1976-1997

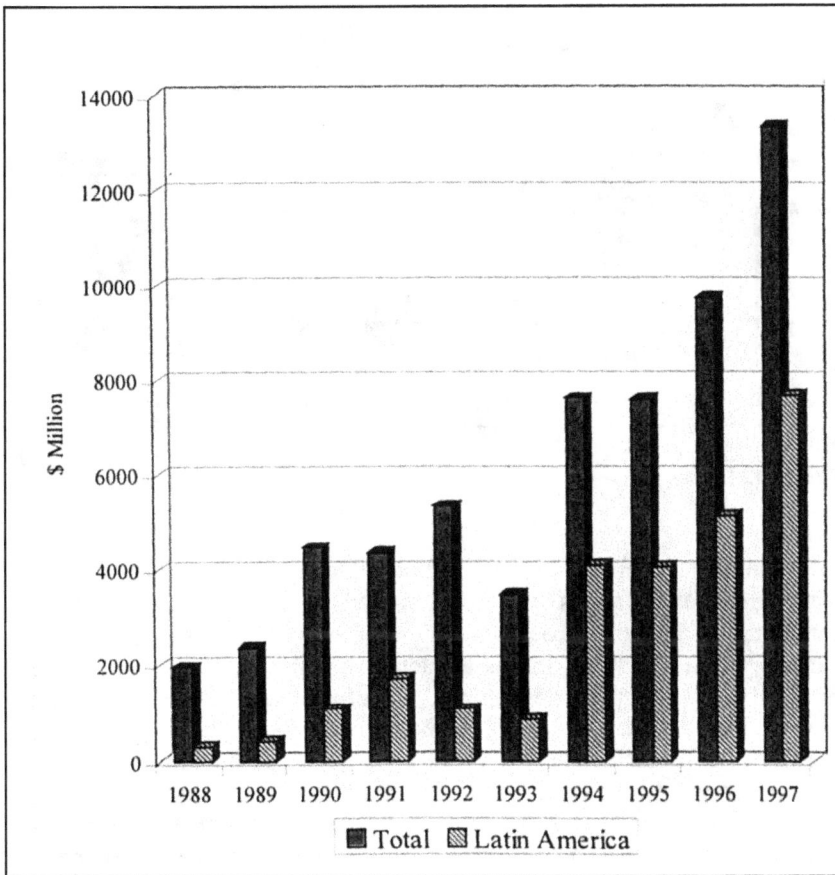

Source: Spanish Ministry of the Economy.

The process of capital liberalization initiated in 1979 caused the overall increase in Spanish FDI rates. In 1979 the Spanish government allowed Spanish citizens to own foreign assets in foreign currency without any extra charge. This eliminated the pre-requisite of requesting permission to invest abroad from the Dirección General de Transacciones Exteriores. After 1986, Spain adapted its legislation to European regulations, emphasizing the need to provide more freedom of operation between residents and foreigners. The culmination of this process took place in 1992, when Spain eliminated all restrictions and limits to capital movements.

Figure 2.2 Spanish FDI in Latin America and the Caribbean as a share of total Spanish FDI, 1976-1997

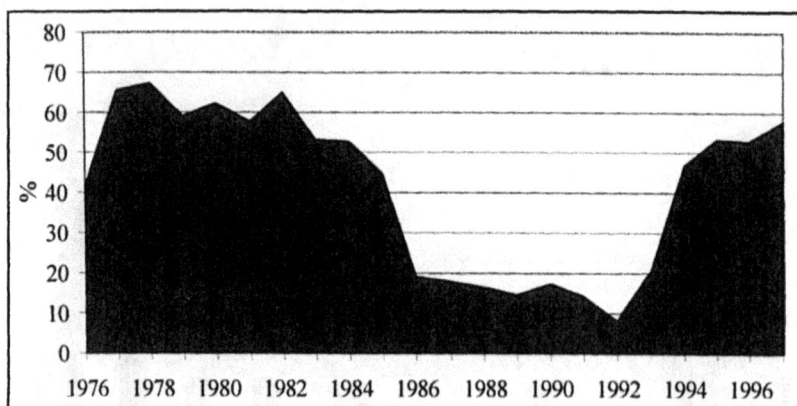

Source: DGEITE.

Spain's membership in the European Union diverted Spanish FDI. Although absolute figures increased, the share going to Latin America fell considerably, bouncing back in the mid-1990s. Argentina, Chile, and Panama, as a result of its fiscal status, became the main recipients, especially from banking institutions. Venezuela, and to a lesser extent Mexico, lost ground. The sectors receiving the largest shares were banking, tourism, manufacturing, and mining and energy. Investment in banking and tourism grew in the late 1980s. Especially notable (from a political standpoint) was the Spanish presence in the tourist industry of Cuba after 1985. Spanish tourist companies invested in Latin America to expand in markets where there was not so much competition, and to provide services to those Spanish tourists who spent their vacations in Latin America.

Figure 2.3 Spanish FDI in a selected group of Latin American and Caribbean countries, 1976-1997

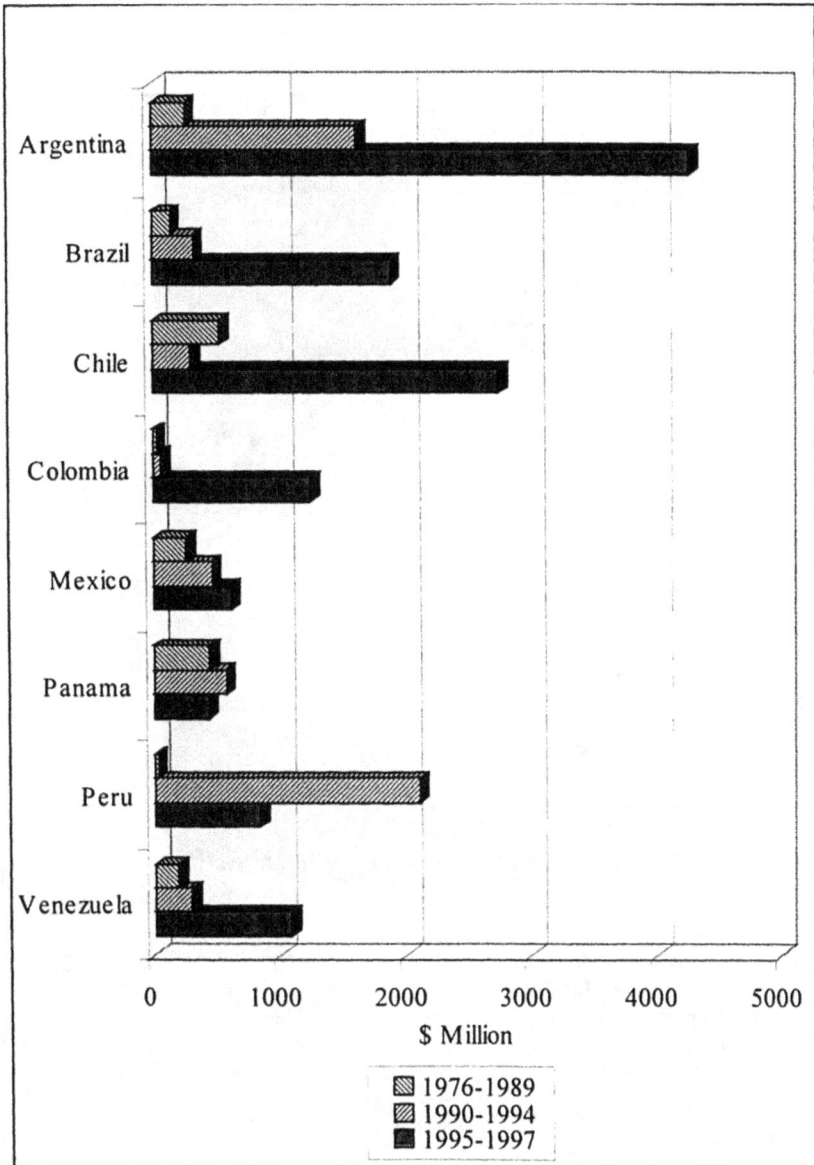

Source: DGEITE.

**Figure 2.4   Evolution of Spanish FDI in Latin America and the
Caribbean by areas of economic activity, 1980-1989**

1980-1984

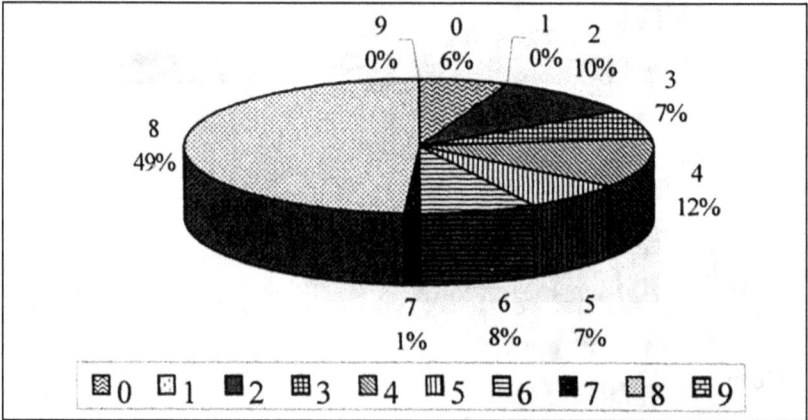

1985-1989

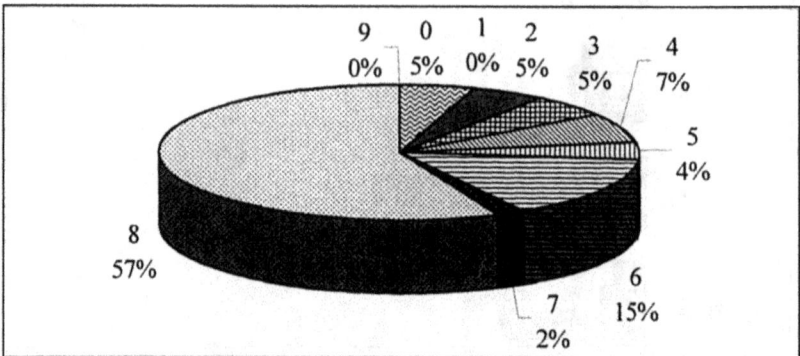

Spanish official statistics divide economic activities into the following areas: 0, agriculture, cattle raising, hunting, forestry and fishing; 1, energy and water; 2, extraction and transformation of non-energetic minerals and products derived from the chemical industry; 3, transformation of metals, precision mechanics; 4, other manufacturing industries; 5, construction; 6, commerce, restaurants and hotels; 7, transport and communication; 8, financial institutions, insurance, services provided to firms and rents; 9, other services.

Source: DGEITE.

Table 2.1   **Spanish FDI in Latin America between 1990 and 1996 by country ($ Million)**

Country	Total Inward FDI	Spanish FDI	Share
Argentina	22,407	4,075	18.18
Bolivia	6.213	679.3	0.91
Brazil	724	23,574	3.07
Chile	1,173.687	10,130	11.58
Colombia	448.788	9,951	4.50
Costa Rica	20	1,905	1.04
Cuba	56.65	1,200[58]	4.72
Dominican Republic	30.23	1,841	1.64
Ecuador	73.78	2,381	3.09
El Salvador	2.62	144	1.81
Guatemala	0.37	593	0.06
Haiti	0	37	0
Honduras	0.08	331	0.02
Jamaica	0	950	0
Mexico	756.33	44,675	1.69
Nicaragua	0	250	0
Panama	943.08	1,239	76.11
Paraguay	17.37	1,005	1.72
Peru	2,814.99	9,151	30.76
Trinidad & Tobago	36.82	1,970	1.86
Uruguay	150.16	673	22.31
Venezuela	716.82	6,999	10.24

Source: CEPAL, IMF, Spanish Ministry of the Economy and UNCTAD.

A large part of the investments in banking were used for the creation of holding societies to channel capital flows from Spain. FDI grew even further in the 1990s, when Banco Bilbao Vizcaya (BBV), Banco de Santander (BS) and Banco Central Hispano-Americano (BCH) (at that point BS and BCH were not merged) embarked on an open war in Latin America to dominate the retail banking. With their aggressive strategies they paved the way for the new flow of Spanish capital.

The significant increase in Spanish FDI in absolute terms was caused by a series of factors: the internal dynamism of the Spanish economy, which in the last years of the 1980s and early 1990s grew at an average rate of 4.2 percent yearly, the gradual consolidation of the process of internationalization of the economy (accelerated by Spain's incorporation to the European Union), and the strength of the Spanish currency, especially against the U.S. dollar.[59]

Notes

[1]   Sebastian Edwards, *Crisis and Reform in Latin America. From Despair to Hope*, World Bank, Washington, D.C., 1995, p. 42.

[2]   Irving Stone, *The Composition and Distribution of British Investment in Latin America, 1865 to 1913*, Garland Publishing Inc., New York, 1987, p. 1.

[3]   H. B. Johnson, "The Portuguese Settlement of Brazil, 1500-1580", in Leslie Bethell (ed.), *The Cambridge History of Latin America, Volume I, Colonial Latin America*, Cambridge University Press, Cambridge, 1984, p. 259.

[4]   Mario Góngora, *Studies in the Colonial History of Spanish America*, Cambridge University Press, Cambridge, 1975, pp. 79-80.

[5]   Ibid., pp.82-83.

[6]   Ibid., p. 85.

[7]   Ibid., p. 86.

[8]   Ibid., pp. 88-89.

[9]   Ibid., p. 93.

[10] J. Stanley Stein and Barbara H. Stein, *The Colonial Heritage of Latin America. Essays on Economic Dependence in Perspective*, Oxford University Press, Oxford, 1970, p. 28.

[11] Irving Stone, *The Composition and Distribution...*, pp. 3-5.

[12] Ibid., p. 5.

[13] D. A. Brading, "Bourbon Spain and its American Empire", in Leslie Bethel (ed.), *The Cambridge History of Latin America...*, pp. 421-422.

[14] Eric R. Wolf, *Europe and the People Without History*, University of California Press, Berkeley, 1990, pp. 135-136.

[15] Murdo J. Macleod, "Spain and America: the Atlantic Trade, 1492-1720", in Leslie Bethell (ed.), *The Cambridge History of Latin America...*, p. 361.

[16] James Lockhart and Stuart B. Schwartz, *Early Latin America. A History of Colonial Spanish America and Brazil*, Cambridge University Press, Cambridge, 1983, p. 101-102.

[17] Ibid., pp. 98-99.

[18] Ibid., p. 152.

[19] Ibid., pp. 152-153.

[20] Stanley J. Stein and Barbara H. Stein, *The Colonial Heritage...*, pp. 47-48.

[21] Ibid., pp. 50-51.

[22] Irving Stone, *The Composition and Distribution...*, p. 10.

[23] James Lockhart and Stuart B. Schwartz, *Early Latin America*, p. 74; Clarence Henry Haring, *Trade and Navigation Between Spain and the Indies in the Time of the Hapsburgs*, Peter Smith, Gloucester (Massachusetts), 1964, p. 124; and Eric R. Wolf, *Europe and the People...*, p. 140.

[24] James Lockhart and Stuart B. Schwartz, *Early Latin America*, pp. 24, 27.

[25] Eric R. Wolf, *Europe and the People...*, p. 140.

[26] James Lockhart and Stuart B. Schwartz, *Early Latin America*, pp. 132-133.

27 Clarence Henry Haring, *Trade and Navigation...*, p. 126.
28 James Lockhart and Stuart B. Schwartz, *Early Latin America*, p. 341.
29 Ibid., pp. 142-144.
30 Ibid., p. 145.
31 Stanley J. Stein and Barbara H. Stein, *The Colonial Heritage...*, pp. 86-88.
32 James Lockhart and Stuart B. Schwartz, *Early Latin America*, p. 340.
33 Herbert S. Klein, "Structure and Profitability of Royal Finance in the Viceroyalty of the Río de la Plata in 1790", *Hispanic American Historical Review*, Vol. 53, No. 3, August 1973, pp. 440-469.
34 Irving Stone, *The Composition and Distribution...*, p. 12; and Stanley J. Stein and Barbara H. Stein, *The Colonial Heritage...*, p. 100.
35 James Lockhart and Stuart B. Schwartz, *Early Latin America*, p. 415.
36 Stanley J. Stein and Barbara H. Stein, *The Colonial Heritage...*, p. 152.
37 Ibid., p. 153.
38 David Bushnell and Neill Macaulay, *The Emergence of Latin America in the Nineteenth Century* (second edition), Oxford University Press, New York, 1994, pp. 38-39.
39 Ibid., p. 40.
40 Ibid., p. 226.
41 Julio Le Riverend, *Historia Económica de Cuba*, Editorial de Ciencias Sociales, Havana, 1985, p. 240.
42 David Bushnell and Neill Macaulay, *The Emergence of Latin America...*, pp. 265-267.
43 Francisco López Segrera, *Cuba: Capitalismo Dependiente y Subdesarrollo (1510-1959)*, Editorial Diógenes, S.A., Mexico City, 1973, p. 144.
44 Julio Le Riverend, *Historia Económica de Cuba*, p. 521.
45 Ibid., p. 406.
46 Ibid., p. 425.
47 Ibid., pp. 423-424.
48 James L. Dietz, *Economic History of Puerto Rico. Institutional Change and Capitalist Development*, Princeton University Press, Princeton, 1986, p. 29.
49 Ibid., p. 17.
50 Ibid., pp. 21-22.
51 Ibid., pp. 26-27.
52 Ibid., p. 28.
53 Laird W. Bergad, *Coffee and the Growth of Agrarian Capitalism in Nineteenth Century Puerto Rico*, Princeton University Press, Princeton, 1983, pp. 81-83.
54 Ibid., pp. 98-99.
55 Ibid., pp. 160-161.
56 Albert Carreras, Xavier Tafunell and Eugenio Torres, "Against Integration. The Rise and Decline of Spanish State-Owned Firms and the Decline and Rise of Multinationals, 1939-1990", in Ülf Olsson (ed.), *Business and European Integration Since 1800. Regional, National and International Perspectives*, University of Göteborg, Göteborg, 1997, pp. 31-49.
57 ICE, various issues.
58 US-Cuba Trade and Economic Council, quoted in Michael Buettner, "Foreign Firms Already Tapping Cuban Markets", *Jacksonville Business Journal*, December 1997, p. 1.
59 Ministry of Commerce, *ICE*, 27 February-5 March 1989, p. 870.

3 Creating Alliances:
Frameworks for Theory

This chapter gives theoretical support to the analysis of Spanish MNEs in Latin America. In the following pages a study of the main theoretical approaches to MNE activity is provided, from international economics to the OLI model. The order in which all these frameworks are presented follows the actual evolution that the theory of MNEs underwent over the years. A close analysis shows a trend from broad sectoral approaches, to firm-specific ones. These theories provide the basis for the ultimate purpose of examining the nature and behavior of Spanish multinationals in Latin America. The empirical analysis is enriched by contributions from several of the following perspectives. The case of the Spanish MNEs tests their validity in predicting and explaining MNE activity.

International Economics

The expansion of U.S. MNEs in the 1950s and 1960s on a global scale led scholars to look for theoretical explanations. The first frameworks were drawn from international economics and international trade in the 1950s. International economics does not study MNEs *per se*. Its focus is on the export of equity capital that occurs when a company starts a foreign subsidiary. International flows of capital are a central concern of international economists, who long explained the MNE as simply an '...arbitrager of equity capital from countries where its return is low to countries where it is high'.[1] There is a strong interrelationship between international trade, international movements of factors of production and the distribution of income. This has empirical implications:

- MNEs should be based in countries best endowed with capital, where its domestic marginal productivity is therefore the lowest.
- They should move capital toward the countries least well endowed with capital (with the highest marginal products of capital).[2]

Richard Caves concludes that the theoretical role of the MNE as a capital arbitrager was neither developed analytically nor tested empirically.[3] Even though international economics does not offer a fundamental explanation for MNEs, it does contribute substantially to explaining their scope of operation through the trade-off between exports and foreign investment and general-equilibrium models. It also provides a framework for understanding the MNEs international movement of resources that are implied by the partial-equilibrium transaction-cost models.

The general-equilibrium approach is based on the Heckscher-Ohlin model of trade, particularly on the interrelationship between a nation's pattern of international trade and its endowment of factors of production. Transfers of capital by MNEs can then be explained as a change in the factor endowments of the sending and receiving countries.[4]

In its simplest form, the Heckscher-Ohlin model of trade assumes that the world consists of two countries -Home (H) and Foreign (F)-. These two countries only produce and trade two commodities -food and cloth-. Each nation has a given endowment of two factors of production -labor and capital. The production functions of food and clothing differ in their requirements of capital and labor. Foreign requires more labor for production because its productivity is lower. A good's production function is the same in each country. A given number of units of capital and labor produce the same number of clothing or food units in every country. The model assumes markets to be perfectly competitive and ignores transportation costs. Production is efficient, in the sense that any increase in the output of one good will decrease the production of the other. In the absence of trade, production equals consumption.[5]

The country that is well endowed with capital realizes an increase in cloth production, and the one endowed with labor, in food. In both, capital rentals relative to wages rise, as prices rise.[6] Without trade, capital yields higher returns in capital-rich Home than in capital-short Foreign. Therefore, capital tends to flow to Foreign, where capital rentals are higher.

Hymer found the capital-arbitrage explanation inconsistent with several patterns of MNEs. He argued that the United States had shown net exports of foreign direct investment but net inflows of portfolio capital. From the international economics perspective, this implies that U.S. equity capital is expensive and portfolio capital is cheap.[7] The model makes no difference between direct and portfolio investment. This point has important implications for this book. First, its goal is to study Spanish direct investment, not portfolio investment. Secondly, Spanish MNEs normally buy large shares of existing local companies (well over 10 percent, which is accepted as the borderline between portfolio and direct investment), in order to gain control over the operations of their subsidiaries.

Hymer also observed that MNEs move in both directions and some nations are both home for many MNEs and host to subsidiaries controlled from overseas. The implication of this is that if MNEs merely arbitrage capital, the rates of return to capital must be high in some industries and low in others, in the same country.[8] In reality, Spanish MNEs invest in Latin America because they believe that their services, technology, and the way they do business meets the need of the local markets, giving them a competitive advantage vis-à-vis their competitors, and thus generating high rates of return. Their returns on investment are not a function of the interest rates, but of the quality of their services and the needs of the market.

If FDI were pure arbitrage of capital, large financial intermediaries would be prominent participants. However, most of the investments are made by non-financial companies (in the Spanish case banks are the most aggressive MNEs, but their investments are based on criteria different from those predicted by the international economics model) and the profits they earn are not related to the long-term rate of interest (which should represent a nation's marginal product of capital).[9] Investment does not depend on capital cost differences. Although banks make a very large share of total Spanish FDI in Latin America, their investment is not motivated by variations of interest rates across countries. Spanish banks invest in the development of infrastructure and services that enables them to provide their services locally. In other words, they make direct investments in order to "sell" a particular product, which generates a return on their investment.

General Equilibrium Theory of International Trade

The general equilibrium theory, also applied to MNEs in the 1950s, rests on two main propositions:

- As patterns of international trade depend on comparative advantage and the factors underlying it, so should the distribution of MNEs. A MNE emerges when an enterprise finds itself with opportunities to start to link up with an establishment in another country. Some countries may be relatively well endowed to support these opportunities. This point fails to explain why Spanish MNEs have invested more than North American ones in Latin America in the 1990s, especially in some sectors where North American firms are better endowed than Spanish ones, such as telecommunications and banking.
- Factor endowments and trade flows are interrelated.

The presence of MNEs in one country does not depend on the country's characteristics. The firm-specific proprietary assets, and transaction-cost factors, among others, led Spanish MNEs to invest in Latin America in the 1990s. The prevalence of MNEs varies systematically among industries. However, those models that consider product differentiation open the possibility that country traits may have an influence on FDI, independent of the industry mix. In these models, some countries' endowments of real resources or culture provide an adequate environment for the emergence of potential MNEs and become home bases for MNEs. Others' endowments lack these traits and become hosts of MNEs' subsidiaries.

Industrial Organization Approach

The industrial organization approach provides the first useful explanation to study the role of Spanish MNEs in Latin America. Developed by Stephen Hymer, the industrial organization approach opened a whole new framework for the analysis of MNEs in the 1960s.[10] In his doctoral dissertation, completed in 1960, Hymer defended a closer analysis of the firm and rejected broader, more sectoral interpretations. Although he finished his dissertation in 1960, the MIT Press did not publish it until 1976, after he died in an automobile accident. The publication committee regarded Hymer's argument as too simplistic.

His point of departure is the distinction between two different types of investment, direct and portfolio investment. If the investor directly controls the foreign enterprise, his investment is called a direct investment. If he does not control it, his investment is a portfolio investment.[11] The US Department of Commerce estimates that there is control when one party owns at least ten percent of the equity.

The basis for the theory of portfolio investment is the interest rate. 'Each investor maximizes profits by investing where returns are the highest. Capital will thus move from countries where the interest rate is low to those where the interest rate is high until interest rates are everywhere equal'.[12] When interest rates become equal across countries, no cross movements of capital would occur. Hymer argues that this theory disregards risk, uncertainty, and barriers to trade. When risk is introduced, cross movements from one country to another result from different risk preferences. For those who divert their portfolio to new areas in order to seek diversification, higher interest rates must be offered. Cross movements also result from uncertainty because investors value the conditions in various markets differently.[13] When initiating foreign operations MNEs are confronted with several barriers:

1. fluctuations of exchange rates increase the risk involved in the investment and engender different returns for locals and for foreigners;
2. they lack information about the market, and the cost of acquiring that information may be considerable;
3. transaction costs are high;
4. local authorities and consumers may discriminate against them. However, once a foreign operation has been established, most of these costs disappear and need not be incurred again.

The risk factor has been a key determinant of why Spanish MNEs took the lead in Latin America in the 1990s. Many potential investors did not believe that Latin American governments were truly committed to implementing serious structural reforms and viewed the reforms undertaken in the late 1980s and early 1990s as temporary adjustments to solve balance-of-payments problems in the short term. Spanish MNEs believed in the seriousness of the policies and estimated that the reforms would stimulate economic growth, which would produce great opportunities for business.

Although interest-rate theory predicts capital investments to occur between industries where the interest rate is low and those where it is high, reality shows that direct investment takes place within the same industry in both home and host countries.[14] Based on these observations, Hymer concluded that the existence of cross movements indicates the inability of the interest-rate theory to explain flows of direct investment and denounces its disregard for the notion of "control".[15] It also disregards other important issues, such as know-how, technology, services, etc., which give firms a competitive advantage in a particular activity. It is not clear that the resources that generate an advantage in one activity would apply in others. Therefore, firms are more likely to invest abroad in the same activities they perform in their home countries. This is the case of the Spanish MNEs in Latin America.

Hymer also differentiated two main reasons why an investor may seek control:

- Direct investment, type 1: the investor seeks control over the enterprise in order to ensure the safety of the investment (prudent use of assets). In this case, as in the case of portfolio investment, the differences in the interest rate drive capital flows. Direct investment of this type will substitute for portfolio investment when the distrust of foreigners is high or when fear of expropriation and risks of exchange-rate changes are high.[16]

- "International operations" or direct investment, type 2: control of the foreign enterprise is desired in order to remove competition between that foreign enterprise and enterprises in other countries, or in order to fully appropriate the returns on certain skills and abilities. In imperfect markets where horizontal monopolies and oligopolies operate, some form of collusion is profitable. Collusion can be achieved by having the various enterprises owned and controlled by a single firm. Moreover, firms have unequal abilities to operate in a particular industry. When one firm has an advantage over the others in the production of a good, that firm may find it profitable to undertake production of the good abroad. In that case, capital movements are needed to acquire a share of a foreign enterprise in order to gain control over it. It becomes clear that the motivation for this type of investment is not the interest rate, but the profits derived from controlling the foreign enterprise.[17]

The second reason, "international operations", is part of the theory of the firm. Its goal is to determine the degree of vertical and horizontal integration of firms on a global scale. Despite the broad scope some MNEs can achieve, most scholars agree that firms have a nationality, determined by three factors: legal nationality, which determines the legal limitations on a firm's behavior; the most common place of residence among the MNE's shareholders, and the currency with which the firm pays dividends; and the nationality of the firm's managers.[18]

Hymer distinguishes two major reasons and a minor one why a firm may want to control an enterprise in a foreign country:

1. It is sometimes profitable to control enterprises in more than one country in order to remove competition between them. Enterprises are frequently connected to each other through markets. They compete or sell to each other. When this connection exists, it may be profitable to substitute centralized decision making for decentralized decision making.[19]
2. Some firms have advantages in a particular activity or industry, and they may find it profitable to exploit these advantages by establishing foreign operations. International operations are motivated by these profits. This explains why there can be direct investment even when there is not enough of an interest-rate difference to induce portfolio investment.[20]
3. The minor reason is "diversification" into different lines of activities. An argument for diversification exists when profits in one line of activity are inversely correlated with profits in another line of activity.

Hymer provides the example of the investment in an aluminum plant in an underdeveloped area. When the cost of energy is low, there is possibility for investment in the electricity sector also. The area may develop in the future, thereby inflating the price of electricity. The investor reduces risk by diversifying.[21]

This book shows that all three reasons apply. The second case most accurately explains the cases of Spanish MNEs investing in Latin America. Spanish MNEs believed they had advantages over their competitors, given their knowledge of the needs of a developing economy. The Spanish local economy served as a training field for Spanish MNEs. Between the mid-1970s and the early 1990s the Spanish economy went through a fast phase of development and rapid growth. Spanish firms learnt the needs of the market and believed they could develop services appropriate for the needs of the developing economies of Latin America better than their competitors from other developed countries or even from Latin America. Nevertheless, most companies preferred to buy local firms already in operation, rather than start through greenfield investments. This allowed them to take over an on-going business, and at the same time remove a prospective competitor from the market. Therefore, Hymer's first reason also applies. Finally, some companies, such as Telefonica,[22] diversified in Latin America into new lines of activities to test new services before introducing them into their home market.

In some cases, firms choose to exploit their advantages themselves. In others, they choose to license them. Hymer (1976) argues that '...the firm is a practical institutional device which substitutes for the market. The firm internalizes or supersedes the market.'[23] Imperfections in the market exist because each firm pursues its own interest instead of joint maximization. Joint maximization would only be achieved through common ownership. Impurities in the market are a reason for internalization. When deciding whether to license or to exploit their advantages themselves, firms have to consider several possibilities. Licensing involves many risks. There may be only a few buyers of the advantage (monopoly or oligopoly) or many buyers who would compete amongst them, driving profits down. Buyers and sellers have different evaluations of the advantage, and agreement over the contract may be difficult to achieve. The licensor may fear that the licensee may discover a process that substitutes for the advantage.[24]

Under all these circumstances, which apply equally to domestic and foreign exploitation of the advantage, a firm will decide to operate itself rather than license. Cooperation with domestic firms in the host country may also make sense when the licensor has little knowledge about that market or when costs are very high. Joint-ventures provide an opportunity to reduce risks. Whereas some Spanish firms chose to operate in Latin America with a local partner, such as Banco Central Hispanoamericano (BCH), others, such as Banco de Santander (BS), chose to operate alone. There may also be a lot of competition. All these reasons call for licensing.

Firms from different nations develop their advantage on the basis of the uneven distribution of skills across countries. Most MNEs originate in the developed world because these countries have more skilled people and their entrepreneurs operate in industries that other entrepreneurs in LDCs may not even have. By evolving in these conditions, firms develop advantages over their counterparts from LDCs.

What determines the extent of control by a firm is the existence or absence of scale economies. The size of the firm is determined by two opposing tendencies. On the one hand, growing size leads to increasing profits owing to scale economies. On the other, the costs of managing and coordinating numerous units increase as the firm grows. 'The firm reaches its optimal size when marginal scale advantages are just overtaken by marginal management costs.'[25]

Scale economies at the level of the firm result from organization (as opposed to scale economies at the level of the industry, which have a technological origin, and result from the division of labor). Hymer defines the firm as an organism that coordinates activities and reduces scale economies to a question of efficiency of information. Firms face the possibility of coordinating their activities through the market or through management. If the market is perfect, there is absolute certainty and the firm can buy at a price that truly reflects substitution costs. The argument for direct investment would then be very weak. Or it may choose horizontal and vertical integration (under vertical integration several stages of the production process are operated as a single unit under common ownership) of its operations, in which case it gains control, order, and predictability.[26] The reasons for vertical integration are:[27]

- To avoid market imperfections. The reasons for which they choose multinational status are the same as those for which they become large-scale firms in one country. In order to reduce costs and inefficiency they prefer coordination.
- Market uncertainty: firms seek to secure access to inputs.
- Financial market imperfections: an increase in demand for a firm's products may not be followed by an increase in production by the firm for lack of inputs, because producers of raw materials may not have enough capital to increase production.
- Lack of information: sellers and buyers hide information to improve the terms of the contract, which leads to inefficient transactions.

When production of inputs takes place in highly concentrated industries, firms are more likely to pursue vertical integration. Direct investment abroad protects a firm against competition and helps it maximize the rents owing to its technological advantages and product differentiation. Horizontal expansion abroad is also justified by the need to avoid transportation costs and barriers to trade, and by the possibility of increasing its share of an industry (which may lead to oligopolistic rents).

From the host country's standpoint, several factors tend to encourage the entry of new firms:[28]

- The supply of local skilled people and capital increases as the country develops.
- The barriers introduced by economies of scale diminish in importance as the market grows.
- Local firms enter the industry when they see that the foreign investors have profits.

'The industries in which international operations occur are often those in which international trade was or is important.'[29] Firms make direct foreign investments to replace exports or to produce imports, when there is actual or potential trade. In fact, there is a direct relationship between trade and advantages. When a firm possesses an advantage in a certain activity, it may export the commodity that embodies its advantages. Trade can lead to further advantages because, through its exports, a firm may establish distribution channels or a differentiated product.[30] This was the pattern followed by many Spanish companies that invested in Latin America in the 1970s and 1980s. They invested to develop their own distribution networks to market their own products in Latin America. In other words, they decided to internalize the distribution process in that region.

Hymer concluded that:

- International operations may occur in those industries in which enterprises of different countries sell in the same market or sell to each other in conditions of imperfect competition. There may be collusion, mergers, profit-sharing agreements or competition. If there is interdependence, some form of accommodation will occur.[31]
- International operations may also occur in industries where some firms have advantages over other firms. When a single firm has a patent, it may use it through licensing (if there are many possible licensors) or more directly through FDI. More common is that several firms have the advantage. They may dominate their domestic markets and share the rest of the world markets. In industries where there is

great competition, FDI only takes place in LDCs, where local
entrepreneurs cannot raise enough funds to face capital investments.[32]

- Diversification across countries is followed in order to achieve greater
  stability in profits (to avoid the fluctuations of particular markets).[33]
- In some cases international operations do not occur for purely
  economic reasons or for lack of integration in the world economy.[34]

Product Cycle Theory

The product cycle theory emerged out of trade theory, but it emphasized
less the comparative cost doctrine and more the timing of innovation, the
effects of scale economies, and the roles of ignorance and uncertainty in
influencing trade patterns. The main advocate of this doctrine, developed in
the late 1960s, was Raymond Vernon. A key concept for him was
"knowledge". Although Vernon believed scientific knowledge is important,
he argued that it is equally accessible to firms in all advanced countries.
Therefore, he focused on knowledge about the needs of the market. He
explained that higher income in the United States and high unit labor costs
create the need to substitute capital for labor. Besides the hope for some
kind of monopoly revenue for the early starter justifies the initial
investment in research and product development. This need for innovation
is generated by the existence of effective communication between the
potential market and the potential supplier.[35]

In the early stages of production of a new good, the manufacturing
process is not standardized. At this stage there is need for considerable
communication between producers and consumers to perfect the product,
and production takes place close to the market. As the demand for that
product expands, a certain degree of standardization takes place while
efforts at product differentiation continue. Variety may appear as a result of
specialization. As the product is maturing, production becomes more
standardized, opening up the possibility for achieving economies of scale
through mass production. There is concern about reducing costs.[36]

When the product appears in the U.S. market, some limited demand
also exists in relatively advanced countries, such as those of Western
Europe. The demand in time will grow rapidly and U.S. producers will
eventually set up a production plant there, when the marginal production
cost plus the cost of transportation of the goods exported from the United
States becomes higher than the cost of prospective production in the market
of import.[37] However, calculation of production costs in a foreign market is
difficult because factor costs and technology are different from those at
home.

Once products and production processes become highly standardized, production moves to less developed countries, which offer lower labor and production costs. At this stage, the home country becomes a net importer of the product, production declines in other advanced countries (they will become net importers eventually) and production for export (as well as for the domestic market) increases in LDCs. Even though LDCs offer cheap labor costs from the beginning, production does not move there initially, because highly qualified labor is needed, in addition to a constant flow of communication between producers and consumers to improve the product and adapt it to the needs of the market.[38]

This theory concentrates purely on manufacturing multinationals and becomes inappropriate to explain the behavior of Spanish MNEs, which are mainly service sector firms. Spanish direct investment in Latin America financed the infrastructure needed for the development and provision of their services. There are cases, however, of Spanish MNEs that invest in Latin America to produce goods for local consumption or for export to third countries, either within Latin America or in North America. Nevertheless, the Spanish pattern bears little resemblance to the model described by Vernon. Production abroad for export back to the home market (Spain), as described by the product cycle theory, takes place in neighboring host countries, mainly Portugal and Morocco.

Location Theory

Raymond Vernon also developed location theory in the early 1970s. He observed that one of the basis on which MNEs built their oligopolistic strength is through the development and introduction of new products and the differentiation of existing ones. For this reason, MNEs invest great amounts of money in R&D. Two locational issues are very important in this regard:

1. The location of the processes of research and development themselves. The goal of industrial R&D is to create something that responds to a specified need at an economic price. In practice, it is necessary to provide swift and continuous communication among marketing specialists, production people, cost analysts and development engineers. This type of communication takes place more efficiently within a single firm than between firms. The implication is that there is a reason to internalize that process and a strong incentive to centralize it.[39] Every area specialist needs to be close to the others. Once grouped, they are more sensitive to the markets nearby (the domestic market),

and develop innovations with sensitivity to the conditions of the home market; i.e., U.S. firms specialize in innovations determined by high labor costs; European and Japanese corporations specialize in innovations that are material saving.

2. The location of production activities: the first production facility is normally a consequence of the development process itself, at a stage when communication among all the departments that are responsible for the innovation is still important. Factor costs are not considered at this stage because the innovator enjoys a period of "monopoly" (until imitators appear in the market). As competitors develop similar products, standardization follows and aggregate demand grows, factor costs become a major concern. Labor intensive products and relatively small economies of scale are the first to move abroad.[40]

Nevertheless, in many industries where MNEs play a leading role, the basis for the oligopoly is not product innovation, but the barriers to entry generated by scale in production, transportation or marketing. When oligopolies mature, the location of facilities is determined by the patterns of pricing and by the stratagems to maintain stability.[41] When a competitor invests in a new market, its rivals may feel that the status quo is being threatened and they will follow the leader and invest in that market too. This practice of risk-reduction explains investments in cases that comparative cost analyses would be unable to predict.[42]

MNEs have access to factors outside the national economy and face different initial costs associated with the application of different techniques of production. These two factors dampen the influence of other local factor costs, and concentrate production in areas whose cost configurations nearly correspond to the environments from which the MNE draws its technologies and its productive factors. When investing abroad, MNEs avoid existing clusters of facilities created by national companies, but they try to avoid remote areas of national economies. When a MNE considers the establishment of foreign plants, it measures the marginal impact of this subsidiary upon the enterprise as a whole. One of the main advantages of MNEs over national competitors is that they have access to cheaper factors that are located outside the national economy.[43]

Location theory bears many similarities with the product cycle theory. It is also very product-specific and views FDI as a function of the several stages of development of new products. Therefore, this model is also inappropriate to explain Spanish FDI in Latin America because it makes FDI a function of the product. On the contrary, Spanish FDI in Latin America shows that many other factors have to be considered. Many Spanish MNEs do not sell goods, but services. Therefore, they must have some infrastructure in the country where they want to operate. Their products are normally geared toward the domestic market. They do not export from the host to the home country, except in the cases of MNEs in the oil and energy sectors.

Theory of the Firm Approach

Out of the industrial organization approach emerged the theory of the firm, in the late 1970s. The theory of the firm puts the firm as the center-piece of its analysis and rejects industry-specific and broader approaches to FDI. The central concept is "internalization," that is to say, substitution of the firm for the market. Internalization theory originated with Ronald Coase in the 1930s but was first applied to international business by Stephen Hymer in the 1960s, who abandoned generalistic approaches that linked FDI to other market structures. Interest for internalization theory grew in the 1970s thanks to the work of scholars such as Mark Casson, John Dunning, Mira Wilkins and Oliver Williamson, among others.

Mark Casson emphasized the need to accept a few assumptions about transaction costs to make internalization theory operational: it is very difficult to license know-how, which leads to internalization of R&D activities; it is difficult to enforce long-term contracts, which causes backward internalization into production of raw materials; and *ad valorem* tariffs, international tax differentials and foreign exchange controls create incentives for transfer-pricing, which are most easily exploited through internalization. However, not all activities in which MNEs operate fulfill these conditions.[44]

As international organization scholars, theorists of the firm stress that in order to compete with indigenous firms, foreign entrants must have some compensating advantage. The advantage can be in technology, knowledge of products and processes, organizational structures or awareness of markets and sources of supply. These advantages are reflected in a trade name that identifies the firm's reputation and the quality of its output. In the case of the Spanish MNEs in Latin America, awareness of the markets is the key advantage. They knew what products and services were needed in developing economies and adapted their supply to the necessities of the Latin American economies.

Theorists of the firm also reject the notion of perfect markets. In a perfect market, companies would not make direct investments across borders because local firms would always be able to outcompete foreign entrants. There are four main areas of internationally transferable advantages resulting from imperfect competition that enable the foreign entrant to overcome its lack of knowledge of local conditions innate in the local firm:[45]

- Departures from perfect competition in goods markets, including product differentiation, marketing skills and administered pricing.
- Departures from perfect competition in factors markets, including access to patented or "proprietary" knowledge, discrimination in access to capital and skill differences embodied in the firm (particularly its management).
- Internal and external economies of scale, including those arising from vertical integration.
- Government intervention, particularly the forms restricting output or entry.

Firm theorists also stress that all market-making activities incur costs that can only be minimized through specialization: the exploitation of economies of scale generated by the increased utilization of purpose-designed indivisible assets, and from the concentration of resources on the activity in which a firm has comparative advantage.[46] Spanish MNEs utilize in Latin America the same services they provided in Spain. Banco Bilbao-Vizcaya, Banco Central Hispanoamericano and Banco de Santander applied in Latin America the same marketing techniques and services they had developed in Spain: aggressive advertising for the promotion of savings and checking accounts, gifts for the bearers of those accounts, etc. In other words, they developed techniques to promote banking services within a public with little bank culture.

Each transaction bears a risk that has to be shared between the buyer and the seller. Instead, each individual could hold a small share of the buyer's and seller's risk associated with all the transactions taking place by diversifying her portfolio of risk. Since individuals have different risk preferences, the least risk-averse individual should be the one to specialize in risk-bearing.[47]

Internalization is a response to imperfections in intermediate product markets that generate transaction costs. The minimization of costs occurs by bringing interdependent activities under common ownership and control. This explains why multi plant firms exist. A MNE is just a type of multi-plant firm.[48] Peter Buckley asserts that foreign direct investment is also a way of seeking diversification. MNEs seek two different types of diversification, product diversification and financial diversification (earning returns in a variety of currencies). Imperfections in the world financial market impede individuals from diversifying satisfactorily and reduce the optimal diversification of intermediaries. Thereby diversification through controlling interests is more efficient than a large number of smaller shareholdings. Transaction costs exist in the equity market in the form of costs of acquiring and disseminating the relevant mass of information, which results in the application by the market of a premium to the equity valuation of diversified firms. Managers may be averse to risk and prefer a diversified company with a higher degree of stability.[49]

Internalization of tangible intermediate product flows between upstream and downstream production in order to guarantee the quality of a firm's goods or in order to reduce transaction costs explains vertical integration between mining and manufacturing, agriculture and food-processing, component production and final assembly and marketing. The internalization of intangible flows of know-how leads to a combination of horizontal and vertical integration.[50] Telefonica's objective is to operate in all the major countries of Latin America in order to install its own fiber-optics infrastructure linking all the countries of South and Central America with North America, and thus internalize the cost of using existing infrastructure. Repsol began extracting oil in several Latin American countries to produce its own oil. By 1998 the company had to buy most of its oil from other oil MNEs.

Peter Buckley explains that the advantages of internalization are given by:[51]

1. 'The increased ability to control and plan production and in particular to co-ordinate flows of crucial inputs;
2. exploitation of market power by discriminating pricing;
3. avoidance of bilateral market power;
4. avoidance of uncertainties in the transfer of knowledge between parties which may exist in the alternative (market) solution;
5. avoidance of potential government intervention by devices such as transfer prices'.

Mark Casson mentions four reasons why a market-making MNE may operate in many different countries at once:[52]

1. There may be economies of scale in production which make it efficient to service several entire national markets from the same point.
2. The buyers of the product may be internationally mobile. They may travel frequently between countries. The existence of a single market-making firm offering its services reduces transaction costs.
3. The buyers of the product may wish to place orders in one location for supply at a different location. Part of the market-making service (contract-making, specification and negotiation) is effected in one

country and another part (exchange and monitoring) in the other country.

4. The firm has an internationally transferable absolute advantage in market-making. The link between the market-making branch plants in the different countries is a common dependence on the firm-specific market-making skills.

Mira Wilkins complements internalization theory with a five-parameter scheme that managers of MNE's follow when they make their investment decisions. Her model provides a more complete examination of the factors that make a firm invest abroad:

1. Opportunity parameter: MNEs expand where there are opportunities to sell and/or to obtain sources of supply. Expansion to sell is a case of market-oriented investment. The host country is seen as the principal market. The larger it is, the sooner it attracts investment. Expansion to obtain sources of supply is an instance of supply-oriented investment. In this case, the MNEs seek raw materials or cheap and disciplined labor. The major market is outside the host country. The managers of all Spanish MNEs with investments in Latin America emphasize the importance of this point. They saw big opportunities for business: growing domestic demand and lack of domestic and international competition.[53]

2. Political parameter: depending on the political circumstances in a particular country, the economic opportunity may or may not exist. This approach considers the nature of government activities, such as rules and regulations, ways of enforcing them, etc. Host government policies can be of three types, namely special treatment, reciprocity (between two countries), and national treatment (however, Wilkins believes that most policies are generally selective and often sectoral). Countries base their attitude toward MNEs on two fundamentals, power and wealth, and seek to maximize national security and economic wealth. The executives of Spanish MNEs believed the new political and economic framework adopted by Latin American governments created the appropriate conditions for investment. They also believed in the commitment of local politicians to push for economic reforms and to respect the privatization agreements and the new investment legislation.[54]

3. Familiarity parameter: the nearer to the home country from a physical standpoint, the greater the shared cultural values, the closer the political relationships, the more congenial the business arrangements, the earlier and greater will be the multinational's interests to invest in that

country. The costs of extending a firm rise as the entity operates under circumstances less familiar. Although Spanish executives emphasize that this factor is secondary to the previous two, they also acknowledged that cultural proximity to Spain made business and communication easier.[55]

4. Third-country parameter: what happens in neighboring third-countries may also have an impact on investment patterns. In most cases, Spanish MNEs invested in Latin America to serve the local market and neighboring economies. The case of Mexico was different. Some Spanish MNEs invested in Mexico after the signature of NAFTA to gain access to the North American markets, benefiting from a culturally familiar environment and lower production costs.[56]

5. Corporate parameter: based on the company's history, set of advantages, strategy and learning process, its managers perceive opportunities, judge political conditions and their firm's familiarity with other nations, and evaluate third-country considerations. Many of the MNEs investing in Latin America in the 1990s had already had investments in that region in the 1970s or had had trade relations. Moreover, the political transition from dictatorship to democratic rule experienced by most Latin American countries, as well as the gradual process of economic liberalization, contributed to increase the similarities between Spain and Latin America in the eyes of the Spanish executives.[57]

Wilkins concludes that a final temporal dimension provides an "overlay" because she believes the history of MNEs is a dynamic one and the conditions influencing them vary constantly. She draws a three-stage model that predicts the evolution of MNEs through time. In stage one a firm decides to invest abroad to sell or to obtain. The firm does not engage in a very complex set of activities. The chief executives of the parent company are involved in the establishment of the foreign subsidiaries and in their financing. The foreign subsidiaries have personnel consisting mainly of salesmen, accountants, and production managers and depend heavily on the parent firm for technology, engineering, product plans, R&D, and added imports (of machinery, components, and related final products). Over time, their functions begin to broaden, even though their operations are still closely monitored and approved by the parent. The subsidiaries begin to develop their own identities as more complete enterprises and may serve more than just the host nation market. Meanwhile, the parent company keeps expanding domestically and abroad, in new markets. An administrative organization to handle foreign operations may emerge, but the company keeps a monocentric structure.[58]

In stage two the foreign units develop their own separate histories and their own satellite activities and gain certain autonomy. Each major foreign unit takes larger functions, integrates its operations and introduces new products. It might expand out of reinvested profits or it might borrow. The management makes certain decisions independent of the parent. When the subsidiary decides to manufacture, it faces several options: licensing an independent foreign firm to manufacture within the host nation; manufacturing through its existing foreign sales units; or buying a foreign manufacturing plant in the same nation. While the MNE expands geographically or diversifies at home, it creates a new administrative structure: a central office and a multi divisional organization. It becomes a polycentric enterprise, characterized by its heterogeneous foreign centers.[59]

Stage three may come early after stage two or may be long delayed. The parent company continues its expansion abroad, starting new foreign units or buying foreign or domestic firms for production of its traditional products or for the marketing of new ones. At this point, the MNE has to accommodate: the parent company's units abroad; new units initiated abroad; new foreign units, representing new products and raw material needs of the expanding parent; companies acquired abroad and their foreign subsidiaries; and existing foreign subsidiaries and affiliates obtained as a consequence of domestic mergers. The polycentric industrial structure breaks down and a new conglomerate entangled structure is created.[60]

Most of the theory of the firm evolved out of the experience of U.S. MNEs (especially in the post-WWII period). Mira Wilkins warns that European and Japanese MNEs have some characteristics that differ from those of U.S. MNEs. For example, whereas U.S. firms learned and gained the advantage at home thanks to their large domestic market, European firms did not have a large market in their home countries (i.e. Nestlé, Match); in some cases they borrowed their "advantages" from firms in other countries (Swedish firms borrowed and extended German technology); whereas U.S. firms set up a plant in each country in stage one, European ones had more.[61]

Wilkins also points out the peculiar case of the British "free-standing" companies. These were British companies that had operations abroad but did not grow out of the domestic operations of existing enterprises headquartered in Britain. They were established to conduct business operations abroad, to manage and to direct a specific business. They were registered as joint-stock, limited liability companies. They had their own board of directors and stockholders, a memorandum of association and articles of association that defined corporate objectives and functions. Their capital was denominated in sterling. They operated in numerous countries, inside and outside the Empire, although initially they were headquartered in the United Kingdom and had operations in one single country. Each firm operated in a single economic sector (agriculture, mining, infrastructure and banking being the main ones, high-tech being the striking exception). They set up their operations through either greenfield investment or acquisition of an existing business.[62]

Their purpose was to obtain capital by bringing together profitable operations overseas, with British investors seeking financial opportunities superior to those at home. Their goal was to attract British and foreign savings and provided an institutional framework that minimized the costs of promotion, legal fees and other payments (which were estimated at 17-33 percent of the amount raised). They had liquidity (their securities were denominated in sterling, consequently they were easy to sell) and were charged by British laws with providing responsible management of capital. These two conditions gave them an advantage over their foreign competitors. The head office was limited to a corporate secretary and the board of directors.[63]

Their activities overlapped at times, which led to the formation of clusters (in order to decrease competition), whose internal connections were very weak: promoters (they played a key role by identifying opportunities to link British capital to overseas investments); investment trust companies; solicitors; accountants; Members of Parliament or other renown directors; geographical locations; mining engineers; non-mining industry networks; trading companies; and merchant banks. Each of these ten clusters had a functional relation to the company and emphasized units rather than packages. Only those free-standing companies that developed their own in-house managerial organizations were able to survive.[64]

Casson calls for a more encompassing theoretical framework to study MNEs and incorporates location theory to internalization theory. For this purpose, he clarifies the distinction between activities and markets on the one hand, and between facilities and linkages on the other:[65]

> A facility is location-specific, whereas an activity is not; a facility is a plant, while the activity is the function it performs... The transfer of resources between two plants is effected by a linkage. A collection of linkages involving the same product constitutes a market. A perfect market contains a large number of linkages. Most markets for intermediate products are imperfect: they contain a modest number of linkages, few of which are perfect substitutes of each other.

Each linkage is embedded in a broader system of linkages. The limitations of the patent system encourage internalization of activities as a strategy to secure secrecy over managerial know-how and to avoid quality uncertainty. These drawbacks provide a strong argument for internalization of the whole system of linkages, due to lack of trust among the contracting units.

Internalization is not a specifically "international business" principle. It first takes place in markets that the firm knows very well. That is why internalization normally takes place in the domestic market first. It can occur through greenfield investment or through acquisition of another firm. The former is more likely when a firm has a distinctive corporate culture. The later becomes unlikely when the expertise of the firm to be bought is difficult to value.[66] Casson defends the dynamic nature of internalization as a principle to explain investment flows. The basis for internalization exists when there is market failure caused by barriers to trade, high transaction costs or because the economies of interdependent activities cannot be fully captured (structural market failure); when there is lack of information about the product (cognitive market failure); or when public intervention distorts the allocation of resources.[67] Through internalization firms can achieve upstream or downstream collusion (market power).

Casson affirms that the transaction cost approach can also explain market strategy and organizational structure. The competitive advantage in the service sector does not stem from a physical attribute of the product, but from superior "standard of service", defined by Casson as better intermediation. This standard of service comprises ease of access, simple specification (no catches about the contract being negotiated), easy negotiation (widely advertised price which is kept fairly stable), and immediate guaranteed delivery and ready enforcement (through a low-cost system of arbitration).[68]

Ownership-Location-Internalization Model (OLI)

When developing the OLI model in the 1980s, John Dunning made an eclectic effort to bring together the coinciding points of several theories. He perceived a growing convergence between the theories of international trade and production and argued that there exists a case for an integrated approach based on the location-specific (or comparative) advantages of countries and the ownership-specific (or competitive) advantages of enterprises. He then developed a systematic explanation of the foreign activities of enterprises in terms of their ability to internalize markets to their advantage.[69]

The capacity of an enterprise to supply a market depends on its possessing certain assets not available to other enterprises. These assets must be capable of generating a future income stream. They can be tangible assets such as natural resources, capital or manpower, or intangible assets, such as knowledge, organizational and entrepreneurial skills and access to intermediate and final goods markets. Such assets could be location-specific in their origin and use (such as resource endowment or the legal, social and commercial environment), or firm-specific, but capable of being used with other resources, such as a legally protected right, or a commercial monopoly.[70]

In some kinds of trade, it is sufficient for the exporting country to have a location-endowment advantage over the importing country. Much of the trade occurring between industrialized and non-industrialized countries is of this kind. The type of trade that takes place mainly between developed countries is of high skill-intensive consumer goods, and is based more on ownership advantages of the exporting firms. The extent to which a MNE engages in foreign production depends on their comparative ownership advantages *vis-à-vis* host country firms, and the comparative location endowments of home and foreign countries.

Ownership-specific advantages are internal to particular enterprises and consist of tangible and intangible resources, such as technology. Dunning distinguishes three types:[71]

1. Monopoly power: access to markets or raw materials not available to competitors; size; and resource capability and usage, such as exclusive possession of intangible assets like patents, trademarks, and management skills, which enable the firm to reach a higher level of technical efficiency and achieve more market power.
2. Ability to co-ordinate the interaction between separate but complementary activities better than other organizational mechanisms, like easier access to financing and resources over a *de novo* enterprise.
3. The ability of the enterprise to adapt to different business environments. This advantage may be a function of the firm's need to operate in a large number of different economic milieus, and facilitates its capacity to take advantage of different country-specific characteristics and risk profiles.

John Dunning agrees with Ronald Coase and the industrial organization school that the growth of firms can be best explained by their efficiency as transaction organizers *vis-à-vis* the market. Relating this thesis to the concept of ownership advantages, Dunning concludes that the propensity of enterprises to engage in FDI is attributable not only to their possession of superior resources, including their ability to internalize markets, but also to their willingness to undertake further value-adding activities embodying these assets. Besides, depending on the firm's reason for internalization, not only do they gain, others may lose, giving way to market concentration.[72]

However, Dunning does not consider other factors external to the firm and to the products they developed. The political and economic environments are fundamental for a firm when deciding where to invest. Mira Wilkins' five parameter model provides a good assessment of the internal and external factors that guide a firms investment decisions.

Alliance Theory

The theory of economies of scale began to provide theoretical arguments against the neoclassical assumption that perfect competition is desirable. The development of economies of scale reduces the number of firms competing in the market. However, the costs of production fall as the number of goods produced increases. As sales increase, firms gain extra revenue that can be used to develop new technologies in order to increase productivity and lower production costs even further. Therefore, a small number of firms competing in a market may lower prices more than many firms competing under conditions of perfect competition.

Alliance theory provides support for this kind of argument. Benjamin Gomes-Casseres gives a good example of the benefits that a situation of non-perfect competition can bring about, in terms of productivity and product innovation. He argues that alliances do not suppress business rivalry. Rather, they transform it and make it more virulent, by increasing the number of competitors of similar capabilities, therefore causing prices to fall. Alliances give way to a new type of competition: "collective competition". He defines an alliance as a '...governance structure involving an incomplete contract between separate firms and in which each partner has limited control'.[73]

Alliances are not the unit of competition, but the links between firms in a constellation. Constellations are varied. Sometimes there are ownership ties, sometimes only contractual agreements, involving all the firms together with a central firm. All of them may be allied to each other. Or all may adhere to a common agreement. Sometimes the constellations consist of a firm that invests in another, and sometimes two or more firms invest in a separate joint-venture. The degree of involvement also varies. Some members are "silent" financial investors and others continually provide technology, production capacity and market access to their partners.[74]

However, in all those cases the firms are bound by various arrangements to compete collectively as one entity. The degree of internal organization that firms achieve within their alliance determines the behavior and performance of the group as a whole. The individual performance of each firm within the alliance is influenced by the organization of the alliance. Constellations become the optimal form of organization under three conditions:[75]

1. There is an advantage to combining the capabilities of two or more firms.
2. It would be costly or impossible to combine the capabilities through pure market transactions.
3. A full merger between the firms must be costlier than a series of alliances as a way to govern the incomplete contracts.

Like Stephen Hymer, Gomes-Casseres explains that alliances are ways of governing incomplete contracts between economic actors. No one firm has complete authority and a process of internal negotiation is always taking place. Firms and alliances are different organizational units that seek to control and organize a set of capabilities so as to maximize their return. Three factors define constellations, identifying their strengths and weaknesses:[76]

1. Capabilities: set of tangible and intangible assets that enable an organization to develop, make and market goods and services.
2. Control: authority of a decision-maker in using and deploying these capabilities.
3. Context: the environment that places demands and creates opportunities for the organization.

The flexibility of their combined capabilities gives alliances two types of competitive advantages:[77]

- Static: they are better equipped than firms to combine inputs from a diverse set of capabilities. Alliances encourage specialization of the member firms.
- Dynamic: they are better equipped than firms to pursue changing opportunities by adjusting their sets of capabilities over time.

The determinants of the spread of alliances in an industry are the pursuit of first mover advantages of scale, scope, and standards, imitation of rival groups in order to reduce the risk of falling behind, and efforts to preempt rivals from linking up with attractive partners. These are external to the constellation. The main internal factor is synergy or the exploitation of complementary capabilities, which leads to specialization. The spread of alliances is limited by a series of factors external to the constellation: scarcity of partners, and the diminishing number of partners with desirable capabilities as alliances grow. Internal determinants are the increasing demands on management to monitor the process of expansion of the constellation; the rising costs of coordination; and rising dependence on the allies (firms have to share control over operations and returns on investment).[78]

Alliance theory provides another useful theoretical tool to pursue the study of Spanish direct investment in Latin America in the 1990s. Many of the main Spanish MNEs that invested in the region in the 1990s formed alliances with other Spanish firms to develop common Latin American ventures. In some cases, firms in an alliance have investments in each other, and both decide to coordinate their operations. Two banks, Banco Bilbao-Vizcaya and La Caixa, were stockholders of both Repsol (oil company) and Gas Natural (gas producer and distributor). Both banks collaborated with these two companies in their expansion in Latin America, by providing funding and by sharing their knowledge of the markets. At a later stage, all four companies collaborated in the creation of a joint-venture to coordinate the operations of both Repsol and Gas Natural in the gas sector in Latin America. The joint-venture was called Gas Natural Latinoamericana. Similarly, Banco Central Hispanoamericano was a stockholder of Endesa and Unión Fenosa, two electricity companies. The bank also provided financial support for both companies when they invested in Latin America.

Nevertheless, Gomes-Casseres constrains his analysis of alliances to firms within the same industry. Spanish MNEs signed collaboration agreements with other firms from the same industry, but this was not always the case. Telefonica, the Spanish telephone multinational corporation, signed an agreement with AT&T and several European telecommunications companies in 1996. In 1997 it broke that agreement to create a new alliance with British Telecom, MCI, and Portugal Telecom. The acquisition of MCI by WorldCom made Telefonica renegotiate the previous agreement, breaking its ties with British Telecom, and reinforcing its alliance with MCI, WorldCom and Portugal Telecom. Banco Central Hispanoamericano's ventures in Latin America were the result of an alliance with Chile's Banco O'Higgins. Endesa and Unión Fenosa, on the one hand, and Repsol and Gas Natural on the other, were cases of same-industry alliances between Spanish MNEs in the energy sector. The alliance between Dragados y Construcciones and Fomento de Construcciones y Contratas was another example of same-industry alliance, in this case in the road construction sector.

The Spanish banks played a critical leading role in the expansion of Spanish MNEs in Latin America. Their successful experience in the early 1990s worked as a stimulus for companies from the energy sector to invest in Latin America. The banks realized there were great opportunities for business in the energy sector in Latin America and, using the power of decision given by the stocks they held in these firms, argued from within them to start new ventures in the Western Hemisphere. The banks contributed with their expertise and financial resources, and gained a share of the profits generated by the new investment, proportional to the amount of stocks they held.

Conclusion

International economics and international trade provided in the 1950s the sole theoretical basis to judge MNE behavior. International economics attributed MNEs the role of arbitragers of equity capital from countries where its return is low to countries where it is high. International trade stated that the emergence of MNEs was a function of the distribution of endowments across countries.[79] On the one hand, international economics failed to explain why MNEs invest in countries and activities that generate low returns, instead of investing in other economic areas and countries where the returns are higher. On the other, international trade did not predict the emergence of MNEs in the same industry in countries with different factor endowments.

Stephen Hymer was the first to prove in the 1960s that these models bore some inconsistencies with the actual pattern of behavior followed by multinationals. The industrial organization approach highlighted that MNEs operate like domestic firms. The only difference between the two of them is the geographical scope of their operations. Hymer resuscitated the concept of "internalization", used by Ronald Coase in the 1930s. Firms substitute for the market. They internalize several stages of production into the firm's structures (those that the market does not price properly) as long as the cost of doing so is lower than the cost of dealing with outsiders in an arm's length basis. The concept of "control" also became crucial in Hymer's discourse: control over new operations in order to ensure the safety of an investment made to exploit a firm's advantage; control in order to remove competition from the market; and control over related industrial activities, when the firm seeks diversification.[80] One of Hymer's great contributions was rather methodological. He put the firm as the centerpiece of the analysis of MNEs, and laid the foundations for later approaches to MNEs. Hymer's theory serves as the point of departure for this analysis of Spanish MNEs in Latin America.

Raymon Vernon provided a new approach in the late 1960s. According to the "product cycle theory" that he developed, those countries that have comparative advantage develop certain products, which can later be exploited on a worldwide basis. For Vernon, "knowledge" is the factor that determines the comparative advantage of firms: knowledge about the market and about the needs and demands of that market. When a product is devised, a gradual process of standardization begins. Once the manufacturing process is fully standardized, it moves to that location where production costs are lower. Product cycle theory was a dynamic one. However, Vernon's approach was not firm specific and was very focused on the U.S. market.

"Location theory" contributed by analyzing the cost structures of where facilities are located. Vernon also explained that when a new product is being designed, proximity to the market is crucial, because there is a great need for rapid and constant communication between the market and the firm. He concluded that there is a strong incentive for the firm to internalize all the processes involved in the design and marketing of a new product, as well as to centralize them in a location close to the market.[81] When the product is broadly accepted by consumers and demand increases significantly, a need to centralize production arises, in order to develop economies of scale.

"The theory of the firm" approach evolved out of Hymer's thesis in the 1970s. Theory of the firm based its approach on key concepts such as internalization, comparative advantage, transaction costs, hierarchy, contracts and imperfect markets. These concepts illustrate the analysis of the expansion of Spanish MNEs in Latin America in the 1990s (Spanish energy MNEs internalized the production stage in order to avoid the transaction costs of dealing with suppliers for their Spanish market). The point of departure is the rejection of the undisputed desirability of perfect competition in the market. This theory accepts that markets are imperfect (lack of optimal information illuminating every transaction) and when firms deal with outsiders (producers of raw materials and components as well as retailers) there are some transaction costs involved.[82]

Casson underlined that firms get involved in FDI to exploit their advantage in a particular industry. They have an advantage in terms of access to resources, markets, technology, management, and more. When the costs of exploiting their advantage on a contractual basis with outsiders are lower than the returns, the firm might decide to license. However, when the transaction costs are very high, the firm will decide to invest and exploit its advantage itself: when the firm cannot fully capture the returns on its advantage, it decides to internalize those activities that the market fails to price correctly, due to imperfections.[83] By doing so the firm retains control over prices. This approach is applicable to both firms operating solely in a domestic market, as well as to MNEs. Mira Wilkins provided specific guidelines that explained the investment behavior of multinationals. She devised five parameters that helped predict FDI: opportunity, political, familiarity, third-country and corporate parameter. Finally, Wilkins explained that the foreign subsidiaries of MNEs gain more autonomy over time and develop their own multinational activities with a higher degree of independence.[84]

Theory of the firm and industrial organization seem more appropriate for predicting the behavior of MNEs, since they put firms in the forefront of their analysis. Earlier approaches such as international economics, international trade and product cycle gave MNEs a very passive role. International economics viewed multinationals as instruments of capital (arbitragers of equity capital). International trade and product cycle considered MNEs a natural consequence of some given structures (distribution of endowments). All three approaches suggest that the autonomy of multinationals is limited, in a highly deterministic way, by certain physical and economic structures. Theory of the firm and industrial organization, on the contrary, gave firms full autonomy. They recognize the dynamic nature of MNEs and FDI and provide the tools to analyze and predict the degree of a firm's integration into backward or downward productive activities.

Many scholars denounce that these two approaches disregard the service sector and concentrate on industrial activities. However, as will be shown in this book, theory of the firm can equally explain backward and downward integration of service activities, as well as FDI in the service sector. They discriminate in terms of the actor (they narrow the scope of their analysis into one single actor, the firm) but not in terms of areas of economic activity.

John Dunning called for a more eclectic paradigm in the 1980s and devised the OLI model (ownership, location, internalization), which he constructed with contributions from earlier theories. He asserts that firms must have ownership-specific advantages embodied in assets not available to other enterprises, such as knowledge, technology, management techniques, or skills. The growth of a firm depends on its efficiency as transaction organizer *vis-à-vis* the market (degree of internalization) and its willingness to develop further value-adding activities. The extent to which a firm gets involved in FDI depends on the comparative location endowments of a MNE, *vis-à-vis* firms in the domestic market.[85] Although Dunning does not come up with an original contribution, the main value of his thesis is the proposition that many factors have to be considered when explaining the behavior of MNEs.

Finally, Benjamin Gomes-Casseres provided a new and useful theoretical framework to illuminate the study of the expansion of Spanish

MNEs in Latin America in the 1990s. He analyzed the virtues of strategic cooperation among firms, which the Spanish firms discovered by cooperating among themselves in their Latin American ventures. Contrary to neoclassical economists, who denounced the "malign" effects of non-perfect competition on consumers and long-term productivity and economic growth, Gomes-Casseres provided evidence that cooperation among firms makes competition fiercer against third parties. He argued that by signing alliances and creating constellations, firms can gain competitiveness, because cooperation within an alliance gives firms the advantage of "flexible capabilities" On the one hand, firms derive static advantages from alliances, in the sense that they pool resources and are better equipped than firms operating alone. On the other, cooperation gives them dynamic advantages, because they are better equipped to pursue changing opportunities by adjusting their set of capabilities over time.[86]

Overall, internal cooperation within a constellation gives firms an incentive to specialize in those activities that they perform better. In the long run, more specialization increases their individual productivity and, in turn, that of the constellation. Although Gomes-Casseres concluded that alliances are created with a specific purpose, his approach is more general than those provided by the product-cycle theory and location theory, which are too product-centered. Alliance theory, however, considers many factors that intervene and influence the decision of firms to cooperate: organization of capabilities, control over authority, and the context in which firms operate.

Notes

[1]   Richard E. Caves, *Multinational Enterprise and Economic Analysis* (second edition), Cambridge University Press, New York, 1996, p. 24.

[2]   Ibid., p. 24.

[3]   Ibid., p. 25.

[4]   Ibid., p. 37.

[5]   Ibid., p. 37.

[6]   Ibid., p. 39.

[7]   Ibid., p. 25.

[8]   Ibid., p. 25.

[9]   Ibid., p. 25.

[10]   After Hymer wrote his doctoral dissertation, his theoretical contributions to the theory of MNEs took on a more Marxian perspective. Some of Hymer's theories expressed in this fragment were taken from Stephen H. Hymer, "On Multinational Corporations and Foreign Direct Investment", in John H. Dunning (ed.), *The Theory of Transnational Corporations* (Vol. 1), United Nations Library on Transnational Corporations, New

York, 1993, pp. 23-43. This article was originally written in 1971 and was included in this collection of articles about MNEs edited by John Dunning and published by the United Nations.

[11] Ibid., p. 23.
[12] Ibid., p. 24.
[13] Ibid., p. 24.
[14] Stephen H. Hymer, *The International Operations of National Firms: a Study of Direct Foreign Investment*, The MIT Press, Cambridge, 1976, p. 19.
[15] Ibid., p. 23.
[16] Ibid., pp. 23-24.
[17] Ibid., pp. 25-26.
[18] Ibid., pp. 27-29.
[19] Ibid., p. 37.
[20] Ibid., pp. 41-43.
[21] Ibid., p. 40.
[22] Telefonica changed its official name in 1999 from "Telefónica" to "Telefonica". The firm's executives decided to eliminate the accent as part of Telefonica's expansion strategy into non-Spanish speaking countries.
[23] Stephen H. Hymer, *The International Operations...*, p. 48.
[24] Stephen H. Hymer, "On Multinational Corporations...", pp. 32-33.
[25] Ibid., p. 35.
[26] Ibid., pp. 35-37.
[27] Ibid., pp. 37-39.
[28] Stephen H. Hymer, *The International Operations...*, p. 75.
[29] Ibid., pp. 79-80.
[30] Ibid., pp. 81-83.
[31] Ibid., pp. 91-92.
[32] Ibid., pp. 92-94.
[33] Ibid., p. 95.
[34] Ibid., p. 95.
[35] Raymond Vernon, "International Investment and International Trade in the Product Cycle", in John H. Dunning (ed.), *The Theory of Transnational Corporations*, p. 45.
[36] Ibid., pp. 47-48.
[37] Ibid., p. 49.
[38] Ibid., pp. 53-55.
[39] Raymond Vernon, "The Location of Economic Activity", in John H. Dunning (ed.), *Economic Analysis and the Multinational Enterprise*, Praeger Publishers, New York, 1974, p. 93.
[40] Ibid., pp. 94-96.
[41] Ibid., pp. 97-100.
[42] Ibid., pp. 102-104.
[43] Ibid., pp. 111-112.
[44] Mark Casson, "Transaction Costs and the Theory of the Multinational Enterprise", in P. J. Buckley and Mark Casson (eds.), *The Economic Theory of Multinational Enterprise*, St. Martin's Press, New York, 1985, p. 20.
[45] P. J. Buckley, "A Critical View of Theories of the Multinational Enterprise", in P. J. Buckley and Mark Casson (eds.), *The Economic Theory...*, p. 2.
[46] Mark Casson, "Transaction Costs...", p. 23.
[47] Ibid., p. 26.

[48] Mark Casson, "Internationalization Theory and Beyond", in John H. Dunning (ed.), *The Theory of Transnational Corporations*, p. 361.

[49] P. J. Buckley, "A Critical View of Theories of the Multinational Enterprise", in P. J. Buckley and M. Casson (eds.), *The Economic Theory...*, pp. 11-12.

[50] Mark Casson, "Entrepreneurship and the Dynamics of Foreign Direct Investment", in Peter J. Buckley and Mark Casson (eds.), *The Economic Theory...*, pp. 186-190.

[51] Ibid., p. 10.

[52] Mark Casson, "Transaction Costs...", pp. 32-33.

[53] Mira Wilkins, "The Evolution of Manufacturing Multinational Enterprise", in Tamás Szmrecsányi and Ricardo Maranhão (eds.), *História de Empresas e Desenvolvimento Econômico*, Editora Hucitec, São Paulo, 1996, p. 99.

[54] Ibid., p. 100.

[55] Ibid.

[56] Ibid.

[57] Ibid., pp. 100-101.

[58] Ibid., pp. 77-78, 101-103.

[59] Ibid., pp. 78-79.

[60] Ibid., pp. 79-82.

[61] Ibid., p. 86.

[62] Mira Wilkins, "The Free-Standing Company, 1870-1914: an Important Type of British Foreign Direct Investment", *Economic History Review*, 2nd series XLI, 1988, p. 262.

[63] Ibid., p. 263.

[64] Mira Wilkins provides a very detailed analysis of the contribution of each of these actors to the free-standing companies in "The Free-Standing Company...", pp. 265-270.

[65] Mark Casson, "Internationalization Theory and Beyond", p. 362.

[66] John H. Dunning, "Trade, Location of Economic Activity and the Multinational Enterprise: A Search for an Eclectic Approach", in John H. Dunning (ed.), *The Theory of Transnational Corporations...*, p. 193; and Mark Casson, "Internationalization Theory and Beyond", pp. 371-372.

[67] Peter J. Buckley, "A Critical View...", p. 14.

[68] Mark Casson, "Internationalization Theory and Beyond", p. 377.

[69] John H. Dunning, "Trade, Location of Economic Activity", p. 190.

[70] Ibid., p. 191.

[71] Ibid.

[72] Ibid., p. 192.

[73] Benjamin Gomes-Casseres, *The Alliance Revolution. The New Shape of Business Rivalry*, Harvard University Press, Cambridge (Massachusetts), 1996, p. 34.

[74] Ibid., p. 36.

[75] Ibid., p. 38.

[76] Ibid., pp. 30-31.

[77] Ibid., p. 44.

[78] For a detailed analysis of these factors, see discussion on pages 142-166.

[79] Richard E. Caves, *Multinational Enterprise...*, p. 24.

[80] Stephen J. Hymer, "On Multinational Corporations...", pp. 24-27.

[81] Raymond Vernon, "The Location of Economic Activity", pp. 94-96.

[82] Stephen H. Hymer, "On Multinational Corporations...", p. 31.

[83] Mark Casson, "Internationalization Theory and Beyond", p. 361.

[84] Mira Wilkins, "The Evolution...", pp. 99-101.

[85] John H. Dunning, "Trade, Location of Economic Activity...", pp. 191-192.
[86] Benjamin Gomes-Casseres, *The Alliance Revolution*, p. 44.

4 Structural Reform in Latin America and the Caribbean: The New Role of FDI

Introduction

Structural reform in Latin America and the Caribbean was one of the main determinants that led to large amounts of Spanish foreign direct investment. Large fiscal deficits, state involvement in production activities, and legal constraints for foreign investors, reduced the attractiveness of these markets for foreign investors. Fiscal deficits promoted governments to print money to finance their debt, which increased inflation (inflation tax). High inflation rates made the returns on investment very unpredictable. To fight inflation, interest rates were raised, decreasing economic activity. The economic performance of state-owned companies was quite poor and contributed to the increase in government deficit. Besides, state companies failed to invest in innovation to raise productivity rates. The incentives to increase economic productivity were scarce, leading most economies into stagnation. Low growth rates, coupled with a debt crisis that broke out in 1982, made foreign investors take their money out of Latin America in the search for safer and faster-growing economies (both portfolio and direct investment).

Gradually, Latin American governments corrected these economic ills through a comprehensive package of deep structural reforms, to regain positive rates of growth. Governments tried to reduce state deficits and, given the low rates of domestic savings, they tried to attract foreign capital too. A new treatment of foreign capital was applied. Reformers realized foreign direct investment was necessary, not only to supplement domestic capital, but also in order to attract competitive firms, capable of generating high value added and eager to increase productivity rates.

Overall, national policies toward FDI have to be viewed in a broad political, economic and social context. The wave of economic liberalization in the 1980s and 1990s was a response to the fiscal crisis that Latin

American governments experienced in the 1970s and 1980s. The crisis triggered a questioning of the development strategies followed by these countries in the post-war years. After the Great Depression of the 1930s, development economics provided strong theoretical support for state involvement in the economy. John Maynard Keynes's approach to the crisis in the 1930s accelerated growth by increasing government expenditures. He believed higher rates of public spending would set a virtuous cycle in motion, increasing overall consumption, which in turn would stimulate economic growth. A new discipline based on these Keynesian premises emerged within economics, "development economics", which took deep roots in Latin America. Advocates of development economics believed that orthodox economics could only be applied under conditions of full employment. Lack of entrepreneurship for large ventures called for a deliberate and intensive guided effort, a "big push", which would accelerate late industrialization.[1]

These policies were very appealing to both the Latin American right and left and, for several decades, provided the theoretical justification for economic populism. After W.W. II, Latin American governments tried to stimulate growth by increasing their expenditures. Many of the public enterprises privatized in the 1990s were nationalized by governments in the 1940s, 1950s, 1960s, and 1970s. Politicians deemed some industries strategic: electric power, air transportation, telecommunications, steel and petroleum were nationalized. Important capital-intensive industries were created and industrialization, overall, grew rapidly (Mexico had rates of industrialization of 8 percent annually in the 1950s).[2] Latin American politicians realized the potential of MNEs to introduce in their countries new technologies, products and efficient marketing techniques, as well as to develop new industries. They also realized the capacity of MNEs to generate cash through the production of goods for export. Thus, in the midst of a period dominated by import-substitution industrialization, they encouraged investments made by foreign companies in those fields that facilitated technology transfers, the development of new industrial activities, and local production for export, through a series of tax breaks and subsidies.

However, the import-substitution development model was feeding some inconsistencies. The industries created by governments were quite capital intensive. Latin American countries had high rates of rural underemployment and urban unemployment, which would have made the adoption of labor-intensive industries more reasonable. As a consequence, employment did not grow considerably, while the population grew rapidly. State enterprises did not face a budget constraint, because their losses were systematically subsidized. Therefore, they did not invest in R&D and their productivity fell over time, decreasing their competitiveness and that of other related industries. Existing private firms did not invest either, because trade barriers protected them against foreign competition and guaranteed them a very large share of the national market. Instead, they engaged in rent-seeking activities to try to gain prerogatives from the government. The productivity of domestic firms fell over time, and in the 1980s economic growth came to a slowdown.[3]

Even though Latin American countries developed important industries, production was generally geared toward the domestic market between the 1950s and the 1970s, because local firms were not competitive in international markets. Most countries remained exporters of raw materials and agricultural goods, while importing capital goods and technology for the local industrial ventures. In the 1950s, economists Raúl Prebish and Hans Singer developed a model that would provide theoretical support for further state intervention in the economy: "Dependency". Prebish and Singer observed that, in the absence of industrialization, a secular deterioration in the international price of raw materials and commodities would result in an ever-widening gap between rich and poor nations. Underemployment in the periphery was creating "unlimited supplies of labor" in the subsistence sector that depressed the real wage throughout the economy. This caused that any gains from productivity increases in the export sector would be likely to accrue to the importing country.[4]

Prebish and Singer concluded that, in order to industrialize, the smaller countries required temporary assistance in the form of protection of the newly emerging manufacturing sectors. Prebish denounced outward orientation because he believed it would never permit full economic development. Instead, he argued that development would involve industrialization through import substitution, which could be stimulated by a "moderate and selective protection policy".[5] Some heavy industries were created with large sums of public investment and protectionism against foreign competition through tariffs on imports and overvalued exchange rates. Eventually, the degree of protectionism increased and expanded to more sectors.

Excessive state protectionism eliminated foreign competition and national firms lost the incentive to invest in R&D, thus their productivity and competitiveness fell considerably. Too much government expenditure led to accumulated deficits and the public debt drained resources away from the private sector. As a result, private investment decreased. In the late 1960s, most of the substitutions of imported goods had taken place and the model was running into difficulties. As economic growth decreased in the late 1970s, some economists began to call for orthodox-type stabilization programs. Dependentists argued that there was still too little government presence in economic decisions and fostered full-fledged Eastern European style planning.[6] Two main differences characterize dependency from the earlier model of development economics: the degree of openness to foreign competition and the degree of involvement of the government in the national economy. Whereas dependentists almost closed national markets to those foreign products that could be produced domestically, development economics believed some kind of foreign competition was beneficial. Besides, the latter defended government investment in those industries where the private sector was not investing, whereas dependency extended the role of the government to an almost totally centralized model of allocation of resources.

Dependency theory impregnated the development strategies of Latin American states in the 1960s and 1970s. However, import-substitution had reached its limits and the rates of economic growth were decreasing. Those industries that grew under protectionism saw how domestic markets were too small to keep generating profits. In the 1960s, Latin American leaders realized that a larger market would help their firms develop economies of scale. Nevertheless, they were not willing to grant North American and European goods free entry to their markets for fear that they would be more competitive than local products.[7]

Instead, efforts for regional integration prevailed and crystallized in the formation of the Latin American Free Trade Area (LAFTA) in 1960 (Argentina, Brazil, Chile, Mexico, Paraguay, Peru and Uruguay), the Central American Common Market (CACM) in 1960 (Costa Rica, El Salvador, Guatemala, Honduras, and Nicaragua), the Caribbean Free Trade Area (Caricom) in 1968, and the Andean Group in 1969 (Bolivia, Chile, Colombia, Ecuador, Peru and Venezuela). All these countries had similar levels of development and the relationships among their firms would be more symmetrical than those between local ones and those from developed countries. Latin governments saw capital inflows from neighboring Latin American countries as a viable alternative to supplement the low rates of domestic saving and investment. However, capital inflows came mainly from multinational institutions rather than private capital. The oil crisis accelerated public borrowing and the role of the state in the economy increased in the 1970s. Inefficient public companies, large public deficits, and the small role of the private sector in production, led to an economic slowdown.

In the 1980s, Latin America went through the worst economic crisis in its history. Economic growth stagnated and inflation reached five-digit figures. Two alternative approaches to the crisis were suggested: the neo-liberal, orthodox or "Washington approach", which called for market-oriented reforms; and the pragmatic or heterodox approach, which evolved out of the dependency school. Not only did they call for different policies and structural reforms, their understanding of the causes and nature of the crisis were also different.

The Orthodox Approach

The orthodox approach was also called "Washington approach", or the "Washington consensus", because its views were shared by multilateral agencies in Washington, the Federal Reserve, the U.S. Treasury, the finance ministers of the G-7 countries, and the chairmen of the twenty most important commercial banks. The origins of this approach lay in the crisis of development economics. As those countries that pursued government-led development strategies failed to achieve significant rates of economic growth in the late 1970s, a new consensus emerged, stressing that the causes of this failure were fundamentally two: (1) excessive state intervention manifested through protectionism, overregulation and an oversized public sector and (2) economic populism or fiscal laxity that translated into the unwillingness to eliminate the budget deficit.

To overcome the crisis, the orthodox approach recommended ten measures, geared toward increasing the role of the market in the allocation of resources: (1) fiscal discipline to eliminate the budget deficit; (2) state expenditures should emphasize education and health rather than subsidies; (3) tax reform to broaden the tax base; (4) interest rates should be determined by the market; (5) free fluctuation of the currency; (6) barriers to trade should be eliminated; (7) eliminate restrictions on inward direct investment; (8) privatization of state-owned enterprises; (9) deregulation of economic activities; and (10) property rights should be made more secure.[8] All these measures can be summarized into two:

- Stabilization by orthodox fiscal and monetary policies, where the market performs the major role.
- Diminution of the role of the state.

The orthodox approach assumed that economic growth would resume once all these reforms were implemented.

Heterodox Approach

The heterodox or pragmatic approach evolved from dependency theory. The main difference between the two is that dependency took the causes of underdevelopment to be structural, whereas the heterodox approach assumed that they were strategic. Its interpretation of the fiscal crisis was radically different from that of the "Washington consensus". It emphasized the positive role played by the state in Latin America between the 1930s and the 1970s in structuring national self-interest and in promoting economic development, when one of the main forces of growth was public savings. Unlike orthodox theorists, the pragmatists believed the fiscal crisis was a structural phenomenon. It was the result of the excessive foreign indebtedness of the 1970s, on the one hand, and the tardiness in substituting an outward-oriented development strategy for the import-substitution strategy, on the other. As a result, the state became unable to perform its traditional role of complementing the market and coordinating the economy.[9]

Unlike orthodox economists, pragmatists believed that the cause of the fiscal crisis was not economic populism, but the decision of taking on an enormous foreign debt in the 1970s (predominantly by military regimes). In other words, the cause was excessive borrowing in international markets. The state was then unable to finance its debt through taxes because the tax system in Latin America was quite inefficient. Wealthy people did not pay taxes, the tax rate was low and most taxes were generally indirect. Since W.W.II, the state had tried to solve its lack of resources through export taxes first, then through indirect taxes and finally, in the 1970s, through foreign debt.[10]

Even though the heterodox approach acknowledged that stabilization and a reduction of the role of the state were necessary, emphasized that these two measures were not sufficient. It was also necessary to solve the fiscal crisis and recover the savings capacity of the state and to define a new strategy of growth in which the state should play an important role.[11] Stabilization involved controlling inflation and the balance of payments. Since prices and wages tended to be informally indexed in Latin America, high inflation had a chronic character. Price-control mechanisms should then include wages and price policies. The heterodox approach coincided with the orthodox approach in the need to control balance-of-payments imbalances, which required restrictive fiscal and monetary policies, and in the necessity to reduce the degree of state involvement in the economy, which should be pursued through privatization of state-owned enterprises, trade liberalization, and deregulation.[12]

Heterodox theorists believed a tax reform was necessary to recuperate public savings. Once this was achieved, they emphasized the importance of devising a new growth strategy that relied on trade liberalization and privatization, where the state played a fundamental role. Public savings should be used to stimulate private investment in strategic industries, such as technology, to protect the environment and to guarantee high education and health standards.[13] This heterodox approach emphasized that economic growth did not necessarily resume after the fiscal crisis was overcome. A development strategy to promote growth was needed.

Even though there were important differences between both approaches, they shared some common aspects, such as the emphasis on stabilization (decrease inflation rates and government deficits) and structural reforms (to increase competition within the economy and levels of direct private investment, both domestic and foreign). They ascertained that the role of the state had to be decreased in favor of the private sector. Direct private investment became one of the most important determinants of economic growth. Since saving rates in Latin America were very low, foreign savings should fill that vacuum and promote the development of productive activities. However, foreign investment could not take place without economic stability, because the high rates of inflation made the returns on investment highly unpredictable and the large government deficits absorbed large amounts of private capital that could have been invested in productive activities. In a closed economy, lack of foreign competitors may result in less competition, which works as a disincentive to invest in R&D, and thus leads to lower rates of productivity. Privatization and deregulation attract private capital (domestic and foreign), thereby increasing competition and accelerating economic growth.

The general tendency in Latin America was to apply heterodox policies first. In the midst of the fiscal crisis of the 1980s, generated by heavy borrowing in the 1970s, governments decided to issue additional public debt, which increased inflation and crowded out private borrowing. Interest rates rose and investment fell even further, contributing to the slowdown of economic growth. Devaluation of the exchange rate contributed to feed inflation and import restrictions decreased trade flows, which kept economic growth at bay. Argentina, Brazil, and Peru tried to stop the upward trend by decreeing wage freezes and stabilizing their currency and deemphasized demand management and fiscal discipline.[14]

However, success did not come about until a mixture of structural reforms, along with heterodox price policies, were implemented.[15] Colombia, Chile, and Mexico were the most successful cases in coping with the crisis in the 1980s. Colombia did not have a fiscal crisis, inflation was never high, and foreign debt was the smallest in Latin America. GDP growth remained steady in the 1980s and 1990s at around 4 percent. Chile stabilized, reduced the state apparatus to lower its fiscal deficit and liberalized trade, achieving annual growth rates of 6 percent after 1985. Mexico adopted fiscal control, credit was constrained and the currency was devalued, but the exchange rate was not fixed. Bolivia fully adopted the orthodox measures, but its growth rates remained either negative or very small in the 1980s, and grew to only 3 percent in the 1990s. Venezuela began implementing reforms in 1994 and economic growth resumed (overall, Venezuela grew at an average 2 percent in the 1980s and first half of the 1990s). Reforms came late to Peru. When president Alberto Fujimori adopted the orthodox package, the economy grew by about 30 percent between 1994 and 1997.[16]

The Argentinean government was one of the first to implement economic reforms. However, economic growth did not resume (Argentina had negative growth rates in the 1980s) until inflation was brought under control in 1991, when the exchange rate of the austral was fixed to the dollar.[17] Brazil began to apply policies to lower the fiscal deficit in the second half of the 1980s. This translated into an average economic growth of around 5 percent in the late 1980s. A new crisis in the early 1990s was not overcome until the administration of Fernando Collor de Mello initiated the privatization process, liberalized trade and controlled inflation through heterodox policies, which stimulated economic growth.[18]

Sebastian Edwards explained that with all these attempts to cope with the crisis (and with the failure of heterodox programs), by the late 1980s there came to be a realization that by emphasizing the role of the state as producers, Latin American governments had deemphasized the provision of social programs aimed at reducing inequality and poverty. As a result, a new view emerged. Economic management required macroeconomic stability, an external sector open to foreign competition, and a smaller role of the state in the production process, along with the implementation of poverty-reducing policies.[19] The pillars of this consensus were:

1. Macroeconomic stabilization was to be pursued through a series of policies.[20] Debt reduction comprised secondary market operations and direct reduction agreements with creditors. Fiscal stability involved improving the efficiency and effectiveness of the tax system and improvements in tax administration to reduce evasion. The price of public services was increased to cover costs, state-owned enterprises were privatized, and credit policies were changed. Instead of increasing government borrowing as in previous years, which crowded out private investment, indirect instruments were used, such as tight monetary policies. Exchange rates were fixed at a set rate to the dollar. Flexible exchange rates had previously allowed the currencies to accommodate inflation and discouraged governments from implementing serious anti-inflationary programs.[21]

2. The opening of the external sector to foreign competition ended four decades of import substitution. Non-tariff barriers were eliminated,

including quotas and prohibitions, the number of tariffs was reduced, and export taxes were either reduced or eliminated. These measures were accompanied by exchange rate devaluations to reduce the anti-export bias and to encourage exports, to help increase the growth of factor productivity through greater competition and enhanced efficiency, and to raise consumer welfare by reducing real prices of imported goods.[22] The formation of trading blocs was a policy for stimulating exports. NAFTA, created by the United States, Canada and Mexico in 1993, gave a big boost to the processes of economic integration. MERCOSUR, established in 1991, included Argentina, Brazil, Paraguay and Uruguay (Bolivia was in the process of joining in 2001 and Peru showed interest). The Andean Community and CARICOM were revitalized in the late 1990s. New prospects also emerged for the Central American Common Market (CACM) after warfare ended in the region in the mid-1990s.[23]

Table 4.1   Process of nationalization and privatization of a selected number of Latin American enterprises acquired by Spanish MNEs in the 1990s

Country	Nationalized in	U.S. Parent	Privatized in	Spanish Buyer
Argentina	1945	ITT	1991	TISA
Brazil	1962	ITT in Rio Grande do Sul	1996	TISA
Chile	1974[24]	ITT	1990	TISA
Peru	1970	ITT	1992	TISA
Venezuela	1976	Mene Grande Oil Field (Gulf)	1997	Repsol

Source: Adeoye A. Akinsanya, *The Expropriation of Multinational Property in the Third World*, Praeger, New York, 1980, pp. 115-146; Paul E. Sigmund, *Multinationals in Latin America. The Politics of Nationalization*, The University of Wisconsin Press, Madison, 1980, pp. 36-39; Daniel Chudnovsky, Andrés López and Fernando Porta, "New Foreign Direct Investment in Argentina: Privatization, the Domestic Market, and Regional Integration", in Manuel Agosin (ed.), *Foreign Direct Investment in Latin America*, IDB, Washington, D.C., 1995, pp. 39-104; Luis Riveros, Jaime Vatter, and Manuel R. Agosin, "Foreign Direct Investment in Chile, 1987-1993", in Manuel R. Agosin (ed.), *Foreign Direct Investment...*, pp. 105-136; *ICE*; and *El País Digital*.

3. Privatization and deregulation reversed a policy of strong state involvement in the economy. Between 1985 and 1992, over 2,000 publicly-owned Latin American firms were privatized.[25] The creation of a substantial state-owned enterprise sector was an important component of the structuralist development strategy. It was regarded as an efficient way of dealing with externalities, especially with natural monopolies and oligopolies. It also was an instrument to serve the public interest and advance social objectives, such as the provision of some services at low prices to the population at large. Finally, it was designed to reduce the vulnerability of the economy to external shocks.[26] Excessive legislation restricted the freedom of the private sector. The public sector became inefficient and lethargic. By the mid-1980s state-owned enterprises were a heavy burden on public finances, provided poor services, and fueled inflation.[27] Within this framework, the private sector was motivated by rent-seeking and corruption. The goal of privatization was to increase revenues for the government, reduce the size of the public sector, increase efficiency as measured by productivity growth, and spread ownership more broadly.[28] Many of the state-owned companies privatized by Latin American governments in the 1990s had been nationalized between the 1950s and 1970s, mainly from U.S. MNEs – see Table 4.1.

4. Capital market deregulation to generate higher savings rates and improve allocation of investment.[29] For many decades, ceilings were set on interest rates and social planners allocated credit to the sectors they deemed important.[30] Since the mid-1980s, reforms included deregulation of interest rates, elimination of direct credit allocation rules, reduction and harmonization of reserve requirements for commercial banks, relaxation of barriers to entry to increase competition, encouragement of security markets and of institutional investors, and creation of modern and efficient supervisory legislation.[31] The role of the government was limited to monitoring and setting appropriate regulation and supervision.

5. FDI was encouraged as a means to allow the host country to come in contact with new techniques and new management styles, help diffuse innovations, encourage the imitation of best practices in more industrialized countries, and accelerate the pace of productivity growth.[32] All the measures analyzed above were necessary to create a more appealing panorama for foreign investors. Within the broader macroeconomic framework, it is easier to understand the role that foreign direct investment played in the new strategy of economic development adopted by Latin American countries in the 1990s. A closer analysis of the policies implemented by some governments is

offered in the following pages. Although the main focus is on national policies toward foreign direct investment, special emphasis is placed on identifying how FDI fits in the overall development strategy adopted by these countries and its relation with other economic factors.

Liberalizing changes were introduced in FDI legislation in Chile and Argentina in the mid-1970s, in Mexico in the mid-1980s, in Colombia, Peru and Venezuela in the early 1990s, and Brazil in the mid-1990s. Some elements were common to all countries: MNEs were granted the same benefits as those enjoyed by domestic enterprises; they were given universal access to the host country's economy, with very few sectoral restrictions; prior authorization for investment was eliminated or restricted to a few categories; unlimited repatriation of capital and profit remittances abroad was allowed; and a policy of "flat incentives" was applied, with exceptions for investment in some priority sectors, such as exports or R&D.[33] What follows is a review of the recent changes in FDI legislation in a group of Latin American countries: Chile, Brazil, Argentina, Mexico and Colombia. The order of this classification deviates from the chronology. It is solely based on the significance of the reforms. Chile was the pioneer in implementing structural reforms, which proved a major factor in attracting FDI.

Chile

Latin American countries regard Chile as an economic success story. Beyond ideological, political and social considerations, Chile's policies after the 1960s were aimed at attracting investment to non-traditional sectors to diversify Chile's economic base, which had been heavily dependent on nitrates in the nineteenth century and on copper exports after the Second World War. Chile's incursion into the flows of international trade and capital came in the nineteenth century when British investors developed the nitrate industry, financial sector, and railway system. At this stage, the small copper industry was in the hands of local entrepreneurs. However, by the turn of the century, the rich copper ore veins had played out and U.S. companies came in to the industry to exploit low-grade ores: Kennecott Corporation controlled *El Teniente* copper mine in 1919 (this mine became the largest underground copper mine in the world in the 1930s),[34] and Anaconda bought the *Chuquicamata* mine in 1923 (ten years later this was the largest open pit copper mine in the world).

These two companies were part of a seven-firm world oligopoly that controlled up to 70 percent of the world's copper supplies outside the communist bloc. Their relations with the Chilean state were cordial in the 1920s and 1930s. However, the Chilean government raised the income tax on copper ores gradually, from 6 percent before W.W.I to 20 percent in the inter-war period. Excess profit taxes and other charges raised the total tax burden up to 70 percent in the early 1950s.[35]

Import Substitution, 1920-1950s

The writings of Raúl Prebish had a tremendous impact on Chilean policies. While working for the United Nations Economic Commission for Latin America and the Caribbean (ECLAC) in Santiago de Chile, he developed a "dependency" model that predicted a deterioration of Chile's terms of trade, resulting from exchanging copper exports (at increasingly lower prices) for imports of manufactured goods (whose prices increased gradually). These notions were exacerbated by the U.S. government's decision in 1950 to set the price of copper at one-half the market price outside the United States, as part of its strategy to manage the Korean War.[36] Between W.W.II and the mid-1950s, the Chilean governments pursued import-substitution policies as a development strategy to cushion the national economy from international shocks and capital shortages.

The Nuevo Trato, 1950s-1964

President Carlos Ibáñez (1952-58) reversed this practice in the 1950s with a package of policies called *Nuevo Trato* (New Deal), aimed at liberalizing the economy. For the first time in Chilean history, a statute (D.F.L. 437) addressed the issue of foreign direct investment. Prior to this statute, foreign investors had to make contracts with the state through individual negotiations that normally focused on tax and tariff relief. The new legislation addressed profit repatriation and the stability of the exchange rate. It also granted equipment importation rights and special tax exemptions for investments in areas that promoted industrial development; authorized investment in transportation and natural resources, including mining, agriculture and forestry; lowered overall taxes and tariffs; eliminated quotas; and adopted a fixed exchange rate. Copper was still the main source of foreign revenue, but its production began to decrease in the mid-1950s, when new copper fields were discovered in Canada and Australia. The government understood that only by creating a favorable investment climate would foreign mining companies increase investment and copper output. Ibáñez also tried to decrease Chile's dependence on copper exports and saw that foreign investors could play a significant role in diversifying the economic base of the country.[37]

Conservative president Jorge Alessandri (1958-1964) decided to deepen Ibáñez's investment concessions. In 1960 he revised the foreign investment statute and passed statute D.F.L. 258, which widened the scope of possible investments to include fishing activities and gave the president discretionary authority to approve or reject special tax exemptions.[38] Between 1960 and 1967, non-copper foreign investment ranged between $150 and $200 million per year. On the contrary, investments in the copper industry did not fulfill the government's expectations and fell from an annual average of around $100 million between 1957 and 1959 to $40 million in the next five years.[39] However, the measures approved by Ibáñez and Alessandri worked as a stimulus. The economy grew and to some degree decreased its dependence on copper exports. Imports soared, causing a trade imbalance, which, coupled with high rates of government expenditures, led to a balance of payments crisis in 1962 and the resurrection of protectionism.

Chilenization of the Economy, 1964-1973

The perceived failure of the *Nuevo Trato* raised spread criticism among some of the most powerful sectors of Chilean society. Besides, the influential landed oligarchy feared that an agrarian reform would come along with economic liberalization and lobbied within the Conservative Party to reverse these policies. The Conservative Party, which had in the agrarian aristocracy its main pillar, blamed Chile's development problems on foreign MNEs, and began calling for the nationalization of their assets. The conservative Christian Democratic Party won the elections of 1964 and the new president, Eduardo Frei (1964-1970), put forward a plan of "Chilenization" that required participation of the government in ownership of the large copper mines (eventually a majority participation of 51 percent) along with commitments to expand production.[40]

The short-term result was positive. Investment in the copper industry increased from $65 million in 1965 to $117 million in 1966, $213 million in 1967 and $507 million in 1968. As a result, government revenue also increased.[41] The main MNEs followed different strategies to cope with the new requirements. In 1967 Kennecott agreed to sell 51 percent of its Chilean subsidiary to the government. Anaconda continued to invest on its own until 1969, when claims for nationalization reached their zenith, and the company also decided to sell 51 percent of its Chilean subsidiary to the government.[42]

Latin American countries tried to promote regional integration into economic blocs as a response to "dependency". The rationale behind this move was the belief that closer economic relationships among countries with similar degrees of economic development would not be so asymmetrical as those between them and developed countries (especially the United States). In 1969 Chile, Bolivia, Colombia, Ecuador, and Peru created the Andean Pact, which set up new restrictions to foreign investment in order to encourage the development of local technology and reduce dependence on foreign capital.[43] The Pact's aims included eliminating barriers to regional trade, erecting a common external tariff and establishing sectoral programs for industrial development that could divide manufacturing operations among member countries in order to gain economies of scale, including provisions that limited foreign ownership to a maximum 49 percent (including a reduction of existing foreign ownership to that level). As a consequence of Chile's allegiance to the Pact, non-copper foreign direct investment in Chile dropped to $197 million in 1966, $24 million in 1968 and $65 million in 1970.[44]

These measures seemed to ignore the crucial role played by MNEs in the Chilean economy in the 1960s, because foreign firms owned large shares of the main economic industries. MNEs controlled one sixth of the manufacturing sector. They were predominant in areas such as electrical machinery (42 percent), rubber (49 percent) and tobacco (57 percent). In 1970, 60 percent of U.S. investment in Chile was concentrated in the mining sector (which was the main industry in Chile), 25 percent in public utilities (primarily the telephone company and electric utilities), 9 percent in manufacturing, and 6 percent in commerce and tourism. However, despite the efforts to diversify the economic base, copper remained the main attraction for foreign capital in 1970. Between 1954 and 1970, mining (other than copper) received 60 percent of non-copper FDI, general industry claimed 38 percent, and less than 1.5 percent went into forestry, agriculture, services or other sectors.[45]

A leftist coalition led by Salvador Allende won the elections of 1970 with 37 percent of the vote and quickly embarked on a program to restructure the economy that included an increase in government spending and nationalization of large private assets. The goal of the new government was to transform the nature of capital accumulation through allocating the role of dynamic agent to the state.[46] Given the importance of copper revenue for the Chilean economy, the three U.S. multinationals that controlled ore industry, Anaconda, Kennecott and Cerro, were nationalized, but only the last two received compensation because they had previously operated in partnership with the government. ITT's facilities were intervened in 1971, as news leaked to the press that ITT managers had tried to enlist the U.S. government and other investors in an effort to prevent Allende's victory.[47] Fear increased among LDCs that MNEs might try to conspire with governments to compromise a host nation's political sovereignty. ITT was finally nationalized by the Pinochet regime in December 1974 and a compensation settlement was agreed between the Chilean government and ITT, to compensate the U.S. MNE for the seizure of its stakes in CTC in 1971.[48]

Other U.S. companies whose assets were also nationalized were General Motors, RCA, Armco Steel, Ralston Purina and Bank of America. By late 1971, the government had taken control over more than 80 key companies that were responsible for 40 percent of the country's productive capacity and one-third of private sector employment, including the most important companies in the mining sector, sixteen commercial banks that represented 90 percent of outstanding credit, and key companies in important sectors such as metallurgy, cement, textiles, fisheries and wholesale marketing.[49] When the nationalization campaign spread into domestic companies, political support dropped considerably.

Economic Liberalization, 1973-2000

A military coup d'état led by General Augusto Pinochet ended Allende's presidency on September 11, 1973. Pinochet immediately put the Chilean economy in the hands of a group of young economists trained by Milton Friedman at the University of Chicago. In 1973 inflation ran wild, international reserves were exhausted and production shut down. The so-called "Chicago boys" removed most non-tariff restrictions and lowered tariff rates progressively from 750 percent to a flat 10 percent by the end of the decade. Many state enterprises were returned to the private sector and budgetary constraints were imposed on those that remained public. Government employment and expenditures were cut. A 20 percent value-added tax was implemented. Foreign investors played a minor role in this period.[50]

However, some policies set the stage for renewed relations between the Chilean state and foreign multinationals. The government returned most nationalized properties, except for the copper mines, that remained in the hands of the state. It also paid compensation to those MNEs whose assets were not returned. The government invited firms to restore and expand previous industrial facilities and to consider new ventures and passed a foreign investment liberal law called Decree Law 600 (D. L. 600), which will be analyzed later on in this chapter. FDI jumped from $100 million annually in the first years of the military regime to an average of $340 million between 1978 and 1982.[51]

The economic conditions improved in 1976, but an overvalued currency (implemented to fight inflation) caused continuous trade deficits and the deregulation of foreign capital flows led to a tripling of Chile's external debt between 1970 and 1982. The financial system collapsed. A new restructuring of the economy was necessary, this time led by Minister of the Economy Hernán Büchi. Five key measures worked as a positive stimulus to attract FDI: internationalization of the economy, promotion of foreign direct investment, debt-to-equity swaps, privatization of state-owned enterprises, and democratization.

Economic Internationalization, 1982-2000

Import-substitution strategies gave way to export promotion policies that stressed non-traditional products and greater reliance on the private sector. These policies became incompatible with the Andean Pact (Chile's Statute D.L. 600 liberalized foreign direct investment, which was incompatible with the restrictions to FDI set by Decision 24 of the Pact) and Augusto Pinochet decided to withdraw Chile from the Pact in October 1976, to strengthen ties with the most developed economies, particularly the United States. Chilean policymakers realized that because of the small size of the Chilean market, import-substitution strategies reached their limit very quickly. Chile was too small to attract significant amounts of FDI.

Besides, Chile had only a few sectorally concentrated large firms with extensive international experience. On the contrary, MNEs had the scale, resources, access, and adaptability to help reorient the economy to overseas markets, and an outward-oriented policy would set a better basis for taking advantage of MNEs. Chile adopted the macroeconomic, trade, investment, and financial policies needed to support an open market reallocation of resources. Consequently, non-traditional product exports grew. While copper production increased by 38 percent between 1980 and 1988, fish, forestry, and fruit production rose by between 200 and 300 percent. Copper's total export share fell from 80 percent in the early 1970s to roughly 45 percent in 1990.[52]

Foreign Direct Investment Rules

A foreign investment statute, D.L. 600 (still in effect in 2001), was passed in 1974. It guaranteed open and nondiscriminatory treatment for foreign investors in both terms of entry conditions and subsequent treatment of business operations. Following implementation of the statute, foreign investors were only restricted in some sectors, such as uranium mining, television stations, coastal shipping, some public utilities and national security industries. Although the statute subjected investments over $5 million, those involving foreign governments, and certain public service projects, to the approval of a Foreign Investment Committee (made up by the ministers of economy, finance, planning and foreign affairs, as well as those whose area was directly affected by a given project), in practice, the Committee, created in compliance with foreign exchange regulations, fulfilled information needs and did not work as a screening mechanism.[53]

The law recognized foreign investment in many forms, including foreign exchange, new or used tangible goods, technology that may be capitalized, loans tied to an investment project, and profit capitalization from earlier investments if the profits were eligible for repatriation. After-tax profits could be freely remitted and capital obtained from the sale of the business may be repatriated after three years from the date of the actual investment. There was no time, nor level of ownership limitations. Foreign investors could choose a 49.5 percent overall tax rate or a 40 percent rate with variable surtaxes for excessive profit remittances, and have a one-time option to shift to the prevailing national rate. Most firms chose the latter option, which was 12 to 13 percent lower than the guaranteed rate.[54] Annual flows of FDI grew from $100 million in the period 1974-1977 to over $300 million between 1978 and 1982.[55] The positive effect of D.L. 600 on FDI was not noticeable until the fourth year, because the investors originally feared that the government may reverse some of the policies.

Debt-to-Equity Swaps

The government also devised a program in 1985 for foreign investors to convert Chile's external debt instruments into local equity investments (Chapter XIX of the Central Bank Foreign Exchange Regulations). Chilean debt could be purchased at discounts that averaged two thirds of the debt instrument's face value. Foreign investors had to provide the Central Bank with information about the nature of the investment and the foreign debt obligations to be used. Once granted authorization, the investor redeemed the debt at the Central Bank for Chilean pesos at a rate closer to the instrument's face value, getting a cash incentive. The government redeemed the debt below its face value, retiring external debt at a discount and increasing capital stock.[56]

One third of Chile's debt ($3.5 billion) was converted to equity between 1985 and 1990 ($2.7 billion of FDI or 46 percent of the total FDI. The other 54 percent was invested through D.L. 600). Three quarters of FDI in mining came through D.L. 600, and one quarter through Chapter XIX (50.9 percent of all D.L. 600 materialized investments between 1985 and 1991 went to mining and 29.8 percent to services).[57] The largest share of investments materialized through Chapter XIX between 1985 and 1991 went to manufacturing (29.8 percent), and export-oriented activities in forestry, agriculture and fishing (30.1 percent).[58]

Agreements with mining companies included exemption from most taxes (except for the gross profit tax), accelerated depreciation of equipment, machinery and installations and the right to deduct from profits any losses incurred in a period of up to five years prior to the tax year in question. However, FDI in mining was low. In 1980, the government decided to approve a new law that gave mining corporations the right over the mineral in the ground, therefore entitling the concessionaire to compensation in case of expropriation.[59]

Debt-to-equity swaps worked effectively in keeping MNEs in Chile and generated FDI that probably would not have occurred. The new investments went to areas different from copper production. FDI thus contributed to diversify the Chilean economy and flowed into manufacturing, forestry, fishing, agriculture, public utilities, commerce and tourism. The Central Bank modified the Chapter XIX program in 1990 to channel the remaining debt conversion funds to priority investment areas. Bank approval was reserved for projects over $5 million in new export and import substitution activities, communications, tourism, energy and environmental protection projects. Some activities in the financial sector were excluded, such as insurance, pension management, investment funds and leasing operations. The goal of these modifications was to deepen the process of modernization of the economy initiated in the 1970s.[60]

Privatization of State-Owned Enterprises

One of the main goals of the whole economic package was to alter Chile's highly statist approach, decentralize decision-making in the economy and open a broad range of new investment opportunities for private investors, both domestic and foreign. Privatization took place in two stages. The first one, between 1974 and 1981. It comprised two types of actions: the return to private ownership of almost all domestic and foreign enterprises nationalized during the Allende regime (except the Kennecott and Anaconda holdings, which were integrated in Codelco, and in the late 1990s produced 50 percent of Chile's copper exports), and privatization of some government functions. The former aimed at regaining private investor confidence and encouraging entrepreneurial initiative. The latter at widening the scope for private entrepreneurship and reducing the fiscal deficit (state enterprises ran a $500 million deficit in 1973).[61]

The privatization process generated enough revenue to turn the deficit of the public accounts into a surplus, enabling the government to create a system of private pension funds in 1981. Between 1982 and 1983 the financial crisis led the government to assume temporary control over most key domestic financial institutions and some corporate enterprises. The privatization process resumed in 1985, when the government returned intervened banks and companies to the private sector. Thirty-three state enterprises were privatized, generating $2 billion of revenue. Among the main state-owned companies privatized were the telephone company (CTC), created after the nationalization of Comapañía de Teléfonos de Chile in 1974 by the Pinochet regime, the power generation firm Endesa, the nitrate and iron producer Soquimich, and the steel corporation CAP.[62]

Especially important was privatization of the steel company CAP (Compañía de Acero del Pacífico), one of the three largest corporations of Chile. While it was in public hands, it was subject to strong competition from Brazilian firms. After privatization, its own workers became its main stockholders (30.5 percent), along with an investment company controlled by the Swiss Schmidheiny groups (29 percent).[63] The new owners invested $800 million into the company to expand its steel and mining activities, to increase its value-added activities, and to improve its competitiveness. Its exports rose by 80 percent and the firm developed a subsidiary for export-oriented forestry products. About 28,000 of their employees and 600,000 Chileans (5 percent of the population) bought shares from the privatized companies. The objective of this so-called "popular capitalism" was to increase the workers' involvement and productivity by giving them a concrete stake in the firm's success.[64]

Democratization

A plebiscite held in 1988 brought as a result the transition to democracy. Fifty-four percent of the vote, with ninety-six percent of the electorate casting ballots, voted for democracy. The role of the business community was crucial to smooth the transition period and sustain similar figures of economic growth. Inflows of FDI continued, including new firms from countries that strengthened bilateral business prospects with Chile. This provided an important boost for the government of Christian Democrat Patricio Aylwin. Preceding the elections of 1989, Aylwin and the members of his center-left coalition reassured the business sector formulating positions that backed retention of the major pillars of Pinochet's economic policy: low inflation rates and stable economic policies to maintain investor confidence.[65]

Brazil

Brazil's post-W.W.II economic history was characterized by major government efforts to industrialize. Four different periods of industrialization can be differentiated, in which FDI played a prominent role. In these efforts, the government's approach to foreign direct investors varied, from periods of distrust to periods of cordial relations.

Import Substitution Period, 1946-1967

After W.W.II Brazil imposed quantitative controls on consumer goods to tackle a deficit in its balance of payments. An import-substitution strategy was adopted, not only to improve the balance of payments, but also to promote industrialization and the development of non-traditional industries. This strategy combined two types of policies: trade protectionism and promotion of foreign direct investment in non-traditional sectors. The "law of similars", implemented in the mid-1950s, allowed trade authorities to block imports of foreign goods when a domestically manufactured substitute was available.[66]

This type of protectionism lured many foreign MNEs to invest in Brazil, attracted by the size of the market. Despite the continuation of balance of payments problems, Brazil's import substitution strategy created a favorable environment for the establishment of modern segments of consumer durables with linkages to basic inputs and capital goods industries. Foreign investors developed an important Brazilian auto industry, with backward linkages with the local mechanical and electrical machinery industries. However, the heavy requirements for foreign companies to use components manufactured by Brazilian firms prevented vertical integration of MNEs.[67]

The Government also implemented special incentives for investment in non-traditional industries. The Superintendência da Moeda e do Crédito (SUMOC), the Brazilian Monetary Authority, approved Instruction No. 113, giving foreign firms exchange advantages to import equipment and machinery.[68] Foreign MNEs invested in non-traditional industries, like mechanical and electrical machinery, transport equipment, and chemicals. Foreign firms also controlled traditional sectors where import substitution was not the motivation for investment, such as food, tobacco, rubber, and textiles.

High rates of government expenditure, coupled with important amounts of FDI (the share of Brazilian manufacturing firms established in Brazil by acquisition of Brazilian firms grew form 9 percent between 1946 and 1950 to 22 percent between 1951 and 1955 and 33 percent between 1956 and 1960, after the application of the export promotion policies),[69] generated high rates of economic growth. However, the maintenance of an overvalued exchange rate, combined with high inflation and large government expenditures, originated balance of payments deficits.[70] The United States and the World Bank refused to finance Brazil's deficits, and local authorities had to find the way to attract foreign capital. They would liberalize the treatment of foreign capital within the country, in order to improve the investment climate.

The "Economic Miracle", 1968-1973

In the early 1960s, the Brazilian economy stagnated. Growth decelerated and inflation ran wild. A military coup in 1964 ended a period of economic and political instability and initiated two decades of military rule (1964-1985). The military leaders implemented a program of orthodox stabilization under IMF guidance that received considerable financial aid from the United States. The key objectives were modernization of the financial sector, fiscal reform, devaluation, and maintenance of "realistic" exchange rates (to increase the competitiveness of local producers in international markets) and promotion of exports. Thereafter, Brazilian policies emphasized neutrality of incentives in Brazilian trade and exchange rate policies. Between 1968 and 1974, economic growth was higher than 10 percent annually. Inflation fell to 20 percent. Manufactured goods replaced coffee as the country's leading export.[71] Annual average growth rates in manufacturing for the period 1968-1973 were 13.3 percent (23.6 percent in consumer durables and 18.1 in capital goods).[72]

FDI played a key role in the orthodox program of economic recovery implemented by the military regime. Brazilian authorities devalued the currency, lifted trade restrictions and initiated new export promotion schemes (production for export). Foreign capital accounted for a third of the increase in capital formation for this period. While the state strengthened its presence in some industries (steel, oil refining and petrochemicals) foreign firms invested primarily in non-traditional sectors for the local market as well as for export to developed countries. This resulted in a diversification of the industrial base toward technologically sophisticated products. Although in absolute terms U.S. firms incremented their investment flows to Brazil, their share decreased due to the large capital inflows from Japan and Europe. European and Japanese firms invested heavily in the chemical industry, mechanical equipment, and precision mechanics and instruments industries.[73]

A peculiarity of this period was the large share of foreign investors that decided to create joint-ventures with local producers. Joint-ventures were more a natural development within industries where the interdependence of firms of different ownership was more pronounced than a governmental mandate. However, the process was triggered by the expansion of the petrochemical industry. The state decided to give the private sector a stake in the national petrochemical company and created a joint-venture with private domestic enterprises as well as with MNEs (the "triple alliance" or "tripod model" of association).[74] The objective was to attract foreign investment and know-how, and to expose domestic producers to the marketing techniques and technology of more advanced MNEs. By creating joint-ventures with local producers, foreign MNEs gained access to the Brazilian market and reduced the risk of expropriation or excessive taxation. In periods of fast economic growth there was a tendency for foreign producers to choose minority participation. This was the case in the early years of the import-substitution period and during the "economic miracle". The share of foreign subsidiaries that were established as joint-ventures grew from 34 percent in early 1960s to over 50 percent after 1968 (that share had been 53 percent between 1946 and 1959).[75]

Adjustment to the Oil Shock, 1974-1985

The military rulers decided to adjust the economic structure to the situation of oil scarcity originated by the shock of 1973 with an ambitious multi-year investment program. Their goals were to move onto a new stage of industrial development, correct imbalances in the industrial structure and save hard currency. The model put forward by the Brazilian government emphasized equilibrium between the state, private sectors and foreign interests. In this scheme, the state would maintain control over some of the key sectors, such as energy, communications and transportation (mainly railways). In the other sectors, the state encouraged the formation of joint-ventures between private parties and between the state and the private sector.[76]

FDI continued to play a fundamental role. Inflows grew by an annual rate of 12.6 percent between 1974 and 1985, and the ratio between the stock of foreign direct investment and GDP rose. However, this time Brazilian law restricted full control of local enterprises by foreign firms. The Second Development Plan (PND II) required foreign investors to form joint-ventures with Brazilian companies. The government had grown concerned about the inability of the domestic private sector to perform its part in the "triple alliance". With the "PND II" the authorities wanted to strengthen the position of domestic capital and maximize gains from technology transfer. Thus, in the Brazilian development model, MNEs played a fundamental role as providers of capital, technology, know-how and access to foreign markets. Protectionism was not geared at reducing the presence of foreign firms in Brazil, but at encouraging production within the country, either by domestic firms, by foreign producers or by a combination of both and the state.[77]

Import substitution accelerated between 1974 and 1983, and exports from the protected sectors increased substantially. These sectors were the same ones that had played a prominent role in previous periods of expansion (in this phase there was no further diversification of the economic base of the country): metallic ore and metal products, other metals, transport equipment, paper and pulp, rubber products, chemicals, textiles, tobacco, electrical machinery and mechanical equipment. Exports helped turn a current account deficit of nearly 8 percent of GDP into a small surplus between 1982 and 1989. Overall, protectionism helped increase the competitiveness of Brazilian firms. The performance of foreign subsidiaries was especially remarkable. Their exports climbed from $2.9 billion in 1978 to $7.1 billion in 1981 with a profit of $3.6 billion, remaining high thereafter.[78]

MNEs benefited greatly from economic liberalization because they possessed comparative and competitive advantages and had easier access to foreign markets, where they could sell steel goods produced in Brazil. Besides, they dominated the most technologically sophisticated sectors and had absolute or majority control over some: transport equipment, rubber products, pharmaceuticals, tobacco, electricity-generating equipment, autos and paints. Between 1947 and 1985, industry increased its share of GDP from 23.7 percent to 35.5 percent, in part thanks to the boost of MNEs, while the share of agriculture fell from 19.5 percent to 10.1 percent.[79]

Economic and Political Liberalization, 1985-1996

Import substitution fostered an explosion of industrial output and improvement of infrastructures. The state developed some public local industries, like steel, electricity and telephone. However, too much intervention promoted the growth of some inefficient local producers over time. Large government deficits made investment figures drop. In 1990, Fernando Collor de Melo embarked on a program of economic liberalization, reducing trade barriers and privatizing state-owned firms. Inflation was out of control until 1994, when the finance minister, Fernando Henrique Cardoso, introduced a stabilization package that included the creation of a new currency, the real, and maintenance of high interest rates. Inflation rates fell from 50 percent for June 1994 to 11 percent for the whole of 1996. Price stability increased the purchasing power of Brazilians, providing a big boost for the consumer market.[80]

The opening of the Brazilian economy prompted a surge of mergers and acquisitions involving foreign firms, which fought to settle in Brazil before their competitors, to profit from the prospects for sustained economic growth. Takeovers of Brazilian companies by foreign firms increased from 185 in 1991 to 318 in 1995. The president of a Brazilian investment bank called Pactual, Luiz César Fernández, said that these figures are so large because 'Brazil differs from other emerging markets in that, for many companies, the market already exists' and 'it is easy to buy market share'. César Fernández estimated that to earn a one-percent market share, a greenfield investment of $60 million was needed. To acquire a company that already controls that share of the market would only cost between 30 and 40 percent of that amount.[81]

The "Real Plan" implemented by Cardoso had two targets:[82]

1. Eliminate indexation. Price stability was achieved by fixing the Real to the U.S. dollar. A floating band exchange system allowed the Real to float in line with wholesale price inflation. Interest rates were extremely high. Although the Central Bank's basic rate oscillated between 4 percent and 2 percent between 1994 and 1996, consumer credit remained above 150 percent and credit card and overdraft rates were even higher. The objective of these policies was to act as a brake on consumer spending and to attract foreign capital in order to cover a current account deficit of almost 3 percent of GDP.
2. Privatization of state-owned firms and liberalization of important economic sectors in order to balance public accounts and attract FDI. For the year beginning in 1996, the government eliminated the legal distinction between foreign and domestic firms and granted foreign firms equal treatment, lifted monopolies over telecommunications, electricity and the oil industry, and private companies were allowed to gain public concessions. These reforms created a great potential for investment. Besides, some state companies were privatized between 1996 and 2000. The expectation that economic growth would increase the demand for electricity beyond the capacity of the energy state-owned enterprises, led the state to privatize existing plants and to grant new concessions. Another big area attracting FDI in the late 1990s was infrastructure. The government planned to privatize the railway companies, to give concessions to operate highways, and to invest in water transportation and treatment.

Argentina

The laws that regulate FDI have been in effect since 1976. They recognize the equality of rights and obligations with local investors and permit incorporation of used capital goods, capitalization of intangibles, profit remittance and unlimited capital repatriation. Nevertheless, the Argentinean government established some sectoral restrictions that were lifted gradually and, since 1993, only the broadcasting and atomic energy sectors were entirely closed to foreign investors. The process of privatization of public enterprises was defined by law via capitalization of external debt and allowed the entry of foreign capital into the privatization of sanitation services, electricity, gas, telecommunications and postal service. The mechanisms of debt capitalization recognized a favorable redemption value, which worked as a subsidy to investment. Most of FDI that came through this scheme went to the industrial sector (especially automotive industries, chemicals and foods). $718 million of FDI out of a total of $3.018 billion came through this mechanism between 1984-1989 and $5.6 billion of a total of $14.7 billion between 1990-1993. Between 1990 and 1995, three quarters of FDI went into the transfer of public assets and subsequent investment or profit reinvestments.[83]

Mexico

Mexico's newest FDI regulation came into effect in 1984. Before 1984, FDI was approved by the government on a case-by-case basis and there existed a 49 percent ceiling on FDI's share in the recipient enterprise's capital. Besides, FDI was barred from sectors such as petrochemicals, financial services and telecommunications. This legal prohibition was eliminated in 1984, along with the ceiling on FDI share in many industries, as part of the plan to solve the debt crisis. The administrative procedure for the approval of investment projects was simplified. FDI liberalization was deepened in 1989, when the creation of enterprises with 100 percent FDI participation was approved for investment projects valued at less than $100 million (with certain exceptions).

Between 1986 and 1987 Mexico operated a program of debt-equity swaps via repurchase of investor-held debt instruments at between 75 percent and 100 percent of face value, depending on the destination of the fund to be invested. The program privileged investments that participated in privatization of public enterprises, and those that increased production capacity (versus the purchase of existing assets), incorporated new technologies or went to the export sector.

This program channeled large amounts of FDI into the manufacturing sector (25 percent of all FDI flows between 1986 and 1990), particularly into the automotive sector. The Mexican government paid an average redemption price of 82 cents on the dollar of debt contracted with those investors that participated in the program. This price represented an average subsidy to FDI of 35 cents per dollar, because these instruments were going for about 45 cents on the dollar of face value on the world market in that period. A second program was implemented in 1990, concentrating on infrastructure projects and the acquisition of public assets, opened to both national and foreign investors.[84]

Colombia

Colombian policy makers recognized the beneficial impact of FDI as a complement to domestic savings and as a technology transfer mechanism in the 1960s. Nevertheless, they were concerned about its impact on the balance of payments and they feared FDI might replace domestic capital. Decree Law 444 (D.L. 444) of 1967 established a National Planning Office (DNP) to channel and plan FDI according to the country's needs. The National Council on Economic and Social Policy (CONPES) was to ensure that the proposed FDI harmonized with the country's economic and social development programs.[85]

Preferential treatment was given to investment leading to export increases or export diversification. Profit remittances were limited to 10 percent of the registered capital and the repatriation of capital was limited to the value of what the investor had imported, with no repatriation allowed on value increases. In accordance with the propositions of the Andean Pact, a new law was passed in 1973 (Decree 1900) that made it necessary for FDI-based companies to be converted into mixed companies. The ceiling on profit remittances was raised to 14 percent.[86]

The fiscal crisis of the 1980s prompted a change in attitude toward FDI. Bureaucratic procedures to formalize an investment were simplified. Colombia applied Decision 220 of the Andean Pact, which eliminated the conversion requirement, liberalized access to domestic credit market (except for development credit), raised the profit remittance ceiling to 25 percent and authorized payment of royalties to the parent companies in the case of new technologies or technologies used for the production of export goods. Sectoral prohibitions were not eliminated, especially in the financial sector. As in the 1960s, the fundamental goal was to use FDI as a mechanism for technology transfer and complementation of domestic savings.[87]

Decision 291 of the Andean Pact was incorporated into Colombian law by CONPES Resolution 49 of 1991, also known as the "Statute on International Investments" (the first Colombian statute incorporating all the existing regulations of FDI), which recognizes equality of treatment to national and foreign investors, universality of access to economic sectors and automatic approval of the investment. The statute also makes foreign investors eligible to all explicit incentives available to locals, access to lines of external credit and to export promotion mechanisms. Resolution 51 eliminated the ceiling on profit remittances and the concept of foreign investment was expanded to include indirect and portfolio investment and all of a company's in-kind capital contributions, including intangibles such as technological contributions, trademarks and patents.[88] However, a system of double taxation remained in effect, which taxed profits and remittances. The profit tax was standardized at 30 percent, and a special contribution of 7.5 percent by all taxpayers was declared for the period 1993-1997 (the overall tax rate in Latin America was 35.4 percent for individuals and 36.3 percent for companies). The additional 22 percent tax on profit remittances was lowered to 7 percent in 1996.[89]

The financial, mining and petroleum sectors received special treatment in Colombian legislation with regard to FDI. Colombia forbade FDI in the financial sector in 1975 by Law 55, following approval of Decision 24 of the Andean Pact. Existing foreign financial firms were forced to convert into mixed enterprises. Following the most severe crisis in the country's history, the financial sector was reformed in 1990 by Law 45, which included new rules on capital amounts, greater flexibility in operational time terms, and expansion of financial service companies' possibilities.[90]

The International Investments Statute, the Petroleum Code, and the Mining Code govern investment in petroleum and mining. The Ministry of Mines and Energy approves investment projects in petroleum and natural gas exploration and exploitation, once the foreign investor has negotiated the contract with the public Colombian Petroleum Enterprise (ECOPETROL). The Ministry authorizes investment in refinancing, transport, distribution, exploration, exploitation, smelting and transformation. The National Planning Office must approve the proposed investment when its value is over $100 million.[91]

Since 1974, foreign investors participate in joint-ventures with the government, which keeps between 81.8 percent and 85 percent of the profit. Taxes are levied on the value of production, not profits. In 1989, the law stipulated that foreign participation would decrease with every discovery of a new field with a cumulative production greater than 60 million barrels. A remittance tax on profits (after deduction of income tax) must be paid, gradually decreasing from 12 percent in 1993 to 7 percent from 1996 onward. If there is reinvestment for ten or more years, this tax does not apply. In hydrocarbon exploration and exploitation, a remittance tax of 15 percent was applied between 1993 and 1995, and a 12 percent tax from 1996 onward. Until 1997, a special contribution was applied, equal to 25 percent of the taxpayer's income tax. A 14 percent value-added tax applies to retail sales, imports and most services.[92]

Rates of FDI remained stable between 1970 and 1993, with a slight surge beginning in 1985, stimulated by petroleum discoveries (the petroleum sector received the largest share of FDI since 1985) and the privatization of financial institutions. In 1993 the stock of FDI was $2.705 billion (8.8 percent of GDP).[93]

Conclusion

Most Latin American and Caribbean countries evolved from a period of protectionism to one of openness in the post-W.W.II era. Chile implemented a strategy of import-substitution after the war that reached its zenith in the early 1970s, when Salvador Allende nationalized the most important industries. In the mid-1970s, Chile liberalized its economy and welcomed FDI as an integral part of its development efforts. Brazil's strategy was not so smooth. Import-substitution was in place until the 1990s. Brazilian authorities tried to control foreign investors. Their policies did not aim at government ownership, but at encouraging domestic production. In the Brazilian model called "triple alliance", authorities encouraged joint-ventures between domestic producers and MNEs, to favor transfers of technology, know-how and managerial abilities.

FDI also played an important role in the economic diversification of these two economies. Through a selective program of privatization and successful debt-to-equity swaps, the Chilean authorities attracted foreign investors to non-traditional economic activities that helped Chile overcome its dependence on copper exports and develop new value-added activities. Capital and trade liberalization also encouraged production for export within Chile. Given the large size of the Brazilian market, protectionism was sufficient to attract FDI. Foreign MNEs wanted to produce in Brazil to sell in its market. However, capital liberalization within the Brazilian economy and an export-promotion strategy lured MNEs to produce in Brazil for export to other markets. This strategy favored the emergence of new economic activities that incorporated more value-added processes. Strategic privatization of several state-owned enterprises also attracted FDI.

Even though Latin American governments were widely criticized for their mistrust of foreign direct investment, a close analysis of the experiences of Chile and Brazil shows that FDI played a fundamental role in their development strategies. The state encouraged new value-added activities and promoted certain industries, either directly with the creation of public firms or by attracting foreign capital where there was lack of private domestic initiative. Reliance on openness to trade and to capital flows, market competition and private enterprise were key characteristics of the models they adopted in the 1990s. Inflows of FDI are likely to increase after 2000, as economic growth is opening up new opportunities for business. There is wide consensus now in Latin America that FDI is beneficial for economic growth, because MNEs bring technology, know-how and management practices that increase the efficiency of their enterprises and thus raise the living standards of society as a whole.

Notes

[1]   Eliana Cardoso and Ann Helwege, "Import Substitution Industrialization", in Jeffry Frieden, Manuel Pastor, Jr., and Michael Tomz (eds.), *Modern Political Economy and Latin America. Theory and Policy*, Westview Press, Boulder, 2000, p. 155; and Sebastian Edwards, *Crisis and Reform in Latin America. From Despair to Hope*, Oxford University Press, Oxford, 1995, pp. 43-48.

[2]   Sebastian Edwards, *Crisis and Reform...*, p. 44.

[3]   Ibid., pp. 4-5.

[4]   Ibid., pp. 44-45.

[5]   Ibid., p. 44.

[6]   Ibid., p. 46.

[7]   Ibid.

[8]   Luiz Carlos Bresser Pereira, "Economic Reforms and Economic Growth: Efficiency and Politics in Latin America", in Luiz Carlos Bresser Pereira, José María Maravall, and Adam Przeworski, *Economic Reforms in New Democracies. A Social-Democratic Approach*, Cambridge University Press, Cambridge, 1993, pp. 18-20.

[9]   Ibid., pp. 20-21.

[10] Ibid., p. 31.

[11] Ibid., pp. 33-34.

[12] Ibid., pp. 21-22.

[13] Ibid., p. 22.

[14] Sebastian Edwards, *Crisis and Reform...*, p. 33.

[15] Ibid., p. 69.

[16] Luiz Carlos Bresser Pereira provides a detailed analysis of the implementation of the reforms in these countries in Luiz Carlos Bresser Pereira, "Economic Reforms...", pp. 36-50.

[17] Ibid., pp. 44-47.

[18] Ibid., pp. 47-50; and The Miami Herald, 20 October 1996, p. 7F.

[19] Sebastian Edwards, *Crisis and Reform...*, pp. 58-59.

[20] Sebastian Edwards gives an excellent recount of the structural reforms implemented in Latin America in the 1990s in *Crisis and Reform...* For more information on macroeconomic adjustment, see pp. 69-114.

[21] Ibid., p. 160.

[22] Ibid., pp. 124-129.

[23] Ibid., pp. 142-163.

[24] ITT's stake in CTC was seized by the Allende regime in 1971, but CTC was not fully nationalized until 1974, during Pinochet's rule. For more information, see Adeoye A. Akinsanya, *The Expropriation of Multinational Property in the Third World*, Praeger Publishers, New York, 1980, pp. 138-139, and Paul E. Sigmund, *Multinationals in*

Latin America. The Politics of Nationalization, The University of Wisconsin Press, Madison, 1980, pp. 148-149.

25 Sebastian Edwards, *Crisis and Reform...*, p. 170.
26 Ibid., p. 171.
27 Ibid., p. 173.
28 Ibid., p. 175.
29 Ibid., p. 201.
30 Ibid., pp. 204-205.
31 Ibid., p. 208.
32 Ibid., p. 246.
33 Manuel R. Agosin, "Foreign Direct Investment in Latin America", in Manuel R. Agosin (ed.), *Foreign Direct Investment in Latin America*, IDB, Washington D.C., 1995, p. 11.
34 Mira Wilkins, *The Maturing of Multinational Enterprise: American Business Abroad from 1914 to 1970*, Harvard University Press, Cambridge (Massachusetts), 1974, p. 104.
35 John M. Kline, *Foreign Investment Strategies in Restructuring Economies. Learning from Corporate Experiences in Chile*, Quorum Books, Westport, 1992, p. 3.
36 Ibid., p. 4.
37 Ibid., p. 5.
38 Stephen F. Lau, *The Chilean Response to Foreign Investment*, Praeger Publishers, New York, 1972, p. 17.
39 John M. Kline, *Foreign Investment Strategies...*, p. 6.
40 Ibid., p. 7.
41 Ibid., p. 8.
42 Mira Wilkins, *The Maturing...*, pp. 358-360.
43 Stephen F. Lau, *The Chilean Response...*, pp. 25-30.
44 John M. Kline, *Foreign Investment Strategies...*, p. 10.
45 Ibid., pp. 8-9.
46 Carlos Fortin, "The Political Economy of Repressive Monetarism: the State and Capital Accumulation in Post-1973 Chile", in Christian Anglade and Carlos Fortin (eds.), *The State and Capital Accumulation in Latin America. Volume 1: Brazil, Chile, Mexico*, University of Pittsburgh Press, Pittsburgh, 1985, p. 151.
47 Adeoye A. Akinsanya, *The Expropriation of Multinational Property...*, p. 138.
48 Paul E. Sigmund, *Multinationals in Latin America*, p. 172.
49 John M. Kline, *Foreign Investment Strategies...*, p. 12.
50 Ibid., p. 14.
51 Ibid., p. 16.
52 Ibid., p. 24.
53 Ibid., pp. 26-27.
54 Ibid., pp. 26-27.
55 Ibid., p. 16.
56 Ibid., p. 29.
57 Manuel R. Agosin, J. Rodrigo Fuentes, and Leonardo Letelier, "Chile: The Origins and Consequences of External Capital", in José Antonio Ocampo and Roberto Steiner (eds.), *Foreign Capital in Latin America: An Overview*, IDB, Washington, D.C., 1994, p. 113.
58 Ibid., p. 113.
59 Carlos Fortin, "The Political Economy of Repressive Monetarism...", pp. 172-173.
60 John M. Kline, *Foreign Investment Strategies*, pp. 32-33.

61 Ibid., pp. 34-35.
62 Ibid., p. 35.
63 Ibid., p. 69.
64 Ibid., p. 36.
65 Ibid., p. 39.
66 W. Baer, *The Brazilian Economy: Growth and Development*, Praeger Publishers, New York, 1989, p. 61.
67 Peter Evans and Gary Gereffi, "Foreign Investment and Dependent Development: Comparing Brazil and Mexico", in Sylvia Ann Hewlett and Richard S. Weinert (eds.), *Brazil and Mexico. Patterns in Late Development*, Institute for the Study of Human Issues, Philadelphia, 1982, p. 139.
68 Ibid., p. 123.
69 Christian Anglade, "The State and Capital Accumulation in Contemporary Brazil", in Christian Anglade and Carlos Fortin (eds.), *The State and Capital Accumulation...*, p. 57.
70 Thomas E. Skidmore and Peter H. Smith, *Modern Latin America*, Oxford University Press, New York, 1997, p. 176.
71 Ibid., p. 185.
72 Christian Anglade, "The State and Capital Accumulation...", p. 67.
73 Winston Fritsch and Gustavo Franco, *Foreign Direct Investment in Brazil: its Impact on Industrial Restructuring*, OECD Development Centre, Paris, 1991, pp. 27-29.
74 Peter Evans and Gary Gereffi, *Foreign Investment...*, pp. 123-125.
75 Winston Fritsch and Gustavo Franco, *Foreign Direct Investment in Brazil...*, p. 29.
76 Ibid., p. 29.
77 Ibid., pp. 29-30.
78 Ibid., p. 31.
79 Ibid., p. 21.
80 Jonathan Wheatley, "Joining the Carnival?", *Accountancy: the Journal of Incorporated Accountants*, London, November 1996, p. 32.
81 Ibid., p. 33.
82 Ibid., pp. 33-34.
83 Manuel R. Agosin, "Foreign Direct Investment...", p. 12.
84 Ibid., p. 16.
85 Roberto Steiner and Ursula Giedion, "Characteristics, Determinants and Effects of Foreign Direct Investment in Colombia", in Manuel R. Agosin (ed.), *Foreign Direct Investment in Latin America*, pp. 138-139.
86 Ibid.
87 Ibid., p. 140.
88 Ibid., p. 141.
89 Ibid., pp. 143-144.
90 Ibid., p. 143.
91 Ibid., p. 142.
92 Ibid., pp. 143-144.
93 Ibid., pp. 146-147.

5 Post-Franco Spain: New Economic Development and Liberalization

Economic Development

Economic liberalization in Latin America alone did not trigger the flow of Spanish direct investment. The Spanish rates of direct investment abroad began to grow significantly in the late 1980s, as seen in figure 2.1, even before Latin American countries began implementing the bulk of their structural reforms. Different developments within the Spanish economy itself took place, which made Spanish companies invest in foreign ventures. These changes can be grouped into two broad categories: "Spain's degree of economic development" and "economic liberalization within Spain". To analyze the first of these variables, it is necessary to understand the relation between economic development and direct investment. Based on this relation, John H. Dunning and Rajneesh Narula provide a division of countries into five stages:[1]

- Stage 1: a country's location advantages are not strong enough to attract FDI, except for extraction and exploitation of natural resources. Income per capita and demand are low. These are LDCs that have abundant poorly-qualified labor and lack transportation and telecommunication infrastructure. FDI is very small and is limited to commercial activities to promote exports.[2]
- Stage 2: the stock of capital in value-added activities and the domestic market are larger than in the first case. Some capital-intensive industries such as steel, shipyards and basic chemicals might appear, as well as labor-intensive manufacturing industries. Inward FDI may take place as a reaction to the import-substitution-industrialization policies implemented by the government, who restricts free trade. Some domestic support industries emerge. Outward FDI starts to grow, either trying to further exports to neighboring countries, or as a

92

strategic move to start production in developed countries.[3] The government gives some priority to education (especially secondary education), transportation, communications and provision of public goods and services. Foreign MNEs invest primarily in the manufacturing sector and in exploitation of natural resources. FDI works as a stimulus for the economy because it increases the capacity and productivity of natural resources. Some industries requiring intermediate technology begin to emerge: consumption goods, leather, textiles, food and electronic goods. At this stage, the government should provide adequate infrastructure and apply coherent macroeconomic policies.

- Stage 3: the standard of living is high, the tertiary sector is large and both consumers and firms give some degree of priority to quality, product differentiation, upper education and R&D. As wages rise (thanks to better education and innovation), the comparative advantages of labor no longer rest on its cost. Inward FDI seeks access to an enlarged market and more efficient production. Outward FDI rests on the possession of proprietary assets similar to those of firms from developed countries, and is directed to countries in stages 1 and 2, in search of cheaper labor and an economy with a lesser degree of development.

- Stage 4: the amount of FDI the country receives is similar to the amount of FDI it sends abroad. The country's comparative advantages rest solely on created factors (derived mainly from their multinationality), not on natural endowments. Domestic companies are able to compete with foreign firms, not only in the domestic economy, but in new markets also. They invest abroad to internalize the market for their ownership advantages by producing abroad. Intra-industry trade and investment takes place. The government tries to phase out inefficient industries, while fostering accumulation of technology in infant industries.[4]

- Stage 5: or information economy. These are postindustrial societies, such as the United States, Japan, Germany, France or Sweden, in which the information sector is very important: telecommunications, computer science, and some others. Their FDI positions become more evenly balanced. MNEs internalize a large share of economic transactions among these countries. The economies of these countries are highly integrated. Industrial strategic alliances and acquisitions pursue higher rates of efficiency. The ownership advantages are less dependent upon the country's natural resources than on the ability of firms to efficiently organize their advantages.[5]

Dunning and Narula point out that their five-stage model is not necessarily the pattern followed by every country in its development path. Nevertheless, based on their model, Durán Herrera analyzed Spain's economic evolution.[6] He explained that Spain went through the first stage in the nineteenth century and first half of the twentieth century. In the 1960s it reached stage 2 and in the second half of the 1980s it entered stage 3. Durán concluded that it entered stage 4 in the 1990s. As seen in table 5.1, in the late 1990s the amount of FDI by Spanish firms was approaching FDI by foreign MNEs within Spain.

Figures 5.1 and 5.2 show Spain's economic growth in the last decades of the twentieth century. The mechanization of industry in the 1960s led to higher rates of growth. That decade Spain initiated a process of slow but gradual liberalization. Imports into Spain grew, as well as FDI. After a slowdown in the late 1970s caused by the oil crisis, Spain resumed growth in the 1980s. In 1979 the government began a process of further liberalization, which opened up the way for quicker exchanges of capital and stimulated economic growth once again. FDI played an important role in this new phase of economic boom. Since the mid-1980s Spain became one of the major recipients of FDI in Europe.

Figure 5.1 Spain's GDP, 1954-1993
(in 1980 Spanish pesetas)

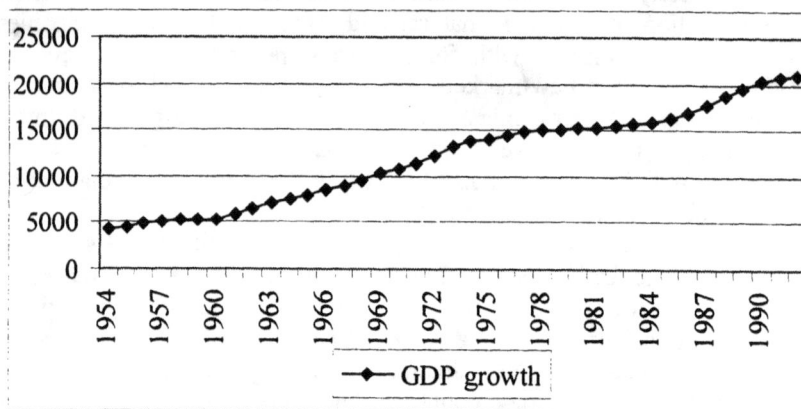

Source: Manuel Román, *Growth and Stagnation of the Spanish Economy*, Avebury, Aldershot, 1997, pp. 10-11.

Figure 5.2 GDP deflator, 1964-1993

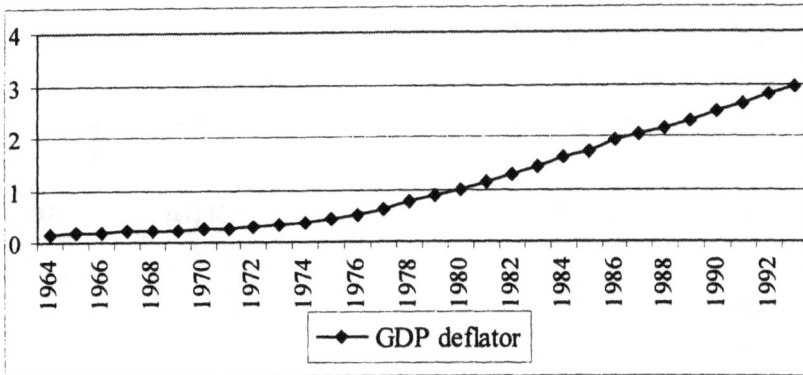

Source: Manuel Román, *Growth and Stagnation of the Spanish Economy*, Avebury, Aldershot, 1997, pp. 160-161.

Economic Liberalization

The government played a crucial role in the process of internationalization of the Spanish economy. The first measure adopted by Spanish authorities to allow freer flows of capital was to eliminate administrative requisites. Up until the mid-1970s, Spain had strong mechanisms to control capital movements, in order to avoid capital flight. When a Spanish company wanted to make an investment abroad it had to request permission from the government. Almost every case was taken to the Council of Ministers. The whole process, from the time the request was made until it was approved, took an average of thirty days.

The first step to liberalize capital movements was adopted on April 14, 1977, when the government passed Royal Decree 1087, regulating Spanish investment abroad. This decree stated that only investments over 50 million pesetas (around 660,000 U.S. dollars in 1976) had to be approved by the Council of Ministers. Investments under 50 million pesetas were approved by the Minister of Trade and Tourism or by the Director General of External Transactions. This whole process took thirty days. A total of 351 investments were approved in 1977 and 485 in 1978.[7]

Royal Decree 2236 of 1979 provided the legal basis to promote Spanish direct investment abroad. The government authorized Spanish citizens to own equity and assets held in foreign currency. Nonetheless, those individuals, firms or organizations making a foreign investment, had to notify the Dirección General de Economía Internacional y Transacciones Exteriores (DGEITE).[8]

Table 5.1   Relation between flows of Spanish direct investment abroad and flows of FDI in Spain, 1979-1994 ($ Million)

Year	FDI in Spain (A)	Spain's FDI (B)	A/B
1979	1,195	332	3.59
1980	1,190	358	3.32
1981	850	325	2.61
1982	1,660	458	3.62
1983	1,102	239	4.61
1984	1,660	304	5.46
1985	1,647	257	6.40
1986	2,862	477	6
1987	5,886	814	7.23
1988	7,289	1,971	3.69
1989	10,511	2,367	4.44
1990	17,848	4,460	4
1991	22,122	4,372	5.05
1992	18,699	5,342	3.50
1993	14,552	3,473	4.19
1994	17,536	7,618	2.30

Source: Spanish Trade Secretariat.

Some conceptual modifications were incorporated to the legislation through Royal Decree 2374 in 1986. Nevertheless, the spirit of the law regulating FDI was not modified until 1992, when Royal Decree 672 reduced the types of investment subject to verification by the DGEITE to three categories: investments over 250 million pesetas (around $2.5 million in 1992), up from the 25-million requirement set in 1990; investments in countries or territories considered fiscal havens (regulated by Royal Decree 1080 of 1991); and investments in societies created to hold stocks.[9]

Spain's incorporation into the European Union in 1986 provided a big boost for the Spanish economy. Before that date, most Spanish products had free entry into European markets. After 1986, European demand stimulated Spanish exports even further. Many foreign firms targeting the

European market invested in Spain, seeking cheaper qualified labor relative to other E.U. countries. As shown in tables 5.1 and 5.2, FDI into Spain increased tremendously since the mid-1980s. The European "cohesion funds" (geared toward the European regions whose GDP/capita was lower than 75 percent of the European Union's average) provided extra revenue for the state and helped fund public works and social programs. These factors contributed to accelerate the rates of economic growth, which in the late 1980s and early 1990s averaged 4.2 percent yearly.[10]

Table 5.2 Main recipients of FDI in the world, inward stock ($ Million)

Host Economy	1980	1985	1990	1995[11]
United States	83,046	184,615	394,911	564,637
United Kingdom	63,014	64,028	218,213	244,141
France	22,617	33,392	86,514	162,423
Germany	36,630	36,926	111,231	134,002
China	--	3,444	14,135	128,959
Spain	5,141	8,939	66,276	128,859
Canada	54,163	64,657	113,054	116,788
Australia	13,173	25,049	75,752	104,176
Netherlands	19,167	24,952	73,664	102,598

Source: United Nations, *World Investment Report, 1996. Investment, Trade and International Policy Arrangements*, New York, 1996, pp. 239-243.

Within the European framework, Spanish firms set up distribution networks to promote their exports in Europe. As integration proceeded, some Spanish firms decided to set up facilities abroad to expand production and increase their sales in the Union. All this process, along with the debt crisis experienced by Latin American nations, diverted Spanish FDI from those traditional markets and from the United States, which was regarded by Spanish investors as a safe haven when investment elsewhere was deemed troublesome.

Figure 5.3 shows how the share of Spanish FDI going to the European Union increased dramatically in the mid-1980s. However, in 1986 Portugal also joined the common market. Since Portugal is Spain's natural neighbor and the single main recipient of Spanish FDI overall, the sharp increase experienced by the European Union area and the decrease of the rest-of-the-world section in 1986 were caused, to a significant extent, by Portugal's incorporation to the European Union. Nevertheless, the important increment in European investment cannot be attributed solely to that factor. Spanish firms diversified their foreign investment and increased their presence in European markets in absolute and relative terms.

Figure 5.3   World distribution of Spain's FDI, 1980-1997

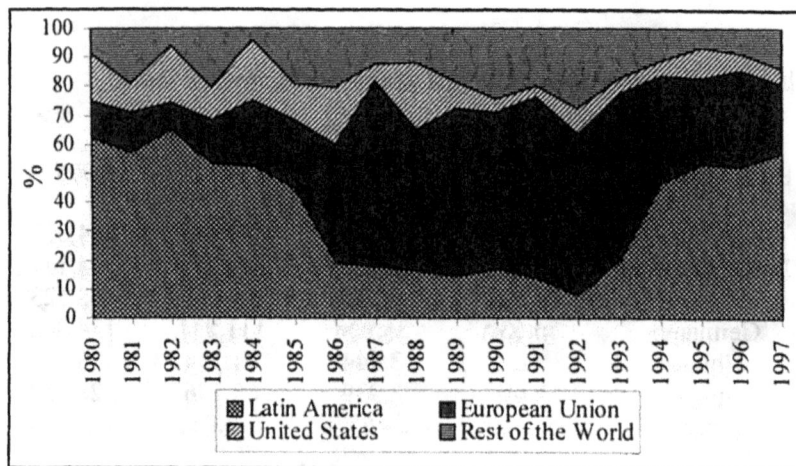

Source: DGEITE.

In the 1990s Spanish FDI concentrated basically in two geographic areas: Latin America and the European Union. The United States had a share of around 7 percent, which began to increase in the year 2000. The process of economic liberalization initiated by the Spanish government in the late 1970s was accelerated after 1986. Nevertheless, European and Spanish authorities negotiated a transition period on a sectoral basis to allow Spanish firms to adapt to broader competition. In general terms, this period ended in 1992. Thereafter, European authorities worked on deregulation procedures to eliminate national monopolies and restrictions to competition from other European companies. Even though some general deadlines were established, as well as guidelines to follow, differences in the degree of competitiveness among firms from European countries made authorities give some countries (including Spain) longer transition periods.

The liberalization of public utilities sectors in the European Union was one of the factors that accelerated Spanish direct investment abroad. The telecommunication sector in Spain was liberalized on 1 December 1997 (1 January 1997 in most E.U. countries), and the energy sector will be liberalized after 2000. Spanish companies in these sectors were afraid to lose a large share of their market to more competitive European firms. FDI was sought as a strategy to grow, to increase efficiency and to learn to operate in liberalized and more competitive markets. This prompted the Spanish telephone monopoly, Telefónica de España, to investment abroad since 1988. The Spanish airline Iberia, the petroleum firm Repsol and the energy distributor Endesa followed the same strategy. Liberalization in Spain coincided with the processes of privatization and liberalization of the telephone, energy and airline sectors in Latin America in the 1990s, giving these Spanish firms terrain to expand their operations, as a defensive strategy against competitors within their home market.

The role played by the Spanish government in this process was very important. Not only by implementing liberalization measures and translating the European Union's policies into Spanish legislation, but also directly by encouraging the process of internationalization of Spanish firms. All of these companies, which were the most visible heads of the Spanish investors in Latin America, were state-owned enterprises at the time they began investing abroad. Even though the Spanish government began privatizing these monopolies in the 1980s, the government still retained a controlling share in most of them until the late 1990s.

The government also devised a patchwork of policies to encourage Spanish firms to invest abroad. These were mechanisms devised mostly in the 1990s to help Spanish companies in their foreign ventures, in order to avoid double taxation, to finance and insure their investments, and to create a favorable investment climate for Spanish firms by signing bilateral investment agreements.

Tax Policy

Following approval of Directive 435 in 1990 by the European Union, E.U. countries did not tax the distributed dividends of those subsidiaries whose parent company was headquartered in other E.U. country to avoid double taxation. Moreover, the home country exempted the company from paying tax on the distributed dividends or deducted from its taxes those already paid elsewhere within the European Union. Even though the European Union did not attempt to harmonize tax systems, it aimed at avoiding cases of double taxation among member states.

Spain's policy applied the same criteria to earnings from other parts of the world. Like most industrialized countries, its policy was to deduct from the taxes on repatriated earnings those already paid abroad, the limit being the tax rate set in Spain for each category. Resident corporations also had the choice of paying the tax that would be payable in Spain if the income had been generated in Spain. Corporate Tax Law No. 43 of December 27, 1995, granted a credit for underlying taxes paid by second- and lower-tier subsidiaries. To benefit from this tax credit, the qualifying parent should hold at least 5 percent of the outstanding shares in its subsidiary for a minimum of an uninterrupted one-year period prior to the date when the dividend became payable.[12] Spanish law also recognized depreciation of the investment, the limit being the cost of the investment, but this deduction was reversed when the subsidiary increased its value again. The losses of the subsidiary could also be included in the balance sheet of the parent.[13]

In 1991, the Spanish Ministry of Trade and Tourism launched the so-called "Internationalization Plan", and in 1994 adopted new "Supporting Measures for the Foreign Activities of Spanish Enterprises" to promote investment abroad. The government believed that 'in the context of open markets, investment abroad allows companies to optimize business opportunities and improve their competitive advantages through direct establishment abroad or through the creation of channels of commercialization that strengthen the presence of Spanish exports abroad'.[14]

The government was especially concerned about promoting Spanish exports. For this reason, it allowed Spanish firms to deduct 25 percent off of the tax on their foreign investment when the investment was related to some export activity (or when it involved tourist services in Spain). This 25 percent deduction also applied to advertising expenditures incurred in the launching of products and penetration or promotion in new markets.[15]

Financial Aid for Spanish Direct Investment Abroad

The government created three credit programs to help Spanish firms finance their direct investments abroad, as part of its broader "Internationalization Plan". The Instituto de Crédito Oficial (ICO) had a fund of 20 billion pesetas (around U.S. $150 million), provided by three government institutions (Ministry of Trade and Tourism, Instituto de Comercio Exterior –ICEX- and ICO), channeled through intermediary financial institutions to finance Spanish investment abroad in the creation or improvement of commercial networks and in production projects in other countries.[16]

COFIDES (Compañía Española de Financiación del Desarrollo), also a state institution, was created to finance Spanish direct investment, particularly in LDCs.[17] COFIDES had financial resources of 2.5 billion pesetas (about $19 million). Its stockholders were two more state institutions, ICEX and a government bank, Argentaria,[18] which had access to extra funding from E.U. institutions. COFIDES only provided funding for projects designed with profitability criteria. In 1994, COFIDES created a new program, along with the Ministry of Trade and ICEX, with a fund of 2 billion pesetas ($15 million) to provide funding for new projects or for expansion of existing ones in LDCs. These projects had to have at least 50 percent Spanish participation.[19]

The third program was implemented in 1997 by the conservative administration of José María Aznar. The government created a fund of 80 billion pesetas (around $570 million) to finance foreign direct investments made by Spanish small- and medium-sized firms. The funds were channeled through ICO. The Spanish Minister of the Economy, Rodrigo Rato, believed then that Spanish small and medium enterprises had great managerial and technological capabilities that made them very competitive abroad.[20] The goal of this program was to promote investment by small and medium enterprises, because until then, most Spanish investments abroad were made by large firms.

As a member country of the European Union, Spanish investors could also benefit from the financial mechanisms created by Brussels to promote direct investment outside the European Union. Even though investment policies were responsibility of the states (not of the European Union), the European Union acknowledged the important role that FDI could play for both the European countries as home, and for hosts of European FDI, primarily developing nations. For this reason, the European Union set up several financial mechanisms to fund European direct investment abroad.

The European Investment Bank (EIB), created in 1958, had four different funds to finance investment in four regions of the world (the EIB was the largest development institution in the world in the 1990s, lending more than the World Bank, and its interest rates were among the most competitive on the international capital markets).[21] The Lomé Agreement created a fund of 12 billion Euros (10.8 billion as subsidies, 1.2 as loans) for the years 1991-2000, to finance direct investment in the ACP region (Africa, Caribbean, Pacific), channeled through the European Development Fund (EDF).[22] The EDF also had 280 million Euros to subsidize part of these credits, as well as 825 million Euros for risk-capital operations.[23] Since 1993, a new fund was designated to finance investments in Latin America and Asia. This fund disbursed 750 million Euros between 22 February 1993 and 22 February 1996.[24]

The European Community Investment Partners (ECIP) program was designed to promote the creation of joint-ventures in LDCs of Asia, Latin

America and the Mediterranean region, with participation of a E.U. firm.[25] It was expected to disburse 50 million Euros yearly for the period 1996-1999. ECIP's goal was to assist companies (particularly small enterprises) to conduct the various stages involved in creating joint-ventures or setting up private infrastructure projects, as well as to support LDCs' governments and public agencies to devise privatization schemes. E.U. officials believed joint-ventures encourage technology and know-how transfers, and contribute to create export opportunities in the host countries.[26]

Al-Invest was created in March 1994 to promote direct investment flows from the European Union to Latin America in all economic sectors. It had a fund of 85 million Euros, provided by the European Union and the private sector on a 50-50 basis. Its second phase was inaugurated in March 1996. It organized 30 biregional business encounters annually, involving 10,000 companies from the European Union and Latin America.

Spanish firms also had access to other multilateral financial instruments. The European Bank for Reconstruction and Development funded up to 33 percent of investment projects for promotion of the private industrial sector. 60 percent of its loans went to private companies, the remaining 40 percent to public infrastructure projects expected to contribute to facilitate the development of the private sector in areas such as telecommunications, transport, energy, and environment. Spain subscribed 3.4 percent of its shares.[27]

Spain was also a significant stockholder in the Multilateral Investment Fund for Latin America (MIFLA) and the Interamerican Investment Corporation (IIC), both financial instruments of the Interamerican Development Bank (IDB). Spain contributed $50 million to MIFLA when it was created in 1992 (the third largest share after the United States and Japan). MIFLA provided financial aid for investments by small enterprises (that promoted participation of women, young people and underemployed labor), working in conjunction with NGOs, foundations and associations and local governments, that fostered the use of appropriate technology and respect for the environment.

Spain was one of the main stockholders of the IIC (3.13 percent), since it was established in 1989. The IIC provided loans and capital investments for small enterprises willing to invest in developing regions (up to 33 percent of the total investment needs). It also created consortia with commercial banks that participated in its loan programs, provided financial and technical consulting for pre-investment surveys, identified and selected investment projects, searched for and selected potential investment partners, participated in the early stages of implementation of the project, and even took part in the administration and management of the business.[28]

Spanish firms could get partial financial support for their investments from the International Finance Corporation (IFC). Its Technical Assistance Trust Funds provided funding for sectoral surveys, technological adaptation and formation of labor in the early stage of the investment. The IFC also had a special program to promote investment in the Caribbean and Central America called "Caribbean and Central America Business Advisory Service".

The UN had trust funds to promote industrial development in LDCs. The United Nations Industrial Development Organization (UNIDO) helped investors find partners in the ACP region and financed training programs and viability reports. The World Bank's International Finance Corporation helped promote development by financing medium- and large-scale projects in LDCs. For each dollar it provided, private investors usually provided 5, but its share never went over one quarter of the total cost. Its contribution ranged between one and fifty million dollars.

All these agencies had some common features. They took a temporary 20 to 40 percent share of the capital in enterprises set up in LDCs but did not participate in the management of the business. They provided loans for between 25 and 50 percent of the cost of projects over $500,000. They required the promoters to provide one third of the capital. They funded, not only new projects, but also the expansion, diversification, modernization and privatization of existing ones.[29]

Between 1988 and 1993, Spanish firms took part in 79 projects arranged through COFIDES. Only 33 of those were funded by the Spanish financial institutions that participated in this program, providing a total of 1.4 billion pesetas. The remaining 46 projects were arranged through COFIDES, but funded by E.U. institutions, which provided a total of 3.7 million Euros.[30]

Protection of Investments

The Spanish government encouraged the use of insurance mechanisms, rather than financial agencies, as an instrument to induce private companies to invest in LDCs. It stressed that if there was a well-crafted coverage scheme to reduce non-commercial risk, institutional financing would be substituted by private financing (protected by multilateral or bilateral insurance agencies). The Compañía Española de Seguro de Crédito a la Exportación (CESCE) played this role. It was created in 1970 to insure credit for exports, and since 1974 it also insured direct investment abroad. Its shareholders were the Spanish state (50.25 percent), banks (43 percent) and insurance companies (7 percent). The Spanish state was the party that paid the investors for the losses suffered in the host country, under the conditions stipulated by its policies.[31]

CESCE provided insurance for the creation of companies, total or partial acquisition of foreign companies, loans with a maturity of five years or longer, and reinvestments. Its insurance protected Spanish firms from the political risks caused by the legislative or administrative action of the host country that implied a change in the conditions and framework that originated the investment and prevented it from completion. There was no limit as to the amount of money to be insured, but CESCE established a ranking of countries into five different categories to determine the cost of the insurance, based on the estimated degree of risk. The insurance was valid for a period of five years, which could be extended thereafter on a yearly basis, for a total period of twenty years. CESCE did not notify the host country of the insurance and obliged the company contracting it to keep it secret. The large companies were the main subscribers of CESCE's insurance, mainly for investments in Maghreb and Latin America.

The Multilateral Investment Guarantee Agency (MIGA) was also open to Spanish firms willing to subscribe an insurance for their investments. It was created by the World Bank in 1988 to promote FDI in LDCs. Its main functions were the provision of guarantees to investors against losses derived from problems of currency convertibility, expropriation, war, civil unrest and failure to fulfill the agreement by the authorities of the host; and the provision of consulting services to LDC member countries as to how to create a more favorable investment climate.

MIGA provided insurance for new projects as well as for expansion, modernization or restructuring of existing ones. It also covered acquisitions in privatization programs and subsidiaries established through direct investment. All of these, however, had to be financially solid, respect the environment and have a positive impact on the economy of the host. MIGA provided insurance for a period of fifteen years, which could be extended five more years, if it was deemed reasonable (the insured could cancel the contract after three years). It provided coverage for a maximum of $50 million. Its interest rate was 0.5 percent.[32]

All Latin American countries except Mexico joined MIGA. Argentina, Brazil and Peru were some of the main recipients of FDI insured through MIGA. Spain held 1.42 percent of the shares ($13.9 million dollars) and had a representative in the Board of Directors, with the support of El Salvador, Honduras, Nicaragua, Costa Rica and Venezuela (Spain also keeps a representative at the Board of Directors of the IMF and the WB with the support of these countries).[33]

Spanish companies, however, did not use these insurance mechanisms very often. The reasons were that Spain was a net recipient of FDI until the late 1990s, the complex exchange rate mechanism that was in place in Spain until the 1980s, lack of information, the concentration of Spanish FDI in OECD countries, where political risk was nonexistent, and the cost of the insurance *vis-à-vis* the appraisal of the profits. Besides, all these mechanisms were designed to provide insurance for large investments. With a few exceptions, most Spanish companies made small investments in Latin America, and did not qualify to take part in these schemes.

Bilateral Agreements

The so-called "Bilateral Agreements for Reciprocal Promotion and Protection of Investments" (BARPPIs) were the main instrument chosen by the Spanish government to create a positive investment climate toward Spanish investors. Spain signed BARPPIs with those countries that received significant amounts of Spanish FDI, purchased a significant amount of Spanish exports or were a potential market for them, those that had a growing economy that offered opportunities for Spanish goods and enterprises, and those that subscribed Agreements of Economic Cooperation (AEC) with Spain and tried to strengthen mutual economic, financial and entrepreneurial relations.

The BARPPIs included protection for investments from the moment they materialized, and obliged the government of the host country to admit the investment and provide all types of technical assistance and licenses to the Spanish investor. The investor also received national treatment and Spain was granted most-favored-nation status. Access to some economic sectors, deemed sensible for national security purposes, was restricted to foreigners in some cases. These restrictions were thus included in the agreement. Free transfer of earnings, profit repatriation, wages and salaries and compensation were guaranteed, as well as loan payments, investments for maintenance and development of the business operation, and transfers for liquidation of the enterprise.

The host country agreed to bear economic responsibility for the loss caused to the investors in cases of nationalization, expropriation, and armed conflicts or equivalent situations. Compensation would be paid at real market value of the investment prior to the announcement of the expropriation, nationalization or armed conflict. Payment was to be in transferable and convertible currency. In case of dispute between the investor and the host country, both parties were referred to the tribunals of the host nation, the International Chamber of Commerce in Paris, the International Court of Justice, the United Nations Commission of

International Trade Law (UNCITRAL) and the International Center for Settlement of Investment Disputes (ICSID).[34]

Table 5.3   Bilateral agreements for reciprocal promotion and protection of investments signed by Spain with Latin American and Caribbean countries up until 1995

Country	Date
Argentina	3 October, 1991
Bolivia	24 April, 1990
Colombia	9 June, 1995
Chile	29 March, 1994
Cuba	27 May, 1994
Dominican Republic	16 March, 1995
Ecuador	25 January, 1994
El Salvador	14 February, 1995
Honduras	18 March, 1994
Mexico	23 June, 1995
Nicaragua	16 March, 1994
Paraguay	11 October, 1993
Peru	17 November, 1994
Uruguay	31 March, 1992
Venezuela	2 November, 1995

Source: José Carlos García de Quevedo and Rosa Hontecillas, "Los Acuerdos Bilaterales de Promoción y Protección Recíproca de Inversiones", *ICE*, No. 735, November 1994, p. 79; and United Nations, *World Investment Report, 1996. Investment, Trade and International Policy Arrangements*, New York, 1996, pp. 312-313.

Multilateral Agreements

Since Spain joined the European Union, it tried to strengthen the economic relationships between the European Union and Latin America in a similar way as France and the United Kingdom institutionalized diplomatic, political and economic relations between the European Union and their former colonies with the celebration of periodical meetings in Lomé: the Lomé Conventions. These efforts began to crystallize in December 1995 with the signature of an economic agreement drafted by Spain between MERCOSUR and the European Union. The accord included provisions on investment signed by all E.U. members and by the E.U. Commission and set out their intention to encourage biregional investment flows and to cooperate on intellectual property matters, to further stimulate FDI flows.

Article 12 dealt specifically with investment promotion. The two sides agreed to create a stable and attractive investment environment to stimulate mutually-beneficial FDI flows, to introduce a favorable legal framework for investment, through bilateral investment protection agreements and double-taxation accords, and to promote joint-ventures, particularly between small and medium enterprises.[35] In 1996, the Spanish government initiated diplomatic contacts with other OECD members to incorporate Latin American countries into the Multilateral Agreement on Investment, promoted by the OECD. Spanish authorities believed this measure would decrease risks for FDI in the area and would stimulate further inflows of direct investment.[36]

Notes

[1] John H. Dunning and Rajneesh Narula, "Transpacific Foreign Direct Investment and the Investment Development Path: The Record Assessed", *South Carolina Essays in International Business*, No. 10, May 1994.

[2] Ibid., pp. 10-11.

[3] Ibid., pp. 11-12.

[4] Ibid., p. 14.

[5] Ibid., p. 15.

[6] Juan José Durán Herrera, "Factores de Competitividad en los Procesos de Internacionalización de la Empresa", *ICE*, No. 735, 1995, pp. 37-38.

[7] *ICE*, No. 1661, 1 February 1979, pp. 349-350.

[8] *ICE*, No. 1765, 29 January 1981, pp. 382-383.

[9] *ICE*, No. 2415, 6-12 June 1994, p. 1403.

[10] Juanita Darling, "Spain Rediscovers Latin America", *Los Angeles Times*, 19 July 1992, pp. D1, D2.

[11] Estimates, based on flow figures.

[12] Price Waterhouse, *Corporate Taxes. A Worldwide Summary*, Price Waterhouse, London, 1996, p. 572.

[13] José Palacios Pérez, "Análisis Comparativo del Tratamiento Fiscal de las Inversiones en el Exterior", *ICE*, No. 735, November 1994, pp. 53-62.

[14] Pilar Morán Reyero, "La Inversión Directa Española en el Exterior: Evolución Reciente", *ICE*, No. 735, November 1994, p. 13.

[15] Ibid.

[16] Loans had to be repaid within a period of five to seven years. The interest rate was half a point over the MIBOR rate. There are no geographical restrictions to the investment. Source: Fernando Aceña Moreno, "Instrumentos de Financiación de Inversiones", and IRELA, *The European Union and Mercosur*.

[17] Between 1988 and 1994, COFIDES approved 79 projects, 33 of them with its own credit, the rest with EU funds, and provided almost 1.5 billion pesetas and 3.7 million ECU worth of credit. Source: Fernando Aceña Moreno, "Instrumentos de Financiación de Inversiones", and IRELA, *The European Union and Mercosur*.

18 Argentaria was privatized in 1998.
19 The limit was 50 percent of the cost of the project or 200 million pesetas, to be repaid in five to eight years. The interest rate could be fixed or variable, and it had a two-percent subsidy, paid by ICEX. Source: Fernando Aceña Moreno, "Instrumentos de Financiación de Inversiones", and IRELA, *The European Union and Mercosur*.
20 *El País Digital*, No. 320, 19 March 1997, "Economía" section, www.elpais.es (observed 19 March 1997).
21 IRELA, *The European Union and Mercosur: Towards a New Economic Relationship? (Base Document)*, Madrid, June 1996, p. 32.
22 Only projects with a cost of more than 20 million ECU were eligible. Funding was available for up to 50 percent of the total cost of the project. Projects had to be of "mutual interest". That is to say, they had to meet one of the following criteria: joint-ventures between Latin American and European Union companies, a high technology transfer, foster closer bi-regional relations (telecommunications and transport projects), incorporate environmental improvements, such as renewable energy sources and anti-pollution measures, encourage subregional integration, or links with other neighboring countries. Source: Fernando Aceña Moreno, "Instrumentos de Financiación de Inversiones", and IRELA, *The European Union and Mercosur*.
23 Loans had to be repaid in ten to twelve years, in the case of industrial projects, or up to twenty years, in the case of infrastructure. The EIB funded under 50 percent of the investment in specific sectors (industrial, agro-industrial, mining, energy, tourism and economic infrastructure), made by a private or by a state-owned company. The loans covered the "fixed asset component". Source: Fernando Aceña Moreno, "Instrumentos de Financiación de Inversiones", and IRELA, *The European Union and Mercosur*.
24 IRELA, *The European Union and Mercosur*, p. 32.
25 ECIP's goal was to assist firms (mainly smaller enterprises) to create joint-ventures or set up private infrastructure projects, to provide training for local employees, transfer of know-how, and to support LDCs' governments and public agencies devise privatization schemes. The European Union provided up to 20 percent of the capital or up to 1 million ECU. A network of E.U. and Latin American intermediary financial institutions had to co-finance the project on a non-repayable basis (ECIP financed up to 50 percent). Source: Fernando Aceña Moreno, "Instrumentos de Financiación de Inversiones", and IRELA, *The European Union and Mercosur*.
26 IRELA, *The European Union and Mercosur*, p. 31.
27 Fernando Aceña Moreno, "Instrumentos de Financiación de Inversiones", *ICE*, No. 735, November 1994, p. 71.
28 Ibid., pp. 68-69.
29 Ibid., pp. 66-67.
30 Ibid., p. 72.
31 Carlos Jiménez Aguirre, "La Protección de las Inversiones en el Exterior. Instrumentos Existentes", *ICE*, No. 735, November 1994, p. 86.
32 Ibid., p. 83.
33 Ibid., p. 82.
34 José Carlos García de Quevedo y Rosa Hontecillas, "Los Acuerdos Bilaterales de Promoción y Protección Recíproca de Inversiones", *ICE*, No. 735, November 1994, p. 79.
35 IRELA, *The European Union and Mercosur*, p. 30.
36 *El País Digital*, No. 320, 19 March 1997, "Economía" section (observed 19 March 1997).

6 The Reconquest of Latin America: 500 Years After

In the mid-1980s, the European Union designed a process of gradual liberalization of many economic sectors, including the telecommunications, energy, banking, and airline industries. This process followed the incorporation of Spain into the European Union. Spanish entrepreneurs realized their companies were too small and less competitive than their European Union counterparts. The latter had operated in a very competitive market and had grown very efficient and competitive. The Spanish market, on the contrary, had only begun to open in the late 1970s and Spanish firms had operated in a protected atmosphere. Spanish firms began to upgrade their management strategies, their technology and their objectives in the 1980s to face increasing competition from Europe.

Even though all industrial sectors liberalized gradually after Spain joined the Union, some industries still remained in a regime of strict protectionism. Those industries that used to be state monopolies, such as telecommunications, air transportation and energy production and distribution, were still strongly protected, not only by Spain, but also by most European states. Monopolies in these industries had been established to protect the sectors deemed important for the country's economy and security. Within the fraternal context created by the European Union, the national security argument was no longer relevant. Rather than in national security terms, European authorities began to look at these sectors in terms of economic efficiency.

State monopolies did not necessarily operate on the basis of economic profit, even though European state-owned enterprises as a whole were more economically efficient than their counterparts in other parts of the world, such as Latin America (as explained in chapter four). The European Union decided to liberalize these industries as part of its strategy to increase integration and economic efficiency among European firms and industries. A date was established for each industry's liberalization, and a period of transition was allowed for governments to adapt their legislation and their state-owned enterprises to competition.

Spanish authorities were especially concerned about liberalization of state monopolies, given the relative backwardness of Spanish state-owned firms, their poor rates of efficiency and technological sophistication, and their modest economic performance. Besides, the size of other European markets, such as Germany, France and the United Kingdom, gave companies in these countries an advantage, in terms of size of their business and revenue. The Spanish government realized the only way of being able to face open competition was for Spanish firms to grow. The response of Spanish firms to liberalization was geographical expansion and gradual privatization. The move toward privatization served two purposes: to increase revenue for the state to lower the government debt, in order to meet the Maastricht Treaty's 3 percent-deficit requirement, and to incorporate profit-driven managers with experience in the private sector to guide the companies in this process.[1] Foreign expansion posed a problem, because the European markets were still closed. Thus, state-owned enterprises had to look for other prospective markets.

At this point, Latin America and the Caribbean as a whole had decided to embark on a process of economic liberalization that included privatization of long-held state monopolies, such as the national airline carrier, telecommunications operator, energy production and distribution enterprises, and other industrial and service enterprises. Privatization gave Spanish firms the opportunity to grow beyond the Spanish market. Besides, the cultural proximity of Latin America gave them the opportunity to operate in a culturally friendly atmosphere. Latin America appeared as the natural market for Spanish firms to expand.

The liberalization of the European markets coincided with the implementation of the structural reforms by most Latin American countries in the late 1980s and early 1990s. Spanish firms were looking for foreign markets to expand their business abroad, and Latin American governments were seeking to attract foreign multinationals to take over the management of former state-owned monopolies in their process of renovation and modernization. Latin America was the most appealing market for Spanish firms. Spanish MNEs were among the most appealing partners for Latin American governments also. Latin American politicians saw in Spain a successful case of fast economic development during the 1980s, and believed Spanish companies could contribute to the development of the Latin American economies with the expertise they had achieved in their home market.

Most Latin American countries returned to democratic rule in the 1980s, after years of dictatorship and in some cases even civil war. The period of transition to democracy was uncertain and many doubts were up in the air about the ability of the new democratic rulers to consolidate democracy and the willingness of the army to retreat from the political domain and subordinate to the civil authorities. The economic crisis had become harsher in the 1980s and deepened economic, social and political inequalities. A new political framework was needed to redefine the relation between the state and its citizens, as well as a new economic agenda that set the basis for an efficient productive structure, capable of generating sustained economic growth in order to alleviate poverty rates and increase formal employment.

Iberian-American countries (those with Spanish and Portuguese heritage) share a strong common historical and cultural tradition that strengthens the bonds between them. Developments within each country transcend its borders and are followed closely within the other Iberian-American countries. Their societies are willing to learn from each other, exchange cultural and political ideas and sympathize with each others' success and misfortunes. The successful Spanish transition to democracy was thus followed very closely in Latin America. Its political and social peacefulness and the high degree of economic welfare achieved by Spain in a few years, turned the Iberian country into a model that provided some insights as to the process to follow by the Iberian American community (the Chilean economic reforms, as well as the South-East Asian tigers, were also regarded as models).

Spanish companies operated in a gradually liberalized economy throughout the 1980s and their performance was satisfactory. Overall, the standard of living in Spain rose considerably and Spanish firms contributed to this process by increasing their efficiency and productivity. Public utilities companies expanded considerably and used a private-sector type of entrepreneurial attitude. They were constrained by the need to run a surplus, improve the quality of their services and satisfy their customers. This attitude was facilitated by the decision of the government to privatize them gradually, in order to give managers from the private sector control over their business strategies and structures.

Spanish firms appeared as an appealing alternative to take part in the process of privatization of state-owned enterprises. They contributed satisfactorily to modernizing the economic sector in which they operated (i.e. by upgrading telephone infrastructure, providing sound credit, increasing the supply of energy at competitive prices, etc.), they were used to operating in a liberalizing economy, and their economic performance was overall satisfactory. The technological needs of Latin American countries were closer to those of Spain than to those of the United States or any other western European country. Besides, Spain was already one of the main providers of industrial machinery and technology to Latin American firms.

In the political arena, consensus among Spanish and Latin American politicians was strong. Their main common objectives were to cooperate in order to strengthen democratic institutions and to set up the economic base for a renewed economic recovery. Political and economic cooperation was constant, not only because linguistic similarities facilitated diplomatic and political interactions, but because the strong presence of Spanish immigrants in many Latin American countries, as well as the growing number of Latin American immigrants going to Spain in the 1980s and 1990s demanded closer relations.

Nevertheless, besides cultural, historical and economic ties, reasons of national security still made Latin American politicians favor Spanish over North American firms. The strong involvement of the United States into the domestic affairs of the countries in this region in the context of the Cold War was still very fresh in the memory of Latin American policy-makers. U.S. troops and the C.I.A. intervened in Latin America, not only for politico-ideological reasons, but also to safeguard the interests of U.S. MNEs. Even though an overt U.S. intervention in the post-Cold War context became very difficult to justify, Latin American politicians still feared U.S. interventionism.

Spain, on the contrary, did not have the potential, the willingness or the tradition to impose strong political pressure on Latin American governments to defend its economic interests. By allowing entry of Spanish companies into key economic sectors, there would be a diminution of North U.S. dominance over the economy overall. Besides, politicians hoped Spanish investors would attract other European companies, which would contribute to increase foreign investment and, at the same time, diminish the historical dependence of Latin American economies on U.S. investors and technology.

The influx of Spanish direct investment into Latin America grew considerably in the early 1990s, attracted by the process of privatization of state-owned enterprises undertaken by most governments and the development of a new legal framework, which gave more freedom to foreign companies. Privatization worked as a powerful stimulus for Spanish investors through the 1990s. In Argentina alone, the state generated a revenue of $10.273 billion from debt reduction schemes. Spain became the single main foreign purchaser, with an investment of approximately $7 billion (for the relative importance of Argentina, see Fig. 2.3).[2]

Figure 6.1   Spanish direct investment in Latin America and the Caribbean by areas of economic activity, 1990-1997

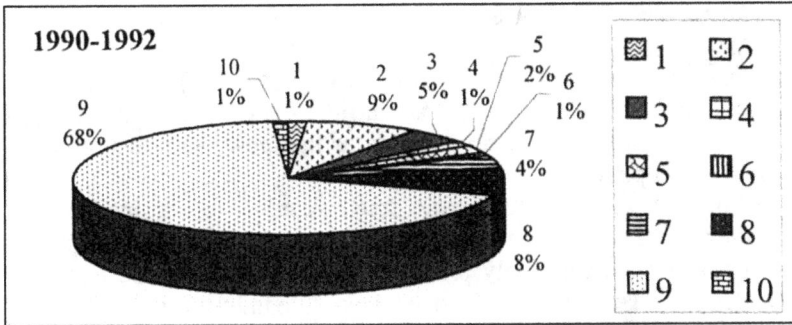

1990-1992

10 1%	1 1%	2 9%	3 5%	4 1%	5 2%	6 1%
9 68%						
7 4%	8 8%					

Legend: ▨1 ▣2 ■3 ⊞4 ▧5 ▥6 ☰7 ■8 ▢9 ⊞10

0, agriculture, cattle raising, hunting, forestry and fishing; 1, energy and water; 2, extraction and transformation of non-energy minerals and products derived from the chemical industry; 3, industries for the transformation of metals, precision mechanics; 4, other manufacturing industries; 5, construction; 6, commerce, restaurants and hotels; 7, transport and communications; 8, financial institutions, insurance, services provided to enterprises, and rents; 9, other services.

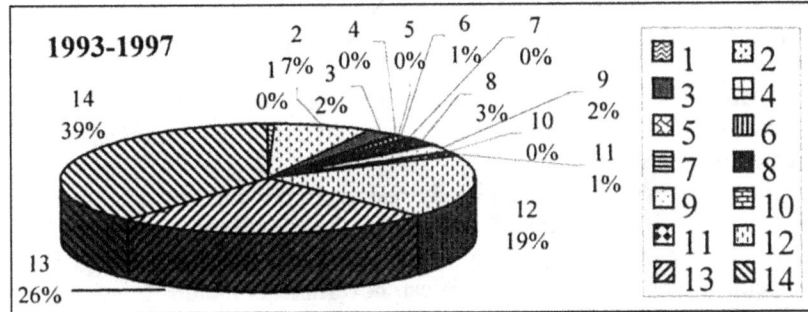

1993-1997

14 39%; 13 26%; 12 19%; 2 7%; 3 0%; 4 0%; 5 0%; 6 1%; 7 0%; 8 3%; 9 2%; 10 0%; 11 1%; 1 7%; 2%

Legend: ▨1 ▣2 ■3 ⊞4 ▧5 ▥6 ☰7 ■8 ▢9 ⊞10 ⊞11 ▢12 ▨13 ▧14

1, agriculture, cattle raising, hunting, forestry, and fishing; 2, production/distribution of electric energy, gas and water; 3, extractive industries, oil refining and fuel treatment; 4, food/beverages and tobacco; 5, textile industry and confection; 6, paper industry, edition and graphic arts; 7, chemical industry; 8, other manufactures; 9, construction; 10, commerce; 11, hotels; 12, transport and communications; 13, financial intermediaries, banking and insurance; 14, holding and others.

Source: DGEITE.

The Airline Sector

Spain's airline company, Iberia, a state-owned enterprise since its creation in 1927, was one of the first Spanish MNEs to make an important move in Latin America. In 1990 it participated in the privatization of Aerolíneas Argentinas and one year later in that of Viasa (Venezuela). In 1993 it also purchased shares in a Chilean private airline, Ladeco. Iberia's managers regarded the expansion in Latin America as the most sensible strategy to survive in a competitive and liberalized market.

In the late 1980s Iberia was small relative to its international competitors, it was in financial trouble, operated limited international networks, and served a highly protected domestic market. The European Union designed a schedule to liberalize the airline industry in the Spring of 1997. Before that date, European airlines were not allowed to transport passengers between two destinations outside the country where they were based. After liberalization, any E.U. air carrier would be allowed to operate to and from any E.U. city, even outside their own country.

The liberalization plans threatened to allow the largest European carriers, especially British Airways, Lufthansa, and Air France, to move into the Spanish market aggressively. Iberia's managers designed a strategy that included expansion outside Spain. This would allow the company, not only to supplement its national revenue with that from its foreign operations, but also to make Iberia an attractive potential partner for other international airlines looking for strategic alliances in Europe and elsewhere. The Spanish government also had plans to privatize the company. A significant presence abroad would thus make it more appealing to potential investors.

In the late 1980s Iberia already had an important network of routes between Europe and Latin America and the Caribbean. Latin America seemed the most likely region for the company to expand and strengthen its competitive advantage. Latin American governments included the national airline among the state-owned enterprises to be privatized early, as part of their privatization schemes. Airlines had accumulated important losses and were an important economic burden for the state. Privatization of the airline would generate revenue directly through the sale of the company, and would also save money indirectly, by relieving the state from the burden of paying the losses contracted by the firm every year.

The decision of the Argentine government to privatize Aerolíneas Argentinas in the late 1980s provided a tempting opportunity for Iberia to initiate its landing in the region. Aerolíneas Argentinas transported 1.1 million passengers on international routes and 2.2 million on domestic flights (68 percent of the Argentinean market).

Figure 6.2   The ten largest airlines and Iberia by volume of sales, 1995

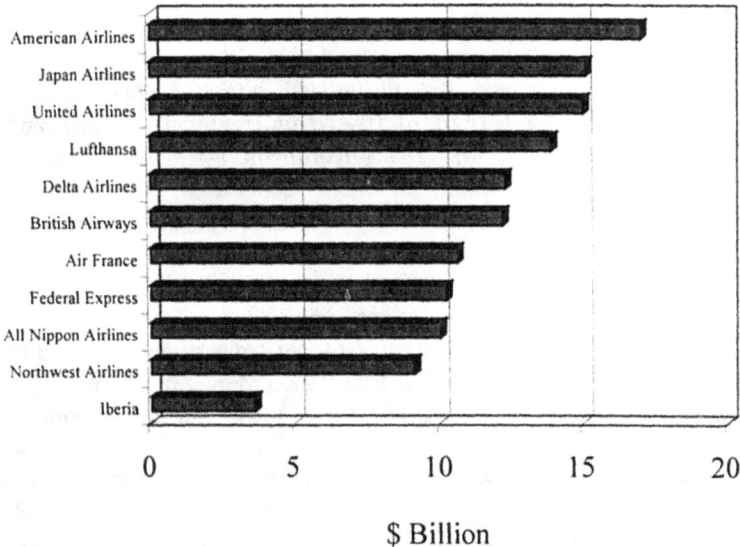

$ Billion

Source: *El País Digital*, No. 415, 23 June 1997, "Economía" section.

In 1988 SAS negotiated directly with the Argentinean Government the acquisition of a large share of the stocks of Aerolíneas Argentinas, but the Argentinean parliament did not authorize this bid of $204 million, and proposed the Government to privatize the airline through an international public auction. Three consortia showed interest: (1) Varig and Citibank; (2) American Airlines and Chase Manhattan Bank; and (3) Alitalia. All of them, however, decided not to bid.

The Argentine government feared the collapse of its privatization plans and initiated negotiations directly with Iberia. In 1990, the Spanish airline agreed to buy 30 percent of the shares directly, its Spanish banking partners (Banco Central Hispanoamericano, Cofivacasa and Banesto) would buy 19 percent, and a group of Argentinean partners another 36 percent.[3] The government decided to keep 15 percent. Mounting losses for the years 1991-1992 required the partners to contribute more funds. The Argentine group was unable to make the required contribution and sold part of its shares, comprising 28 percent of Aerolíneas Argentinas to the government, whose participation rose to 43 percent. In the end, the purchasing consortium was awarded 56.28 percent of the shares. The privatization agreement included an initial cash payment of $130 million; an additional $130 million to be paid in 5 years; and $1.61 billion in debt paper at nominal value (equivalent to $490 million in cash). The total was $750 million ($652.95 million of which was provided by the Spanish consortium). The privatized assets included all properties owned by Aerolíneas Argentinas and the designated airway rights for landing international traffic for periods of five years (regional services) and ten years (international services). The government assumed all the firm's liabilities, with the exception of labor debts and some commercial liabilities. Iberia would be directly responsible for the management of Aerolíneas.[4]

In 1991, Iberia also participated in the privatization of Venezuela's airline Viasa. Iberia created a consortium with a domestic bank, Banco Provincial, and offered $145 million. Another consortium, made up by the Dutch airline KLM, Northwest Airlines, Banco Mercantil of Venezuela and two private investors, had shown interest in Viasa, but decided not to bid, because they estimated that the company had a net worth below the minimum sale price of $135 million. As in Argentina, Iberia was the only bidder. The Spanish airline bought 45 percent of the shares, Banco Provincial 15 percent, 20 percent was given to the employees and the government kept 20 percent, to be sold later in the stock exchange.[5] With the acquisition of 38 percent of a private Chilean airline company, Ladeco, in 1993, Iberia completed its expansion in Latin America.

These three acquisitions gave Iberia control over 32 percent of the Latin American market in terms of passengers. The Spanish airline reorganized all its Latin American flights and those of its subsidiaries as a single company and made efforts to increase their productivity. In Viasa, for instance, the labor force was cut by a third, while occupancy rose by a fifth and the number of flights rose by almost 50 percent. Profits, however, never came. The bad performance of Latin American airlines was a carryover from the 1980s, made worse by the use of leased aircraft, which lowered barriers to entry into the industry. The deregulation of the domestic airline service market in the United States led to attempts by the U.S. government to liberalize and deregulate international bilateral air service agreements. This paved the way for U.S. carriers, such as American Airlines and United Airlines, to fly to Latin America.

Iberia could never turn its Latin American ventures into a profitable business. In fact, Iberia itself was losing money since the late 1980s. In 1992 it required a government bailout of $770 million and another cash infusion of $690 in 1996.[6] The European Commission authorized the 1996 subsidy on condition that Iberia sold its stakes in its Latin American subsidiaries. Iberia sold most of its shares in Aerolíneas Argentinas to

"Andes Holding", a society created by Bankers Trust, Merril Lynch and Sociedad Española de Promociones Industriales (SEPI), a Spanish government's enterprise that grouped most Spanish state-owned firms, including Iberia.[7] Viasa was closed down in February 1997. After its privatization, Viasa had accumulated a debt of $200 million. Iberia's venture in Chile was also unsuccessful. Ladeco canceled all its international flights in 1995, and in 1997 Iberia sold its 38-percent share to Ladeco's main local competitor, Lan Chile, for $8 million.[8]

As of October 2000, Iberia still retained a 10 percent share in Aerolíneas Argentinas. In December 1997, American Airlines signed an agreement with Iberia to purchase 10 percent of Aerolíneas' shares from Andes Holding, and committed to find financial investors and other airline carriers to buy the remaining 80 percent of the shares of the Argentine company.[9] The Spanish authorities were preparing Iberia for privatization. A three-year plan aimed at cutting costs and raising productivity was devised. In 1996 the airline was back in black numbers, with a modest profit of $20 million.

Table 6.1 Main proposed airline groups, as of June 1997

American Airlines	Lufthansa	Delta Airlines	Air France	KLM
Aerolíneas Argentinas	United Airlines	Air France	Alitalia	Northwest
British Airways	SAS	Swissair	Continental	Kenya
Japan Airlines	Air Canada	Singapore Airlines	Virgin	Garuda
Iberia	Thai Airways	Sabena		
Canadian Airlines	Varig	Austrian Airlines		
Avianca				
Lapsa				
TAM				

Source: El País Digital, No. 415, 23 June 1997, "Economía" section.

Iberia's long-term strategy aimed at integrating itself into one of the large world airline groups. The interest of American Airlines in Latin

America brought Iberia closer to the potential AA-British Airways alliance. Even though Iberia was only the twenty-first largest airline in the world in 1995 in terms of revenue, it still had powerful tools to negotiate with AA and BA. Iberia still owned majority stakes in Aerolíneas Argentinas, it was the main passenger carrier between Europe and Latin America, it had a prominent presence at Madrid airport, one the fastest-growing European airports, and the Spanish domestic market was growing at an annual rate of 12 percent.

In the late 1990s, the airline industry was going through important changes in facing a liberalized market. The airline companies were negotiating among themselves to create large groups, capable of operating around the whole world. This outcome provides empirical proof to Gomes-Casseres' theory of alliances. Gomes-Casseres explained that alliances are creating a new type of competition (collective competition), rather than suppressing it. Liberalization of airways will open the way to competition among airlines worldwide after 2000. Only those firms offering good services at a lower price will be able to survive competition. Iberia was negotiating the creation of an alliance with American Airlines (AA) and British Airways (BA) in the late 1990s.

Table 6.2   Flights between Europe and Latin America, share of the market by occupancy, 1996-1997

Airline	January 1997	January 1996
Iberia	14.51	14.24
British Airways	13.49	16.00
Lufthansa	9.37	9.39
Air France	8.60	6.95
KLM	7.87	7.87
Alitalia	4.90	5.86
American Airlines	4.67	6.21

Source: Iberia.[10]

The alliance would allow these airlines to share their infrastructure and personnel, to use common trade codes and to combine their routes. Iberia's contribution to the alliance would be its infrastructure in Madrid's airport (in terms of space and flying rights), the growth of Spain's domestic market, and its leading position in the transportation of passengers between

Europe and Latin America. If the alliance is finally established, Iberia is likely to specialize in the transportation of passengers between Europe and Latina America. Iberia's incorporation to the AA-BA alliance would allow it to expand its travel destinations worldwide, by combining its flights with those of the other airlines. This may allow Iberia to attract more customers, both in Spain and in Latin America. Similarly, AA and BA would be able to incorporate Iberia's routes to their own services. Cooperation would therefore increase their reach and lower their costs, which may translate into cheaper prices. Overall, the group would increase its competitive advantage *vis-à-vis* other airlines.

Telecommunications Sector

Telefonica became one of the most prominent Spanish MNEs in Latin America in the 1990s, not only for its presence in most countries in the region, but also for the large amounts of money it paid in the privatization of some of the national telephone companies ($2 billion for the Peruvian telephone company, which more than doubled the second bid, and $4.965 billion for Brazil's Telesp), and the high rates of return its investments generated (40 percent annually in Argentina in the first four years of operation).[11]

Telefonica's investment in Latin America was triggered by a conjunction of factors. On the one hand, the Spanish telecommunications sector was liberalized in December 1997, when a second operator began to operate in Spain. Secondly, the long process of privatization of Telefonica, initiated in the 1970s, was culminated in 1997. Finally, developments within the telecommunications industry triggered a process of internationalization of companies in this sector after the mid-1980s, which led in the late 1990s to the creation of large multinational telecommunications groups (following the pattern described by Gomes-Casseres).

The deregulation of the telecommunications industry was made possible by a significant change in the perception that governments had about this sector. Although the telephone industry was started in Latin American countries by the concessions granted to foreign MNEs (in most cases ITT), governments nationalized the assets of ITT between the 1940s and the 1970s, following the beliefs of dependency theory (Argentina in 1945, Brazil in 1962, Peru in 1970, Chile in 1971,[12] and Venezuela in 1976).[13] The politicians claimed that the state had to provide this strategic public service, which the market did not price correctly. This interpretation justified the classification of the telecommunications industry as a "natural monopoly" of the state. The same pattern took place in Spain. Telefónica de España was the Spanish subsidiary of ITT. Created in 1926, it was nationalized by the Franco regime in 1944 under national security claims. In the 1970s the Spanish government decided to initiate a gradual process of privatization that ended in 1997.[14] Economic interdependence and the process of regionalization of the economy increased in the 1990s, and with them the needs of firms to enjoy good and efficient telecommunications services. At the same time, technological innovations such as digitalization, fiber optics, mobile telecommunications and satellite communication increased the variety and quality of telecommunications services that operators can provide as well as their reach. This meant that telecommunications was no longer a "natural-monopoly".

Deregulation involves the elimination of legal barriers to entry into the industry and the redefinition of a new legal framework that defines the pricing policy, the charges applied by the owner of the basic network to other operators competing in the market and the privatization procedures. The privatization of national telephone companies was caused by the governments' dissatisfaction with the state enterprise's past performance: long waiting lists, outdated technology, poor service, artificially low prices and the excessive power of the workers and unions in the firms.[15] The state-owned telephone company had been unable to keep technology up with the needs of sophisticated users, who demanded cheap, reliable, high-speed networks for transmitting data, voice, text and images.

The privatization of the telephone company also served to maximize the proceeds from its sale to help end the country's fiscal and balance of payments crises and to send a positive signal to private investors. This latter reason was very important. FDI played a fundamental role in the development strategy devised by Latin American politicians in the 1990s. Latin markets became less interesting for foreign investors after the debt crisis and Latin American politicians believed they needed to call their attention again. The sale of the telephone company would serve that purpose. Its strategic importance would make the governments appear as truly committed to their structural reform program. By privatizing a "plum" rather than a "lemon", foreign investors would regain their interest in the market.[16] The telecommunications industry was highly attractive to foreign investors because at that point it had great opportunities for growth.

The telecommunication's companies from more industrialized countries were ready to take part in the privatization of these Latin American state-owned enterprises. They had the proper technology to upgrade the system. Telephone companies need large markets to make their investment profitable. Liberalization in the industrialized world was forcing (or threatening to force) national operators to compete with foreign firms in their countries. Thus, they sought abroad new markets to increase their sales and make their business profitable overall. In the United States, Japan and some European countries, the ratio lines per inhabitant was very high and had reached its limits to growth.

Table 6.3 Lines in service per 100 residents in a selected group of countries

Country	Lines in Service per 100 residents (January 1, 1989)
United States	52.7
France	45.6
Japan	41.7
Spain	28.1
Portugal	17.8
Uruguay	11.3
Argentina	9.9
Costa Rica	9
Venezuela	7.8
Colombia	6.8
Brazil	5.8
Mexico	5.1
Chile	4.9

Source: Manuel Sánchez, Rossana Corona, Luis Fernando Herrera, and Otoniel Ochoa, "The Privatization Process in Mexico: Five Case Studies", in Manuel Sánchez and Rossana Corona (eds), *Privatization in Latin America*, IDB, Washington, D.C., 1993, p. 156.

The process of internationalization of telecommunication companies can be in the form of exports of services and/or technology or through direct investments abroad. FDI in this industry can be divided in the provision of three main types of services: basic telephony, mobile communication and advanced business communication services. The first option implies the acquisition of the network from the government privatizing the industry. LDCs need the managerial and technological capabilities of some of the most advanced international companies to upgrade their telecommunications infrastructure. The second possibility is the development of mobile telecommunications. In this case, the network is rarely acquired because this is a very new service, and the telecommunications operator normally develops the infrastructure, once it has been granted a license by the government to operate in the market. The third alternative is the provision of sophisticated business services. Most of the firms demanding these services are located in industrialized countries. Opportunities for this sub-industry in LDCs are very small. A telecommunications company that has not internationalized its operations can only provide services to its customers within its domestic territory. Many firms internationalize their operations and need efficient communication among its centers, scattered around the globe. The leading telecommunications companies try to develop large international networks to provide these services among a larger number of countries and thus capture all the benefits generated by every single service.

Telecommunications companies can pursue their internationalization strategy individually, through alliances with other firms (in a hierarchical fashion, with the telecommunications operator being the leading partner: vertical internationalization) or through consortia (in a relation of cooperation: horizontal internationalization). This latest option was the one most commonly utilized by Telefonica for its overseas expansion. Juan José Durán and Fernando Gallardo define an international consortium in the telecommunications sector as a process of entrepreneurial cooperation with a temporal horizon (*a priori* unlimited) among several firms (at least one of them being a telecommunications operator) for the development of a large telecommunications venture that requires large financial and technological resources (provided by the partners). The rules guiding the consortium are pre-established by the partners and are not necessarily those guiding their regular individual operations.[17]

A telecommunications consortium is made up of a main technological partner, other minor telecommunications operators, financial parties and local partners. The formation of the consortium is led by the main telecommunications operator, who seeks new foreign markets as a defensive strategy to overcome competition in its domestic market or as an offensive tactic, to exploit its competitive advantage in other markets. As the leading partner in the consortium, it provides financial, technological and human resources, as well as managerial expertise. It is also responsible for the management of the new enterprise and its financial realization. When a telecommunications operator decides to participate in a consortium as a minority partner, it seeks to expand in new markets, as well as to learn and gain experience in the operation of particular services. It also provides resources and partakes of the management, but to a lesser extent. Financial partners only seek financial profitability. They do not provide resources apart from access to financial markets. The local partners seek to benefit from the venture as suppliers of equipment and/or services, or because they have great demand for telecommunications services for their particular businesses. They cooperate with their knowledge of the domestic market and contacts in the local economy. The relationship among all partners must be predefined, in order to maximize their contributions and smooth the development of the venture. The new enterprise has to be given an organization and personality of its own, independent from those of each member.

Governments are key agents in the process of creation of a new telecommunications enterprise. Even though they might not participate directly in the consortium, they must interact with it very closely. In the process of privatization the government defends the national interest, versus that of the foreign operators. It might also subsidize the enterprise, if the expectations of profit are too low, or it might require the licensee to extend its service to all areas in the country (even to underpopulated rural sectors where investment is not attractive). Moreover, the government is the ultimate agent deciding which consortium is awarded the service. Its criteria are not solely based on the offer made by each consortium, but also on their international prestige. A good relationship with the government might influence its decision when granting the license, as well as some future rewards, such as subsidies, fiscal exemptions, a fixed tax rate, or protection against political risk.

Telefonica had no previous experience outside Spain when it submitted its bid in the process of privatization of the Chilean telephone company in 1987. In the 1980s, it had been upgrading its services and expanding its lines inside Spain, keeping up with the growing demand. Even though its domestic growth was larger than that of telephone companies in other industrialized countries, the ratio lines per inhabitant in Spain was still lower (see table 6.3). In the late 1980s the Spanish domestic market still had enough potential for Telefonica to grow. Nevertheless, the company perceived attractive investment possibilities in the privatization process that was beginning in Latin America and decided to invest there. Chile in 1987, Argentina in 1988, and Mexico in 1990 were its first foreign bids.

Stephen Hymer's industrial organization approach provides the theoretical basis to understand Telefonica's expansion outside Spain. The liberalization of the Spanish market in 1997 became an immediate threat to the Spanish monopolist. Telefonica decided to explore international markets as part of its strategy to compensate for the decrease in revenue from its domestic market when the monopoly was lifted, and as a way to grow in order to increase its financial resources to withstand competition. Hymer cites three reasons why a firm may decide to initiate foreign operations: to remove competition, to exploit their advantages in new markets, or to diversify into different lines of activities.

Table 6.4   Telefonica's direct investments outside Spain in August 1998

Country	Subsidiary	Consortium	% owned	Main Partners	bought in
Argentina	Sintelar	Yes	25	Sintel	1990
Argentina	Telefónica de Argentina	Yes	19.38	Citicorp, Technint, Banco Río de la Plata, BCH	1990
Brazil	CRT		35		1996
Brazil	Embratel	Yes	20	MCI	1998
Brazil	Tele Leste Celular	Yes		Iberdrola	1998
Brazil	Telesp	Yes	65	BBV, Iberdrola, Portugal Telecom, RBS	1998
Brazil	Telesp Celular	Yes	38	Portugal Telecom	1998
Brazil	Tele Sudeste Celular	Yes	75	Itochu, NTT	1998
Chile	CTC	No	43.6	Chilean Pension Funds	1990
Chile	Publiguías	Yes	51	CTC, Publicar, Ed. Lord Cochrane	1990
Colombia	Codelco	Yes	31	Grupo Sarmiento, Ardilla Lule, CTC Celular	
El Salvador	INTEL		51		1998
Peru	CPT	Yes	35	Graña y Montero, Banco Wiese, State of Peru	1994
Peru	ENTEL Perú	Yes	35	Graña y Montero, Banco Wiese, State of Peru	1994
Portugal	Contactel	Yes	15	Marconi	
Puerto Rico	TLD	No	79	Autoridad de Teléfonos de P.R.	
Romania	Telefónica de Romania	Yes	60	Romtelecom, Radio-Communicatil	
Venezuela	CANTV	Yes	6.4	GTE, Electricidad de Caracas, AT&T	1991
	Infonet	Yes	7.29	DBT, FT, KDD, Swiss PTT, PTT Netherland, Telecom Singapore, RTT	
	FNA	Yes		MCI, Mercury, France Télécom, DBT, others	
	JNI	Yes		AT&T, BT, KDD, France Télécom	1995
	Unisource	Yes	25	Telia, PTT Netherland, Swiss PTT	

Source: Juan José Durán Herrera and Fernando Gallardo Olmedo, "La Estrategia de Internacionalización de las Operadoras de Telecomunicaciones", *ICE*, No. 735, November 1994, p. 97; and Telefonica.

In the case of Telefonica, all these three reasons applied: the privatization of telephone companies in Latin America was to be followed by a period of monopoly, which would insulate the awardee from competition. Telefonica estimated that it would not need to adapt its products to the language of the host countries, thus diminishing the cost of its original investment, and it would be operating in a familiar environment, given the linguistic and cultural similarities. Finally, its long-term strategy emphasized the diversification of its services from basic telephone into other related activities, and Latin America could be a testing ground for the new products.

Telefonica's strategy was not limited to a few countries. Its long-term goal was to operate across Latin America, which would allow it to coordinate its activities and develop its own infrastructure. The immediate goal was to develop a network of optical fibers connecting all the countries where its subsidiaries operated, which would eliminate the cost of renting the existing infrastructure and would increase the capacity of the existing network (therefore, increasing its overall total revenue) and the quality of its services. In other words, Telefonica contemplated the possibility of integrating backward (internalization, in the terminology used by theorists of the firm). The development of its own supranational infrastructure is a way of overcoming a market deficiency, the high cost of existing obsolete technology.

Mira Wilkins's parameters also provide useful guidance to frame the analysis of Telefonica's expansion in Latin America. The need to improve the obsolete telephone systems of Latin American countries, the increasing needs for fast and efficient service, given the prospects of economic growth that accompanied the process of structural reform, led Telefonica's executives to conclude that there was an opportunity for business in Latin America. Privatization of the public utilities state-owned enterprises was interpreted as a sign of the strong commitment of the governments to push the reforms through to the end. In other words, the prospects of political change were low. Cultural and linguistic similarities made the region more appealing to the Spanish MNE. The fact that all Latin American countries committed themselves to implement drastic economic reforms in the 1990s increased the appeal of the region as a whole (third-country parameter). Telefonica's gradual process of privatization also contributed to increase the familiarity of this company with privatization processes (corporate parameter). The need to work closely with the government, the need to provide periodic rewards to its new stockholders, the need to show its customers a significant improvement in the quality of the service with respect to the period of public ownership were fresh issues in Telefonica's past experience in Spain.

Telefonica's lack of international prestige and experience were liabilities that the company had to overcome. In December 1987, the

Spanish monopoly lost the concession over the Chilean company to The Bond Group of Australia, despite presenting a strong bid. Telefonica's offer was not so appealing to the cash-starved Chilean government because its bid relied more heavily on debt-to-equity swaps, whereas the Australian group offered to invest capital through D.L. 600. In 1988, negotiations between the Argentine government and the Spanish company to sell 40 percent of Argentina's Entel and its management to Telefonica faced political opposition and the legislature did not ratify the deal.[18]

In 1990 in Mexico, Telefonica's offer was very close to the winning bid. Telefonica's group (also integrated by GTE and a domestic group called Acciones y Valores) presented a bid of $1.687 billion for 20.4 percent of the capital of the Mexican telephone company (Telmex), which fell short of the $1.760 billion offered by the group led by France Cable et Radio. Moreover, in the eyes of the government officials, the Spanish bid did not have technological guarantees. Although the Spanish system was ranked ninth in the world in terms of lines per resident and efficiency levels, density of lines in Spain was lower than in other industrialized countries, and Telefonica's technology was deemed obsolete by the privatization authorities.[19] In Argentina, Telefonica was not the favorite candidate of the government either. The Argentine authorities preferred to grant the concession to U.S. companies, not only for the quality of services and technical expertise of U.S. firms, but also because officials believed private U.S. firms could offer a better financial deal than state-owned European enterprises. As a consequence, the process of privatization was designed so that it would comply with U.S. FDI legislation. The investment requirement for foreign telephone companies was lowered from 10 percent of the bidding consortium's equity to 4.9 percent, so that Bell Atlantic could be eligible (U.S. legislation barred Bell Atlantic from investing more than 4.9 percent).[20]

Telefonica learned a lesson from its Mexican and Chilean failures. Since it did not have international prestige, it had to pay a higher price for entry. Thereafter, Telefonica increased its economic offers. The Argentine government split the national telephone company, Entel, into two for their privatization. One would be granted a monopoly over the northern part of the country and the other over the southern part. In 1990, Telefonica presented the largest bid for both areas, and chose to take on the latter (which comprised Buenos Aires), for which it offered $2.720 billion. Bell South was the second largest bidder for the northern area, but it had to back out because its financial partner, Manufacturers Hanover, could not acquire the required amount of Argentine debt. The third bidder, a group led by Italy's Stet, now Italia Telecom, and France Télécom, was awarded the concession. They paid $2.308 billion.[21]

In Chile, Telefonica initiated a second offensive. In 1989, it acquired 10 percent of Entel Chile, a provider of international and long distance services. In 1990, The Bond Corporation faced financial difficulties to raise cash to meet creditor demands and sold all stock in Compañía de Teléfonos de Chile (42.8 percent) to the Spanish company in April, for $392 million (the Bond Group paid $130 million two years earlier).[22] In 1994, Telefonica's $2 billion bid in cash and investment commitments for a 35 percent stake in the Peruvian telephone company was more than twice those of U.S. companies GTE Corporation and Southern Bell Corporation.[23] In 1996, Telefonica also submitted the highest bid to the first privatization in Brazil: Companhia Riograndense de Telecomunicações (CRT).

Telefonica's biggest acquisition took place on 29 July 1998, through the privatization of the Brazilian national telephone company, Telebras. Telefonica paid $4.965 billion for Telebras's largest regional subsidiary, Telesp, which operated in São Paulo, and $1.174 billion for Tele Sudeste Celular, a cellular telephone company that operated in Rio de Janeiro and Espíritu Santo. Telefonica's ally Iberdrola (a Spanish electricity generator and distributor with investments in Brazil and Latin America) paid $366.45 million for Tele Leste Celular, the cellular company that operated in Bahia and Sergipe. Portugal Telecom acquired São Paulo's cellular telephone company, Telesp Celular, for $3.099 billion dollars, and MCI acquired Embratel, Brazil's sole long distance operator, for $2.245 billion.[24]

Through its alliance with MCI and with PT, Telefonica planned to own control equity in all of these companies. However, the privatization regulations stipulated that none of the major partners could own more than 20 percent equity in more than one of them. In 2000, Telefonica and its allies rearranged their participation in each one of their new Brazilian subsidiaries. Telefonica's original stakes were 75 percent in TeleSudeste Celular, 63 percent in Telesp, 38 percent in Telesp Celular, and 20 percent in Embratel.[25] Two of Telefonica's allies were also involved in its Brazilian expansion, Iberdrola (which submitted the largest bid for Tele Leste) and Banco Bilbao Vizcaya (which provided financial support).[26]

Telefonica's last acquisitions in the 1990s were Internacional de Telecomunicaciones (INTEL), the public telephone company of El Salvador, and Telefónica de Guatemala. The Salvadoran government sold 51 percent of its national phone company to Telefonica on 14 August 1998 for $41 million, in a public auction.[27] In March 1999, Telefonica won a license to provide cellular phone services in Guatemala and, in July, Telefónica de Guatemala began to operate its service of fixed telephony.[28] To prevent takeovers over its subsidiaries, in the Spring of 2000, Telefonica offered to purchase 100 percent of the stocks of Telesp, Telesudeste Celular, Telefónica Argentina, and Telefónica del Peru.[29]

The governments reformed the telecommunications sector before privatizing the telephone operator to make it more appealing to the foreign investor, and to facilitate its job in upgrading the network. To increase profitability, they raised prices for regulated services (95 percent in Argentina, 65 percent in Mexico), streamlined the workforce at the government's expense, and wrote off or transferred to another state organization part or all of the outstanding debt ($1.757 billion in Argentina, $500 million in Venezuela). Special taxes on telephone users were lowered sharply or scrapped altogether.

The telephone company was insulated from competition in basic and long-distance service (which made up 90 percent or more of the sector's revenue) for periods ranging from six to twenty-five years (seven years in Argentina, extended for a further three years if the companies met a series of operating targets; ten years in Peru, that could be extended to five more years; and eight years in Venezuela). To protect investors from the risks of inflation and price regulation, the governments adopted the price-cap method of rate regulation for the period of monopoly concession. Firms were allowed to raise prices automatically for regulated services to offset the effects of inflation, less an adjustment for anticipated productivity improvement (Venezuela, Argentina and Mexico assumed very little or no productivity improvement). The potential for productivity growth in this industry was great, so the pricing regime was deliberately generous, to offset the risks of doing business in Latin America and to finance rapid expansion of the network.[30]

The governments required the formation of a core investor group referred to as "strategic investor", who would be responsible for running the firm after privatization. Reputable foreign firms from the industry and local firms should be present in the group. This way, the government would avoid charges that it was giving away the national patrimony to foreigners. Foreign participation would raise foreign exchange, send the right signal to international investors and provide access to foreign technology and expertise. The licensee was also granted one of two concessions to provide cellular telephone service, a rapidly growing and highly profitable business. Competition was allowed in all other "peripheral activities", such as value added services, trucking and paging, and firms were not barred from diversifying into these other services.

Telefonica saw in the privatization of Latin American telephone companies an opportunity to expand abroad and gain new markets. When the liberalization of the telecommunications industry in Spain was set for December of 1997, Telefonica was smaller (in terms of sales) and had lower efficiency rates than other European telecommunications operators. Expansion in Latin America provided the possibility of increasing the size of its business and gain efficiency, in order to face competition from other European operators in the Spanish market. Ignacio Santillana, Telefonica's chief executive, explained that within this framework of privatization and liberalization of telecommunications services and networks, Telefonica devised a strategy that comprised expansion in European and American markets, including the United States, to achieve its maximum competitive advantage in terms of potential market and in terms of synergy of international traffic and common systems of exploitation of the network. Telefonica's investment strategy comprised an analysis of the profit-risk relationship of each project to find profitable investment opportunities and potential markets.

Telefonica's long-term strategy comprised several factors: macroeconomic, social and political stability, a legal framework defining the rules of the game, dynamic business networks, availability of qualified labor, the government's economic policies, the potential for growth of the economy, especially the telecommunications and export sectors, credibility of the government's reform programs, and the synergy that a particular investment may generate for the firm as a whole.[31]

"Potential growth", rather than risk, was the main characteristic of Telefonica's strategy. U.S. firms were willing to take up very little risk in Latin America in the early 1990s. They had lost a lot of money in this region during the debt crisis. The economic slowdown made many borrowers unable to repay the debt contracted with U.S. and European creditors, and many North American and European firms deemed investment in Latin America as very risky. Telefonica's evaluation of potential over risk was positive. Ignacio Santillana told a story to explain the difference in perception between Spanish and U.S. investors. The day the bids were to be submitted for the privatization of the Peruvian telephone company, the five-member Telefonica team went for a stroll in downtown Lima and stopped for a shoe shine. By contrast, the U.S. bidders arrived in armored cars, protected by bodyguards. Santillana's conclusion was that "Telefonica had a very different idea of risk" and concluded that where the North Americans saw risk, the Spaniards saw potential.[32] This explanation refers to two different types of risk: personal and political. Santillana's point was that in all senses, the Spanish company felt much more comfortable in Perú than its U.S. counterparts, because cultural and historical affinity gave Telefónica's executives a better understanding of the locals and local politicians.

Telefonica initiated its foreign expansion in 1990. Most of its ventures were established through consortia, in which the telephone company was the leading telecommunications operator, the exception being CANTV in Venezuela, where it was a minority technological partner of GTE.

Telefonica provided the technology and was responsible for the management of its ventures. Among its financial partners, there was usually a Spanish bank, such as Banco Central-Hispanoamericano (BCH) in Argentina, and Banco Bilbao Vizcaya (BBV) in Brazil (BBV was a stockholder of Telefonica) and a local financial institution, such as Banco Río de la Plata in Argentina and Banco Wiese in Peru. The relation between Telefonica and the Spanish banks BBV and Argentaria will be explained in more detail in the next section.

In spite of the linguistic and cultural similarity between Spain and Latin America, Telefonica's main competitive advantage was not its ability to operate in a Spanish environment, similar to that of its home country. Doing business in the Spanish language and sharing some of the cultural codes of Latin American countries made interactions easier. Argentina and Chile have a large European population and their cultural similarities with Spain are many. However, Peru is mainly populated by non-European people, and most Latin American countries have large segments of society of native and African descent, with traditions and beliefs different from those of Spain. Spanish companies had to adapt to this environment, which was not exactly that of Spain.

Telefonica's main competitive advantage resided in its ability to develop both basic telephone infrastructure and new telecommunications systems, such as mobile telephony, as well as to extend the number of lines to new large segments of the population that did not have it before. In other words, to upgrade the telecommunications infrastructure. Since the early 1980s, Telefonica was forced to expand the telephone network in Spain at a very fast pace, as well as to make significant improvements in the overall quality of the service, including the introduction of the latest technology available in the market. The economic boom of the Spanish economy in the 1980s increased the needs of firms and individuals for reliable and efficient telecommunications. The internationalization of the Spanish economy also demanded fast and efficient communication to and from Spain.

Telefonica's performance in Spain was quite successful in the 1990s. In the ten-year period between 1989 and 1999, the number of lines per 100 inhabitants grew by 45.9 percent, from 28.1 to 41, and the quality and variety of service increased.[33] The needs that Telefonica had to satisfy in Spain in the last twenty years were the same it faced in Latin America: fast-growing economies with the need for efficient communication. The company had the technology and the expertise required to meet these demands. It improved and extended the telephone infrastructure, as part of what one of the company's executives defined as "trench strategy": to earth existing aerial cables, improve the overall quality of infrastructure, and increase the number of lines.

Table 6.5 Telefonica's direct investments abroad in December 1998

Country	Company	Activity
Argentina	Multicanal	Cable television.
Argentina	Sintelar	Engineering, telecommunication equipment and line installation.
Argentina	Telefónica de Argentina, SA	Cellular and regular telephony, telephone directories, public telephones, international telephony and data services.
Argentina	Tyssa	Personalized service to preferential clients.
Brazil	Companhia Riograndense de Telecommunicações	Local, interstate and long distance telephony, public telephones, telephone directories, data transmission and cable television.
Brazil	Embratel	Long distance telephony.
Brazil	Tele Leste Celular	Cellular telephony.
Brazil	Telesp	Regular telephony.
Brazil	Telesp Celular	Cellular telephony.
Brazil	Tele Sudeste Celular	Cellular telephony.
Chile	Compañía Telefónica de Chile	Cellular and regular telephony, telephone directories, public telephones, international telephony, cable-multimedia, data transmission and equipment.
Chile	Publiguías	Telephone directories.
Colombia	Codelco	Cellular telephony.
El Salvador	INTEL	Cellular telephony.
Peru	Sintel Perú	Engineering, line installation, telecommunication equipment.
Peru	Telefónica de Perú	Mobile and regular telephony, telephone directories, public telephones, international telephony, cable-multimedia, data transmission.
Portugal	Contactel	Mobile telephony.
Puerto Rico	TLD	Long distance telephony with the United States and international telephony from Puerto Rico and the U.S. Virgin Islands to the United States.
Romania	Telefonica Romania	Mobile Telephony.
USA	Infonet	Data transmission.
Venezuela	CANTV	Mobile and regular telephony through subsidiaries, telephone directories and data transmission.

Source: *El País Digital*, No. 347, 15 April 1997, "Economía" section; Miguel Ángel Patiño, "El Único Operador Global en Latinoamérica", *Gazeta Mercantil Latinoamericana*, 10 August 1998, pp. 6-7; Miguel Ángel Patiño, "Telefónica y Sus Socios Invertirán Dos Billones en Brasil", *Expansión*, 30 July 1998, p. 3; Carmen Jiménez, "Telefónica Se Convierte en el Mayor Operador de Brasil", *El País*, 30 July 1998, p. 30; and *El Nuevo Herald*, 14 August 1998, p. 5B.

Telefonica made it very clear from the beginning that its strategy would be development from the bottom: expansion of telephone services to all sectors of society. U.S. firms, on the contrary, focused their plans on their better ability to introduce the latest technology in Latin America, which would not fulfill the most immediate needs of Latin American societies, of universal access to communication facilities.

The economic performance of Telefonica in Latin America was also successful. In Argentina, the annual return on investment was 40 percent in the first four years. Telefónica del Perú had a profit of $29.1 million in 1994, and $318.9 million in 1995. Overall, Telefónica Internacional, S.A. generated 15.2 percent of the total income of the company in 1996.[34]

Telefonica's strategy for the year 2000 and beyond is the development of a Panamerican network of fiber optics to link all its Latin American subsidiaries and thus achieve a higher degree of synergy among all its ventures (internalization of infrastructure). The company would thus capture all the revenue generated by international calls among those nations. At the same time, Telefonica considered expansion into new markets in the region that offered great growth opportunities, such as Mexico and Brazil. Telefonica's will to incorporate the United States and Mexico to its network made its executives consider the creation of a multinational telecommunications group. On 9 March, 1998, Telefonica reached an agreement with WorldCom and MCI to create a comprehensive telecommunications group to coordinate their activities in Latin America, Europe and the United States.

The telecommunication industry was moving in the late 1990s toward the formation of multinational groups by domestic operators in order to provide worldwide service and thus achieve synergy to increase efficiency and reduce cost. The four main groups that emerged by March 1998 were Uniworld, led by AT&T, Global One, dominated by France Télécom and Deutsche Telekom, Concert, led by British Telecom, and the new group created by MCI-World Com, Telefonica, Portugal Telecom, and maybe NTT of Japan.

Telefonica tried to join one major international telecommunications operator to gain financial support for its Latin American ventures, especially for the privatization of the largest Brazilian telephone company, Telebras, in July of 1998. Telefonica joined Unisource on 25 June 1995, a group made up by smaller European operators, which united forces with AT&T to operate in the European market. Unisource's failure to obtain the concession as the second telephone operator in France in 1996 was attributed by Telefonica's executives to AT&T's disregard for foreign markets. At that point, the U.S. operator was more concerned about the shrinking of its market share within the United States, when the so-called

Baby Bells were about to be allowed to process long-distance calls. Telefonica estimated that AT&T did not have a clear strategy of overseas expansion, while it believed its other partners within Unisource were more enthusiastic about expanding in Europe than outside.

Thus, as Telefonica searched for reliable partners to consolidate its long-term strategy of expansion, primarily in Latin America, it realized Unisource was going in a different direction. British Telecom was absent from Latin America but was eager to operate there, given the possibilities for growth of these markets, and saw in Telefonica the best-possible ally to enter that market. An alliance with British Telecom would also have given Telefonica its long-wanted key to the U.S. market and Mexico, through BT's then partner MCI and the latter's Mexican subsidiary, Avantel.

Should the arrangement have gone through, MCI would have benefited from Telefonica's infrastructure to process its international calls with Latin America. On 18 April, 1997, BT, MCI and Telefonica agreed to an alliance. Under that plan, BT would have bought a 2 percent stake in Telefonica, and the Spanish company would have a 1 percent stake in BT. Telefonica and MCI were to create a pan-American joint venture to be managed by the Spanish operator, which comprised an investment of $1 billion to develop a fiber optics network among all their Latin American subsidiaries. The arrangements were that Telefonica would have management control over MCI's Avantel joint venture with Grupo Financiero Banamex and Accival S.A. in Mexico (MCI owned 45 percent of Avantel) and would have had the option of buying 33 percent of MCI's interest (Avantel was Mexico's second-biggest telephone company after Teléfonos de México, S.A. at that point). British Telecom-MCI were to have an option to buy 10 percent of the stakes of Telefonica's subsidiary TISA, to be fully privatized by the Spanish government in the fall of 1997, and Telefonica was given the option of buying 10 percent of Concert.[35]

Telefonica's interest in Brazil put PT in the picture too. Telefonica bought 35 percent of the first Brazilian state telephone company privatized in 1996, Companhia Riograndense de Telecomunicações, and in the first half of 1998, Telefonica prepared its bid to participate in the privatization of Telebras, the national telephone company (the Brazilian market generated 40 percent of Latin American phone revenue in 1998). Portugal Telecom had a good relation with the Brazilian government and had signed an agreement with Telebras (called "Atlantic Alliance") to develop an ambitious project to install a system of fiber optics for Transatlantic communication between Latin America and Europe.

On 16 April, 1997, Telefonica and Portugal Telecom sealed their alliance. The accord included linking the Brazilian fiber optics infrastructure to Telefónica's pan-American network. PT was given the option to buy 10 percent of the consortium that held 35 percent of the stakes in CRT.[36] Portugal Telecom also was to become Telefonica's partner in its expansion in Brazil and northern Africa. Both companies were to define a joint strategy to participate in the privatization of telephone companies and the concession of telephone licenses in those regions.[37] As a consequence of the alliance, Telefonica acquired 3.5 percent of PT's shares and PT bought 1 percent of the Spanish company.

The decision of WorldCom (based in Jackson, Mississippi) to improve on BT's offer for MCI on October 1997, froze the Concert alliance. On 12 February, 1998, BT decided to break its pact with Telefonica, which was already conducting negotiations with WorldCom, and especially with MCI, to save the parts of the earlier agreement that had linked MCI and Telefonica. The new agreement of 9 March, 1998, established that MCI would provide financial support for Telefonica's Latin American ventures; Telefonica would provide logistic and financial support to MCI's campaigns directed to the Hispanic market in the United States; Telefonica would have the option to buy a share of MCI's Avantel subsidiary in Mexico; Telefonica would cooperate with WorldCom in its expansion in Europe through the development of a joint-venture; the three companies would integrate their infrastructure by the year 2001 to provide comprehensive services to their clients across Latin America, the United States and Europe (see table 6.6 for more specifics).[38] This strategy would allow MCI-WorldCom to market its products in Telefonica's markets (MCI's takeover by WorldCom was approved by the Federal Commission of Telecommunications on 15 September, 1998).[39] Telefonica would gain financial support for its ventures in Latin America, and access to the Mexican and U.S. markets, where it was trying to enter since the early 1990s.

The prospects of operating in Brazil also shaped Telefonica's long-term strategy. The need to increase its financial resources to participate in the privatization of the largest state-owned telephone company in Latin America, Telebras, forced Telefonica to seek foreign allies. Portugal Telecom became a key component in Telefonica's strategy in the Spring of 1998. The Portuguese telephone operator had very good relations with the Brazilian government. It developed a joint project with Telebras in 1998 to build a fiber-optic network linking Europe and South America. For this reason, Telefonica wanted to involve Portugal Telecom in its venture. On 27 March 1998, the executives of Portugal Telecom agreed to create a joint company with Telefonica (50-50) to provide mobile telephony in Eastern Europe, Africa and Asia. Telefonica also offered Portugal Telecom the possibility of buying a ten percent stake in TPAM.[40] PT gave Telefonica the option of increasing its stake in PT from 3.5 to 5 percent.[41]

Table 6.6   Telefonica's-MCI-WorldCom agreement of 9 March 1998

- Telefonica would buy 10 percent of Eurocom, WorldCom's operator in Europe.
- Creation of a joint-venture between Telefonica (49 percent) and WorldCom (51 percent) to operate in Eastern and Southern Europe.
- Telefonica would have the option to acquire 40 percent of the company that WorldCom would create in Italy.
- Telefonica would distribute Eurocom's products in Spain. Telefonica and Eurocom would study the possibility of creating a joint-venture in Spain to distribute voice and value-added products in Spain.
- Telefonica had the option to acquire 10 percent of the new MCI-WorldCom.
- MCI and Telefonica would create a joint-venture (70-30), managed by MCI, to adapt its services and promotions to the needs of the Hispanics living in the United States.
- Formation of a joint-venture between Telefonica (51 percent) and MCI (49 percent), called Telefónica Panamericana MCI (TPAM), controlled by Telefonica, to manage Telefonica's Latin American subsidiaries. TPAM would build a digital network to link the main trade capitals of Latin America. This network would use high-speed fiber optic materials and commutation equipment to allow the simultaneous flow of greater amounts of conventional phone calls and Internet services. In 2001, they hope to link up the main Latin American cities, the United States and Europe.
- MCI had an option to buy 10 percent of TISA before June 2000.
- MCI and Telefonica would merge their activities in Puerto Rico.
- Telefonica had the option to buy a share of Avantel (controlled by MCI and Banamex) in Mexico.
- The president of Telefonica, Juan Villalonga, would join MCI-WorldCom's council, and Bert Roberts, MCI's president, would join Telefonica's executive council.
- If the merger between WorldCom and MCI does not materialize, Telefonica and WorldCom would maintain their accord of 9 March 1998.

Source: El País Digital, No. 676, 10 March 1998, "Economía" section.

Figure 6.3   Main proposed telecommunications groups, as projected in August 1998

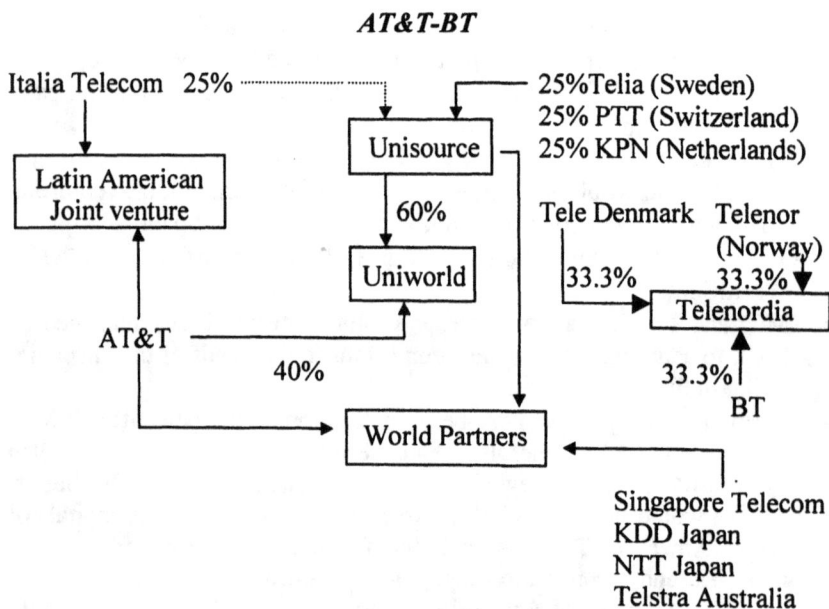

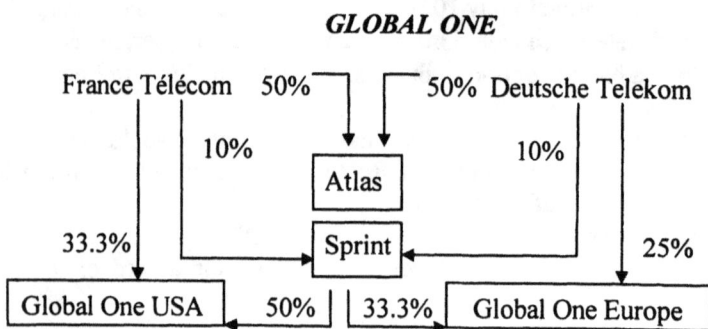

AT&T-BT

Italia Telecom   25% .... ─── 25%Telia (Sweden)
25% PTT (Switzerland)
Unisource ─ 25% KPN (Netherlands)

Latin American
Joint venture

60%   Tele Denmark   Telenor
(Norway)

Uniworld   33.3%   33.3%
Telenordia

AT&T ───

40%   33.3%
BT

World Partners ◄───

Singapore Telecom
KDD Japan
NTT Japan
Telstra Australia

GLOBAL ONE

France Télécom   50%   50% Deutsche Telekom

10%   10%

Atlas

33.3%   Sprint ◄   25%

Global One USA   50%   33.3%   Global One Europe

WorldCom-MCI-Telefonica-Portugal Telecom

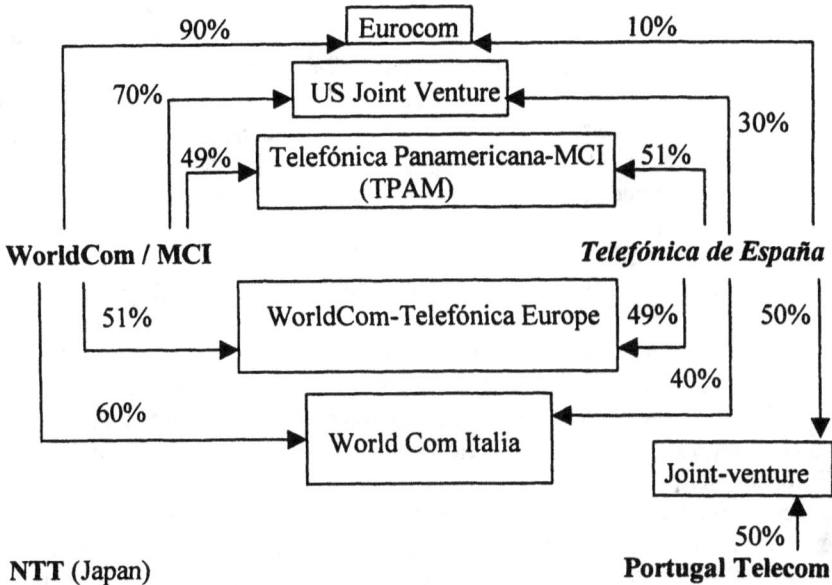

Source: El País Digital, No. 318, 17 March 1997, "Economía" section.

In 1998 it seemed clear that the internationalization of the telecommunications sector would accelerate, and that the small domestic operators would have a clear disadvantage against the largest international consortia and groups. Telefonica's strategy was no longer confined to the Spanish market. The revenue from its international ventures was 15 percent of total in 1996, but it was expected to rise, as Telefonica operated its new foreign alliances. With its new partners, Telefonica tried to consolidate its Latin American network, comprising most American markets. Its medium-term goal was to incorporate Mexico and the United States into its network. The planned partnerships with MCI-WorldCom could give Telefonica the opportunity to enter those markets.

Expansion into Africa was another new venture for Telefonica. The privatization of the Moroccan telephone company in 1999 could serve as Telefonica's bridge to Africa. In 1990 Spain was one of the main foreign investors in Morocco. The significant presence of Spanish and European firms in that country was a strong incentive for the Spanish firm that aimed at channeling calls between Morocco and Europe. Spain also increased its presence in Algeria and other Maghrebian countries in the 1990s, and

Telefonica also aimed at incorporating them in its Mediterranean network. Telefonica was also investigating investment possibilities in South Africa. PT's experience in Africa was seen by Telefonica's executives as an opportunity to learn about African markets for future expansion. In 1990 PT was present in São Tomé and Principe, Cape Verde, Guinea-Bissau, Kenya, and Mozambique, and also in Macau. Southeast Asia was another booming market totally unknown by the Spanish company. PT and MCI-WorldCom appeared as the appropriate partners for its future joint-ventures in these areas. Thus the relationships set up for Latin America provided a springboard for further international expansion.

Despite the relative success of Telefonica in the 1990s, the way ahead has many uncertainties. Its expansion in Latin America and its aborted agreement with Concert brought it into a broader world of telecommunications. AT&T showed its clear intention to expand in Latin America and may become Telefonica's main contender in that area. AT&T reached an accord with Italia Telecom (IT) on 2 July 1997, the only big European telephone operator that had remained out of the large world telecommunications groups. This alliance would serve AT&T's purposes of expansion in Latin America, including "retaliation" against Telefonica. IT submitted the largest bid for the second telephone operator in Spain, which began operating in December, 1998. AT&T participated in this consortium as the technological and financial partner to compete with the Spanish company within its domestic market.

AT&T's purpose of expanding in Latin America may also be served by the creation of a pan-American joint-venture with Italia Telecom to manage IT's existing Latin American subsidiaries. These ventures included Telecom Argentina (the operator that won the concession for the northern part of the country), 50 percent of Entel, 25 percent of Impsat Corporation (a satellite communication network) and the Bolivian telephone company. Even though IT owned 29.9 percent of the stakes in the Cuban telephone company, this venture remained out of the joint-venture for political reasons.[42]

AT&T was also considering expansion in Europe and South East Asia. With that goal in mind, AT&T signed an agreement with BT in the Summer of 1998. Moreover, AT&T created a consortium in East Asia with a number of Asian companies and an Australian company. AT&T saw BT as the best partner for expansion in this region, if the proposed arrangements were consummated. For Europe, AT&T was ready to use its venture with several European operators (Unisource), in which IT could take up Telefonica's place. There, AT&T-BT would face competition from WorldCom-Telefonica, and Global One, the other large world operator, constituted by France Télécom, Deutsche Telekom and Sprint.

The prospects for the creation of large telecommunications consortia illustrates Gomes-Casseres' argumentation of a new type of competition in an industry dominated by a small number of "constellations" or groups of firms. A smaller number of firms (oligopoly) dominating a market does not necessarily tend to increase prices in that market. This type of market structure may lead to fiercer competition and may lower prices, as companies combine their resources to lower the costs of production and pool resources to innovate, specialize and increase the technological complexity of their products, producing higher quality services or goods for lower prices. Antitrust regulators are monitoring these arrangements very closely. Telefonica moved very actively in the late 1990s to create an alliance that would strengthen its position in Latin America, where it became one of the leading telecommunications providers.

Banking Sector

Spanish banks were the most aggressive Spanish MNEs in Latin America in the 1990s. Although their investment in Latin America fell in the 1980s after the debt crisis, they took the lead after the structural reforms began in the late 1980s. They invested over $6 billion between 1995 and March 1997 and accumulated a stock of $5.3 billion in Latin America and assets for the value of $62.9 billion, until 1997.[43] More than 50 percent of total Spanish FDI in Latin America occurred in the banking sector. In Chile, Colombia, Peru, Puerto Rico, and Venezuela, Spanish banks Banco Bilbao Vizcaya (BBV), Banco de Santander (BS) and Banco Central Hispanoamericano (BCH) controlled more than 20 percent of the domestic banking system in 1997.[44] In Argentina, BS and BBV controlled 14 percent of the market.[45]

Margin compression (decreasing profit margins) in Spain encouraged Spanish banks to seek markets with higher returns. The average margin between the cost of borrowing and the interest earned on loans fell from 7.39 percent to 4.38 percent between 1991 and 1995.[46] The government's commitment to meet the Maastricht Treaty's criteria of macroeconomic stability drove inflation and interest rates down. To meet the 3 percent public deficit criterion, the Socialist government first and the conservative administration after March 1996, cut the fiscal deficit from 6.2 percent of GDP in 1995 to 2.6 percent in 1997. Inflation fell from 6.5 percent in 1992 to 2 percent in 1997. The Bank of Spain pursued a tight monetary policy based on high interest rates to curb inflation. As inflation decreased, interest rates fell from over 14 percent in 1992 to 5.5 percent in June 1997.

In this environment, based on lower inflation and lower interest rates, Spanish banks redefined their business policies and diversified their operations, geographically as well as in terms of business activities. Geographically, they invested abroad, especially in Latin America. In terms of business activity, they followed the German model, where banks invest in industrial enterprises, over the English model, where banks stick to banking and financial activities. The result was that all of the large Spanish corporations investing in Latin America had at least one of the major Spanish banks among their main stockholders. In fact, the successful experience of the banks, which came to Latin America earlier, was the force pushing some of these companies to follow and invest in Latin America too.

Bank executives perceived that the telecommunications and energy sectors had great opportunities for growth, and concentrated their investments in these sectors. Two great financial groups controlled equity in the main telecommunications and energy sector enterprises, one of them dominated by BBV and La Caixa, the other one by BCH and Argentaria. On the one hand, BBV and Argentaria bought five percent of the stakes of Telefonica each. BBV was also the main stockholder of Iberdrola (11 percent of the equity[47]) and Repsol. La Caixa, a regional savings bank based in Barcelona, also had significant participation in Repsol and Gas Natural.[48] On the other hand, BCH was part of the consortium that submitted a bid for the concession of the second telephone operator in Spain, which began to operate in December 1998. BCH and BS had stakes in the Spanish electricity distributor Endesa, which initiated ventures in Latin America too.[49]

Table 6.7   BBV's participation in a selected group of Spanish MNEs in April 1998

Investor	BBV	Argentaria	Repsol	La Caixa
Gas Natural			45	25.5
Iberdrola	7.7			
Repsol	7.54			N/A[50]
Telefonica	6.12	5[51]		5

Source: BBV.

Table 6.8 BCH's participation in a selected group of Spanish MNEs in April 1998

Investor	BCH	Endesa	Dragados y Construcciones
Endesa	3		
Unión Fenosa	9.91		
Cepsa	8.15	8.1	
Retevisión	10	22.2	
Airtel	14.09	8.14	
FCC	3		3
Dragados y Construcciones	18.93		

Source: BCH

Table 6.9 Spanish energy MNEs in which BS had control equity in April 1998

Cepsa
Endesa
Unión Fenosa

Source: BS.

The process of geographical expansion of Spanish banks in Latin America was facilitated by the similarity of the process of banking and financial liberalization that Latin American countries underwent in the 1990s, and the process underwent by the Spanish firms since the early 1980s in their home market. In those twenty years, Spanish banks went through a continuous process of adaptation to a liberalized, modernizing and more competitive banking and financial environment. Until the 1970s, banks were the principal financial institutions. Several innovations appeared in the financial market that forced them to adapt their products to a more sophisticated and demanding clientele, in order to attract their savings. Competition arose from pension and investment funds, public bonds, equity markets, corporate bonds, etc.

A similar process of disintermediation was under way in Latin America in the 1990s. The creation of pension funds in many countries, the appearance of a corporate bond market in Chile, money markets in Mexico and equity markets in a number of countries, increased the possibilities of people to invest their savings and, at the same time, diminished the traditional role of banks as the only financial institution. This process was in part the culmination of a series of policies implemented by Latin American governments to face the debt crisis that erupted in 1982, geared to increasing the strength of the banking sector. The weakness of the Latin American banking sector became manifest during the debt crisis in the 1980s. The lending boom that preceded the crisis left the financial system in a very weak state when the economy decelerated, which further amplified the downside of the economic cycle. In LDCs, bank deposits are the most important form of household savings and bank loans are the main source of external finance for firms. The bank crisis undermined the ability of banks to provide credit to firms and individuals.

The governments' policies were partly responsible for the crisis that broke out in the 1980s.[52] Most countries had a regime of financial repression that restricted the creation of new financial institutions, set ceilings to interest rates below ongoing rates of inflation (generating negative real interest rates and thus capital flight) and established strict guidelines regarding the sectoral allocation of credit through four channels, to prevent specific sectors from receiving a volume of loans below what was deemed as socially optimal by the government. The four sectors were government-owned development banks, which lent to certain sectors at below-market interest rates, commercial banks were required to lend a certain portion of their portfolio to specific sectors, the central bank provided preferential rediscount rates to commercial banks for loans provided to specific industries and commercial banks were subject to differential reserve requirements, depending on the characteristics of their loan portfolios.

The lack of an adequate supervisory framework and lax supervision also contributed to the encouragement of excessively risky behavior by commercial banks. The magnitude of the banking crisis that erupted in 1982 was exacerbated by the high franchise value of many banks, as well as by the lack of soundness of their credit policies. The franchise value is an indicator of the quality of banks and their ability to issue liabilities that are accepted as means of payments. The credibility of banks as issuers of liabilities is higher than that of other institutions, because they maintain deposits at the central bank and have access to the central bank's credit facility. When banks borrow excessively from the central bank, inflation tends to increase, since there is more money in circulation, and their liabilities lose real value. This makes restriction of lending necessary. Banks should provide credit only to those customers capable of repaying their loans.

The banks' franchise value is measured both as the loan-to-asset ratio and as the cash-to-deposit ratio. In other words, the ratio of loans provided to their customers with respect to their assets and the ratio of their cash assets in relation to their deposit liabilities. If the amount of cash assets they hold is very high relative to their deposit liabilities, banks enjoy high liquidity and do not need to discipline their borrowers to remain liquid. Therefore, they can provide them long-term loans. They do not need to restrict their credits, feeding inflation, and thus undermining the value of their liabilities. If borrowers default, banks have to absorb the losses either through confiscation or through inflation (new loans). A high ratio of cash assets (cash and deposits at the central bank) to deposit liabilities thus represents a weak franchise and shows little market discipline exerted by banks on borrowers.

When reserve requirements are high, banks normally show a high ratio of non-loan assets to assets. They hold government bonds, development bonds or central bank bonds, and use the proceeds to provide long-term credit to borrowers. Under these circumstances, banks are not helping borrowers solve their credit problems, and when a credit crisis arises, bankers expand credit without working out a sound loan repayment scheme that helps borrowers solve the deficiencies that led to the crisis.

Banks cannot rely solely on their loan customers for liquidity. They must have access to funds through the banking system to solve problems of lack of liquidity. Inter-bank markets are not competitive in industrializing countries. Therefore, banks must resort to the central banks for credit. Central banks then have to play the pivotal role of guaranteeing liquidity in the system. They have to provide credit only to banks that ensure sound and strict repayment schemes with their clients. Thus, when the banks borrow from other banks (mainly from the central bank), they have a high ratio of loan to assets, increasing the power of the central bank to supervise their credits. A low ratio of cash assets to deposits and a high ratio of loans to assets make banks dependent upon the central bank for credit, enabling the central bank to maintain a close supervisory relationship with banks to ensure that liquidity persists in the banking system.[53]

The debt crisis hit most Latin American banking systems very severely. Following a period of large capital inflows in the 1970s, in late 1982 the creditworthiness of Latin American borrowers deteriorated in the eyes of both domestic and foreign creditors, initiating a period of large capital outflows that continued in 1983 and 1984. Governments had to either change these perceptions to stop capital outflows, or generate sufficient cash flow on their trade accounts to compensate for the outflows.

Table 6.10 Indicators of bank franchise value for a selected group of Latin American countries, 1982 and early 1990s

Country	Cash Assets to Deposits		Loans to Assets	
	Percent			
	1982	*Early 1990s*	*1982*	*Early 1990s*
Argentina	76.19	20	48.57	75
Chile	21.13	10	63.42	51
Colombia	20.96	21	58.66	50
Mexico	65.13	5	45.82	64
Peru	55.32	50	45.82	42

Source: Liliana Rojas-Suárez and Steven R. Weisbrod, *Financial Fragilities in Latin America. The 1980s and 1990s*, IMF, Washington, DC, 1995, p. 14.

In 1982, banks had large ratios of cash assets over deposits, which gave them high liquidity. Under these conditions, they did not need to apply strict repayment schemes to their borrowers in order to remain liquid. Borrowers thus did not invest the money in sound projects, which made them default. Foreign financing stopped in 1982 and many local firms could not pay their loans. The total of non-performing loans exceeded 20 percent of total portfolios in some cases. However, liquidity allowed banks to provide extra credit to their clients, who needed extra capital for their unsound projects. These projects never became profitable and increased the crisis even further. In Argentina, the largest private commercial bank and 42 small and medium-size financial institutions had to be liquidated between 1980 and 1982; eleven in Chile between 1981 and 1982, whose portfolios represented almost 15 percent of total loans. Seven insolvent banks were taken over by the government in 1983. Two were liquidated and the other five rehabilitated.[54]

When the crisis broke out, Chile and Colombia had relatively low ratios of cash assets to deposits and high ratios of loans to assets. Their central banks sought the way out of the crisis by providing credit to banks. Since banks had their central banks as the sole providers of credit, central banks were able to establish repayment programs that made them responsible for repaying and thus forced the banks to monitor very closely how their borrowers used the money they were credited. Money was thus made available to finance businesses and monitoring guaranteed investment in sound projects, which made economic growth resume.

Argentina, Mexico and Peru decided to solve the crisis by expanding credit to government institutions. These institutions were too large to be monitored by banks, and the governments failed to work as supervisors. Credit was not invested in profitable activities and borrowers could not repay their loans. Economic activity did not grow and inflation rose, undermining the value of assets held in domestic currency.

The bailout programs succeeded when the supply of central bank credit to distressed institutions was based on an appraisal of the borrowers' possibility of returning to solvency. Governments tried to improve the quality of banking practices by forcing banks to monitor their borrowers, to work out repayment schemes based on sound investment. They achieved this goal by lowering the ratio of cash assets to deposits and increasing the loans to assets ratio, which gave central banks more control over the liquidity of banks, and allowed them to monitor credit closely.[55]

Major reforms were introduced in the financial system since the mid-1980s to increase the degree of financial intermediation and raise the efficiency of investment. Deregulation of interest rates, elimination of direct credit allocation rules and reduction and harmonization of reserve requirements for commercial banks helped expand the degree of intermediation, pressured firms to increase the quality of their investment projects and forced banks and other lenders to make a greater effort to identify promising investors. Relaxation of barriers to entry was adopted to increase competition. Encouragement of security markets and institutional investors was implemented to create new credit alternatives. The creation of modern and efficient supervisory legislation should help to allow the performance of financial institutions to be monitored closely.[56]

The foreign commercial banks were crucial to develop an efficient banking system. Nevertheless, in the late 1980s many U.S. and European banks, including Spanish ones, were weary of Latin America because they had lost a lot of money during the debt crisis, when their borrowers defaulted. Many banks left the region and were not willing to come back. Spanish commercial ones were the first to return to Latin America.

The liberalization of the banking sector took place in Spain in the 1980s. New financial services emerged, such as investment and pension funds, which also contributed to revitalize the equity market. De-regularization eliminated legal operating barriers among different types of financial institutions, allowed foreign entrants into the market, and liberalized capital flows and eliminated restrictions on interest rates, making the Spanish market more contestable, and overall reduced the financial margins for banking institutions. Within this framework, Spanish banks had to adapt to a new environment, in which a larger number of competitors were offering a wider variety of services.

One of their key competitive advantages to survive in this environment was their universal character. Unlike most of their European competitors, Spanish banks provided all kinds of financial services, such as deposits, pension and investment funds, mortgages, insurance, etc. The emergence of new financial products threatened to weaken the role of banks as main providers of credit, both to firms and individuals. The ability of Spanish banks to provide other services, besides purely banking products, as well as their role as intermediaries among their customers and issuers of liabilities, and operations in the equity markets, allowed them to retain a large share of the market.

Within this framework, only the firms that could evolve from mere banks into "financial conglomerates" or "providers of financial services" could survive. The banks that were unable to adapt were absorbed by larger institutions or went out of business. The most competitive banks grew to capture larger shares of the market. Two Basque banks merged in 1987, Banco de Bilbao and Banco de Vizcaya, creating Banco Bilbao Vizcaya (BBV), the largest in Spain. In 1991, Banco Central and Banco Hispanoamericano also merged, creating Banco Central Hispanoamericano (BCH). In 1993, Banco Santander (BS) surpassed BBV when it presented the winning bid for Banesto, which had been temporarily taken over by the Bank of Spain for its financial difficulties. In March 1998, BS achieved control over 100 percent of Banesto. In 1999, BS and BCH merged, becoming the largest Spanish bank, Banco Santander Central Hispano (BSCH). The rates of banking concentration in Spain in the late 1990s were among the highest in Europe. BS, BBV, BCH and Argentaria had 50 percent of bank deposits, a share similar to the top five banks in France, but larger than Germany, where the top five banks had 25 percent, 43 percent in Italy and 35 percent in the United Kingdom.[57]

Spanish banks began to invest large amounts in Latin America again in the mid-1990s. Profit margins were shrinking in their domestic market, but rates were considerably higher in Latin America. Besides, the possibility that Spain would meet the requirements set by the Maastricht Treaty to join the European Monetary Union in 1999 resuscitated the fear of foreign competition. Even though Spanish banks were able to retain 88 percent of deposits in the Spanish market vis-à-vis foreign financial institutions after liberalization was implemented, the relatively small size of the Spanish market and the need to operate in pesetas might have worked as a deterrent, keeping many foreign banks away. The monetary union would force Spanish banks to operate in Euros, and the elimination of the currency deterrent would facilitate the penetration of European and U.S. banks into Spain. The fear of growing competition from larger European financial institutions mainly led Spanish banks to look for markets to grow.

The banking and financial sectors in Latin America were in a process of growth and development of new services in the 1990s, and governments were welcoming institutions with high competency in traditional banking, as well as in the new financial products being developed. U.S. and European banks were still suspicious about the possibilities for growth of these markets and showed distrust for the smoothness of the reforms. Spanish banks saw in Latin America virgin terrain to be explored, with great opportunities for growth in many areas and little competition from local banks, which were still too small and lacked competency in many of the new financial services being developed. Latin America offered Spanish banks a very similar panorama to that in which they operated for two decades: the need to develop new financial mechanisms, market concentration in the banking sector, and growing competition.

Spanish investment in banking mounted in the 1990s. By 1997, BS had invested $3.5 billion ($1 billion in Chile alone), it had assets of $45 billion, and 57.6 percent of its employees worked in its Latin American subsidiaries. In 1997, BS controlled 10 percent of deposits in Argentina, Brazil, Colombia, Mexico, Peru, Puerto Rico, Uruguay and Venezuela,[58] and 47 percent of its profits were generated by its Latin American subsidiaries.[59] By 1997 also, BBV had invested $1.6 billion[60] and its assets were worth $25.7 billion.[61] That year, 27 percent of its income came from its Latin American subsidiaries.[62] BCH had invested $487 million in Latin America, mainly through its Chilean subsidiary O'Higgins Central Hispanoamericano, S.A. BS and BBV ranked third and fourth in assets in Spanish-speaking Latin America, after Mexico's Banamex and Bancomer groups.[63]

Table 6.11 Main subsidiaries of Spanish banks in Latin America in September 1998

Argentaria

Country	Subsidiary	Number of Offices
Argentina	Siembra AFJP	
	Sur Seguros de Retiro	
	Sur Seguros de Vida	
Bolivia	Fondo de Pensiones Argentaria	
Brazil		
Colombia	Colfondos	
Mexico		
Central America	Banco Exterior de España	10 offices
South America	Banco Exterior de España	16 offices

Banco Bilbao Vizcaya

Country	Subsidiary	% Ownership
Argentina	Bco. Francés del Río de la Plata-Crédito Argentino	52.4
Bolivia	AFP Previsión BBV	
Brazil	Banco Excel Económico	100 [64]
Colombia	Banco Ganadero	59
Mexico	Banca Cremi	
	Banco Oriente	
	Banco Probursa	70
Panama	BBV Panamá	100
Peru	Banco Continental	37.57
Puerto Rico	BBV Puerto Rico	100
	Banco de Ponce	100
Uruguay	Banco Francés Uruguay	
Venezuela	Banco Provincial	49

Banco Central Hispanoamericano

Country	Subsidiary	% Ownership
Argentina	Tornquist	100
Bolivia	Banco del Sur	98.42
Chile	O'Higgins-Santiago-BCH	50.03
Colombia	Banco de Colombia	35
Mexico	Banco Bital	8
Paraguay	Banco Asunción	77.7
Peru	Banco del Sur	98.42
Uruguay	Banco Central Hispano	100

Banco de Santander

Country	Subsidiary	% Ownership
Argentina	Banco Río de la Plata-Banco Santander Argentina	41.2
Brazil	Banco Geral do Comercio	50
	Banco Noroeste	25
Chile	Banco Santander Chile	65.15
	Pensiones Chile	Majority
Colombia	Banco Comercial Antioqueño (Bancoquia)	55
Mexico	Banco Santander Mexicano	68.5
	Banco Santander de Negocios de México	100
Peru	Banco Santander Perú (Banco Mercantil – Banco Interandino)	100
Puerto Rico	Banco Santander Puerto Rico	99.6
	Leasing Puerto Rico	Majority
Uruguay	Banco Santander Uruguay	100
Venezuela	Banco de Venezuela	93.6

Source: El País Digital, No. 852, 2 September 1998, "Economía" section.

Retail banking was the main bet of Spanish banks in Latin America. Their universal character allowed them to provide an array of financial services to meet the necessities of a developing market. BS's experience in Chile was an illustrative example. Banco Santander provided leasing services, administered mutual funds and pension funds, and had stock brokerage services, through Santander Merchant provided credit to finance trade, and Inversiones Bansander financed investments. It also had a real estate division called Inmobiliaria Santander and a life insurance company.[65]

The competitive advantage of Spanish banks laid in their expertise in working in developing financial markets. The Spanish experience in the 1970s and 1980s, which resembled that of Latin America in the mid-1990s, allowed Spanish banks to make an evaluation of business possibilities. Their conclusion was that potential for growth outweighed risk. The universal nature of Spanish banks also allowed them to gain expertise in several financial services, which was later applied in new markets. Latin American banks were forced to adapt to a liberalized financial market abruptly and provide new services to which they were not accustomed. Spanish banks, on the other hand, were familiar with the needs of the market and offered products that met the financial needs of the public: sound credit, pension funds, intermediaries in equity markets, and more.

There was agreement on the side of Spanish bankers and on the side of Latin American politicians that Spanish banks played a crucial role in the development of the banking system in the region, which helped overcome the banking crisis of the 1980s. Spanish bankers emphasized that the importance of their investment did not lie in their cash contributions to the host countries' economies, but on the services they provided to the public in general and to the local businesses in particular. The top executives of BBV, BCH, and BS claimed that their investments in Latin America should be regarded as the "export of a way of doing business".[66]

Their goal was to create a new banking culture. Latin American banks normally served as intermediaries collecting the payments of purchases made on credit. Many Latin Americans did not keep their savings in the bank and normally showed up personally at the bank when they had to make their payments (electricity, telephones bills, etc.), either using cash or checks. The short-term goal of the Spanish banks was to do this service automatically, utilizing the offices only for the negotiation of other products, such as mortgages, insurance, pension funds, and loans. Their long-term project was to develop their investment funds, life and home insurance, and leasing services, which had not achieved a large degree of penetration in the market yet. This would allow the banks to reduce the size of the offices, the amount of employees, and overall operating costs, providing more personalized and faster services to their customers. BBV, BCH, and BS had already launched campaigns to promote their savings and checking accounts, in order to gain customers. The promotion included a daily lottery among those who had an account in their bank, giving presents and cash rewards to the winners. BBV gained 1.6 million customers between 1996 and 1997.[67]

The strategy of Spanish banks to gain market share was to present themselves in the eyes of locals as local banks. In spite of cultural proximity and a common language, BS's executive Francisco Martín López Quesada acknowledged that every country has cultural differences. However, he claimed that BS tried to overcome this drawback by hiring a group of managers, mainly locals, who knew the peculiarities of the market. They diversified and adapted BS's services to the needs of its customers. BS's executives called the BS's subsidiaries "franchises".[68] This team of managers was integrated in the international organization that devised the bank's strategy. Their objective was to make the banks appear to the eyes of locals as a domestic group with foreign capital, not as a foreign group.[69] Nevertheless, each bank pursued a different expansion strategy.

BBV sought a powerful local partner. Its participation in the local banks varied between 30 percent and 40 percent. BS sought majority ownership (in some cases even 100 percent). BCH expanded through its Chilean subsidiary, O'Higgins Central Hispano, in Chile, Argentina, and Paraguay, allying with a local partner in each country (in Mexico, however, it only had a 10 percent stake in Banco Bital). However, BCH had control over management in all cases.[70]

Argentaria redefined its strategy. Prior to 1996, its subsidiary Banco Exterior de España (BEX) had sixteen branches in South America and ten in Central America, providing credit and insurance to medium-size and small-size enterprises. In March, 1998 it acquired 50 percent of Citibank's subsidiaries in Argentina (insurance and pension fund services) and both companies began to contemplate the possibility of formalizing an alliance to operate in Latin America (Argentaria and Citibank also had a joint-venture in Colombia, Colfondos). Citibank was one of the main competitors of BBV, BCH, and BS in Latin America and Argentaria was one of their main competitors in Spain. Argentaria was partly owned by the state, until its full privatization in 1998.

The expansion of Spanish banks in Latin America can be explained from the theoretical perspective provided by the theory of the firm approach, as well as by the industrial organization approach. On the one hand, Spanish banks decided to expand in Latin America, not because interest rates were higher there, *vis-à-vis* Spain (even though that was the case), but because they believed they had a competitive advantage and wanted to exploit it in new markets. Internalization was the drive behind foreign direct investment. It was not upstream internalization into the provision of inputs (none of the Spanish banks began to expand in Latin America to gain access to inputs), but downstream internalization into marketing of their own products. The Spanish banks tailored their products for the Spanish market and believed the same services would be adequate for the developing markets of Latin America. The reason behind their move was to be present in the markets where they believed they would be able to exploit their advantage. To avoid the risks of franchising their products, Spanish banks chose to commercialize them directly by being present in the market. In most cases, they chose to buy a local bank, with ongoing operations, rather than start anew through greenfield investment. Stephen Hymer's theory of industrial organization also provides an explanation. By buying a local firm, Spanish banks removed direct competition from the market.

"Theory of the firm" provides further insight to understand their strategy. Mark Casson argued that the emergence of economies of scale gives an advantage to firms developing those economies of scale. The similarity of the Latin American markets and their banking necessities reduced the need to develop country-specific strategies and products. The lack of banking culture in Latin America as a whole, rooted in years of economic problems, poverty and hyperinflation, made Spanish banks define a common strategy. This was the development of a "popular banking culture". In other words, the banks tried to make people familiar with the use of banks and increase the range of banking services available to the bulk of the population.

Mira Wilkins's five parameters also contribute to shed light on the expansion of Spanish banks in Latin America. The banking sector was underdeveloped in most Latin American countries, and people were not familiar with the wide variety of services that banks provided. Moreover, economic instability and hyperinflation made saving almost impossible, because money lost its value very quickly (in some cases even overnight). The structural reforms initiated a period of sustained economic growth and stability that reduced the risk of saving. Spanish banks realized there was "opportunity" for business. The commitment of governments to achieve sustained economic growth became evident with the implementation of structural reforms under the auspices of the World Bank and the International Monetary Fund ("political" parameter).

The cultural "familiarity" was guaranteed by a common linguistic, historical and cultural heritage. The fact that all countries embarked on structural reform and the similarity of their banking structures provided

Spanish banks the opportunity to integrate their operations globally and reduced the need to introduce big modifications in their products ("third-country" parameter). All of the main Spanish banks had been operating in Latin America before the debt crisis erupted in 1982, and many of them had had some kind of relationship with Latin America since the nineteenth century, such as BS, which was established in the 1860s to fund trade between Spain and Latin America, as well as BCH. Their "corporate" history had a tradition of involvement in this region.

The performance of Spanish banks in Latin America is reflected in their economic results. In 1996 BCH's Latin American ventures generated a profit of $32.5 million and the prediction for 1997 was to increase that figure by 25-35 percent. The profit of BBV's Latin American subsidiaries in 1996 was $74 million, which was expected to grow in 1997 to $464 million. BS's expected profit in Latin America in 1997 was $408 million, double the amount of the previous year.[71] The estimated return on investment for both BBV and BS was 20 percent.

Spanish banks contributed to the process of financial development in Latin America with the expertise they gained in their local market. Many government officials and representatives of several multinational institutions, such as the Inter-American Development Bank, acknowledged the contribution of Spanish banks to the development of contestable and reliable financial and banking markets in Latin America. They contributed to increase the quality of credit (based on the percentage of non-performing loans), by working out with their customers repayment programs and restricting their loans to sound investments. They also contributed to develop new financial mechanisms, which increased the confidence of the public in their financial institutions and thus raised savings rates.

The period of large investments in Latin America was coming close to an end for the main Spanish banks in 1998. Argentaria had a $2 billion package ready to be invested in Latin America before it was taken over by BBV in 1999 (the Spanish state held 29.2 percent of the equity of Argentaria until 1998). BBV, BCH, and BS had already set foot in the main markets and were starting to restructure their subsidiaries and define their strategy in each country. Brazil appeared, however, as likely terrain for further expansion. BCH did not have a subsidiary in the largest Latin American country, BS entered late, in 1997, and BBV made an acquisition in April 1998. BBV executives announced that they had been studying several banks in Brazil and Chile, and allocated a fund of between $2.5 and $3.5 billion for this venture.[72] BBV received authorization in July 1998 from the Brazilian Monetary Council to increase its share of equity in Banco Excel Económico up to 100 percent. In 1998, BBV also negotiated the purchase of control equity of Banco Wiese of Peru. BS was considering to buy a second bank in Brazil to gain a larger share of the market, and BCH announced its interest to acquire the largest Argentine bank, Banco de Galicia.[73]

The strategy of expansion followed by BCH and BBV also illustrates Gomes-Casseres' alliance theory. However, a major qualitative difference exists between his theory and the type of constellations these Spanish banks developed. Gomes-Casseres constrains his analysis of constellations and alliances to firms operating within the same industry. The Spanish banks did not normally form alliances to extend their banking operations in Latin America. BCH allied with Chile's O'Higgins group to devise its expansion in Latin America. BBV's strategy was country specific, seeking a local partner in each new market where it initiated operations. Nevertheless, in all cases the expansion took shape through a takeover, rather than as an alliance. Both BBV and BCH bought large shares in each of their new Latin America subsidiaries, in order to have control over management. Although Gomes-Casseres acknowledges that the firms creating an alliance might buy shares in each other, he does not contemplate the possibility of a major takeover, as in the cases described here. It could be argued that the acquisition of Latin American subsidiaries was an "internalization" of the alliance. By taking a majority share, the Spanish bank took automatic control over the main management decisions, even though the local partners contributed with their knowledge of the market to inform the decisions taken by the Spanish parent.

Argentaria's alliance with Citibank in Argentina and Colombia was a different case. Argentaria understood that it could gain from Citibank's resources and financial services, and Citibank thought it would gain expertise from Argentaria's cultural familiarity with the environment, in order to design a strategy to adapt better to the institutional, economic, political and cultural conditions of Latin America. Argentaria became a fully private bank in 1998, when the Spanish government sold its remaining stake. However, the state retained its "golden share" for eight more years, that is to say, the Spanish government will be able to veto certain decisions over that period. In October 1999 Argentaria was taken over by BBV.[74]

A growing number of alliances involving Spanish and U.S. firms were created in the second half of the 1990s (i.e. Telefonica-WorldCom-MCI, Iberia-American Airlines-British Airways, Argentaria-Citibank, and many others involving firms in different sectors). In all cases, the common denominator was, on the one hand, the interest shown by Spanish firms in gaining management expertise, and technological and financial resources from U.S. corporations. On the other, the interest of U.S. firms to take advantage of the penetration of Spanish corporations in Latin American and European markets, and the knowledge of Spanish firms about Latin

American markets and the conditions of operation in the Latin American business environment.

However, Gomes-Casseres ignored the alliances created by firms in different sectors, which were very important for the expansion of some Spanish companies in Latin America. The alliances involving Spanish firms from different sectors have to be viewed, from the perspective of the events that took place within Spain in the mid-1990s, not as a strategy for expansion outside. The liberalization of the telecommunications sector in 1997, and the elimination of geographical restrictions within Spain for energy firms (prior to overall European liberalization in 2007) led to the formation of alliances involving at least a bank and several companies from both the energy and the telecommunications sector. The objective was to create constellations of firms from these sectors that could pool resources and benefit from the synergies that would emerge, therefore developing competitive firms able to withstand fiercer competition.

Two main groups were created in 1995, one involving BBV, La Caixa, Argentaria, Iberdrola, Repsol, Gas Natural, and Telefonica, the other one involving BCH, Endesa, Unión Fenosa, Retevisión, FCC, and Dragados y Construcciones. In each case, there was a major bank (BBV vs. BCH), one major electricity provider (Iberdrola vs. Unión Fenosa), one oil company (Repsol vs. Cepsa), and one telecommunications operator (Telefonica vs. Retevisión). In the case of BBV, the Catalonian savings institution La Caixa also played a leading role. In the group led by BCH, two contractors were included, with important road concessions in the Western Hemisphere, from Canada to Patagonia: FCC and Dragados y Construcciones. Because these strategies were devised for competition within Spain, some of the firms involved did not have a notable presence outside Spain and some did not even have any presence at all (Retevisión was the second telephone operator that began to operate in Spain in December 1997, competing against Telefonica). As opposed to the other main Spanish banks, Banco Santander did not have a great direct presence in the executive councils of key Spanish companies in the telecommunications and energy sectors. Its president, Emilio Botín, affirmed that Banco Santander's investments in industrial corporations were purely financial. BS did not want to have control over management.[75]

Nevertheless, BBV cooperated with Iberdrola, Telefonica, Repsol and Gas Natural, by providing financial resources for their expansion in Latin America. Similarly, BCH provided financial support to Endesa, Unión Fenosa, FCC and Dragados y Construcciones. BBV and BCH played a leading role in convincing the executives of these companies that there were investment opportunities in Latin America. These two banks provided their market analysis, their risk assessment and their estimates of growth opportunities to the executives of these energy firms to convince them to invest in Latin America. The presence of some managers of the banks in the executive council of these firms (the share of ownership of BBV and BCH in these companies gave them some degree of control over the executive decisions taken by the council) was important in deciding to invest in Latin America.

An illustrative example was the alliance between Endesa and BCH, signed in June 1995. In August 1997, Endesa bought 27.9 percent of Chile's electricity company Enersis. In December 1997, BCH's Chilean partner in O'Higgins-Santiago-BCH, Grupo Luksic, acquired an extra 5 percent to increase Endesa's decision power within Enersis. An agreement was finally reached between Endesa and Enersis in March 1998, to expand together in Latin America thereafter.[76] BCH played an active role in mobilizing its allies within Chile to support its partner Endesa. In September 1997, BCH led a group of banks that funded the acquisition by Endesa of 49 percent of two Colombian electricity companies, Codensa and Emgesa. Endesa created a fund of almost $3 billion for investment and acquisitions in Latin America for the period 1997-2001. BCH provided funding for some of those acquisitions.[77]

The emergence of four large Spanish banking groups engaged in aggressive competition in Latin America provides support to Gomes-Casseres' claim that alliances stimulate fiercer competition. A reduced number of groups pool resources to provide cheaper and better goods or services. The presence of Spanish groups in Latin America increased the complexity of the services provided by local banks, which were therefore forced to upgrade the quality of their goods to keep up with their foreign competitors.

The creation of multi-sector alliances, as described above, also reinforces Gomes-Casseres' idea that alliances cause fiercer competition. However, Gomes-Casseres did not explore these types of constellations. The formation of alliances of groups involving firms from different sectors (banking, energy, and telecommunications) in this case study was caused by factors internal to Spain. The liberalization of the telecommunications and energy sectors made firms from these sectors look for partners to increase their capacity to withstand fiercer competition. Banks saw the potential for growth of the telecommunications and energy sectors in Spain and decided to create alliances with firms from those sectors, to diversify their sources of revenue and invest in areas where returns were expected to be high. Indirectly, these alliances became operative in Latin America, when the Spanish banks, telecommunications and energy sectors began to invest significant amounts of money in the acquisition of local firms. These multi-sector alliances also contributed to increase the competitive character of every group.

Energy Sector

The investment of Spanish MNEs in the energy sector (by energy, I refer broadly to all types of energy, from electricity to oil) in Latin America was also caused by a series of factors: on the one hand, the liberalization of the Spanish domestic market and, on the other, the privatization of state-owned energy companies by the Latin American governments. The liberalization of the electricity sector in Spain will take place in the year 2003. Until 1998, production and distribution was primarily in the hands of regional companies (partly owned by the state and regional governments) that enjoyed a monopoly concession for a particular geographical region. These companies will be gradually privatized and, after 2003, they will face competition from European entrants. This time horizon stimulated some of them to invest overseas, not only to grow in size, but also to learn to operate in a competitive environment. Liberalization in Latin America provided the appropriate ground to test their competitiveness.

The liberalization of the energy sector in Latin America was the response of the governments to the growing needs for energy generated by higher rates of economic growth in the 1990s. Energy was one of the sectors deemed "strategic" by Latin American governments since the 1950s. Politicians believed their states would have better control over their national sources of energy with a nationalized energy industry, therefore having a continuous and sufficient flow of energy to satisfy the needs of domestic industrial companies. Moreover, state-owned firms served social and political objectives rather than entrepreneurial ones, and provided electricity at below-cost prices. In 1989, 79 percent of the people in Latin America and the Caribbean had access to electricity. Without the profit motive, state-owned firms failed to update their technology, which caused inefficiencies. Lower efficiency rates raised costs.[78]

The amount of energy generated by local producers under state control was not sufficient to fulfill the extra demand triggered by accelerated economic activity in the 1990s, forcing governments to liberalize the industry and privatize some state-owned enterprises. In Latin America and the Caribbean alone, an additional generating capacity of 70,000 megawatts was required to keep up with the needs for the period 1994-2000 only. Meeting this demand required an investment in the electric power sector of $20-25 billion dollars. In the midst of adjustment and debt-reduction schemes, states could not afford that amount. The only solution was to allow the private sector to provide it. A significant structural reform was implemented to increase efficiency and maximize the proceeds from privatization, which involved dividing the energy firms between energy production activities and distribution. Chile began its liberalization and privatization in the early 1980s and 85 percent of the firms operating in the energy sector were in private hands in 1995. Argentina began in 1990 and in 1995 private firms generated more than 50 percent of domestic energy production.[79]

Foreign firms were ready to invest in the liberalization of the energy sector, seeking higher returns and better opportunities for growth. In the United States, the demand for electricity was estimated to rise 1.9 percent between 1995 and 2000, with returns on investment ranging between 8 and 12 percent annually. For the same period, demand was expected to grow 5.5 percent in Latin America and the Caribbean, with a return on investment in that region varying between 20 and 25 percent.[80]

FDI in the energy sector in Latin America was mainly North American until the mid-1990s. Spanish energy firms did not have a strong tradition of investment in Latin America. The most important Spanish MNE in this sector was CHADE, which had investments in several countries, especially in Argentina, and was nationalized by the Perón Government.[81] Nevertheless, as the liberalization horizon in the domestic market approached in the mid- and late 1990s, Spanish firms were increasing their overseas investments, and Latin America was one of their main targets, not only for reasons of cultural affinity, but also for the potential for growth of Latin American markets. Between 1995 and 2000 Spanish firms invested considerable amounts of money in the energy sector in Latin America. The leading enterprise was Repsol, Spain's main MNE in the oil sector. Established by the state in 1987 as part of a reorganization of an older state-owned oil company (Instituto Nacional de Hidrocarburos), it became fully private in April 1997, after the culmination of a privatization process that began in 1989. In 1997 Repsol ranked sixth among European oil companies.

Repsol had a long-term strategy to diversify in two fronts. On the one hand, it aimed at diversifying its business operations away from oil distribution to oil production. In its origins Repsol was basically an oil distributor. In 1996, refining and marketing still generated 78 percent of the company's revenue, whereas exploration and production accounted for 14.3 percent.[82] Profit margins in refining and marketing activities were very small. In 1997, Repsol produced only 25 percent of the oil it processed. This decreased its profit margins, because it had to buy 75 percent of its oil from other producers.[83] For this reason, the Spanish company did not benefit from the rise in oil prices of the mid-1990s as much as its North

American and European competitors. On the other hand, Repsol planned to seek new foreign markets to overcome its dependence on Spain, where it generated 85 percent of its revenue in 1996.[84]

Latin America served Repsol's strategy in both senses. It provided new markets for Repsol's products. Privatization of oil fields gave the Spanish company an opportunity to expand its production business. In 1996 Repsol bought 47.5 percent of Argentina's Astra for $488 million. This company exploited oil fields in Argentina and Venezuela.[85] On 4 June 1997 Repsol paid $330 million (Repsol more than doubled the second bid, submitted by the Chevron-Statoil consortium) for the privatization of Mene Grande oil field, one of the richest in Venezuela, which used to be exploited by Gulf before its nationalization by the Venezuelan government in 1976. Repsol planned to increase production there from 5,500 barrels daily in 1997, to 65,000 in 2002. The Venezuelan government granted exploitation of the field for twenty years, and decided to pay for all investment costs and to buy all the oil extracted.[86] In 1999, Repsol purchased YPF from the Argentinean government for $15.540 billion.[87]

Figure 6.4   Largest European oil companies in 1997, by volume of sales

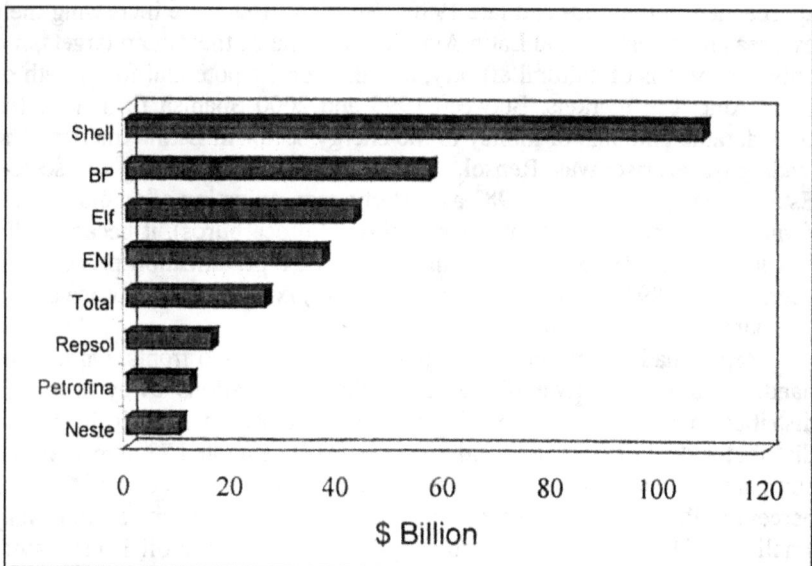

Source: Luis Aparicio, "Repsol, en Manos Privadas", *El Pais Digital*, No. 346, 14 April 1997, "Economía" section.

In July 1997 Repsol operated in some Latin American countries and had very ambitious plans of expansion. Between 1995 and 1997 it gained control over 42 percent of the Peruvian market of bottled gas and 15 percent of the gasoline market in both Ecuador and Argentina. It had plans to keep expanding in the future in several activities, such as oil and gas production and distribution, and bottled gas. In June 1996 Repsol's investments in Latin America had reached the amount of $1 billion and its president Alberto Cortina announced a plan to invest $11.5 billion in Latin America alone in the five-year period between 1997 and 2001, for development of new natural gas plants, gas distribution infrastructure, electric energy generators in refineries and commercial development.[88]

Table 6.12 Repsol's subsidiaries in Latin America in July 1997

Country	Subsidiary	Percent Ownership	Activity
Argentina	Astra [89]	47.5	Oil exploration and extraction, production of lubricants and asphalt.
	Metrogas		Gas distribution.
	Grupo Comercial del Plata		
	JME Inversiones		
	Isaura		
	EG3	32.5	
	Refinería San Lorenzo (Refisan)	42.5	
	Refinerías Argentinas de Petróleo (Dapsa)	50	Oil refining.
	Parafinas del Plata	50	Oil refining.
	Pluspetrol	45	
Colombia	Gas Natural ESP * [90]		Natural gas extraction. Natural gas distribution.
Ecuador	Repsol Ecuador		Natural gas distribution. Service stations. (Plans to expand into refining and bottled gas).
Mexico	Nuevo Laredo *		Gas distribution.
	Saltillo *		Gas distribution.
Peru	Repsol Perú (former Corpetrol)	80	Gasoline stations.
	La Pampilla		Oil refining.
	Solgás		Bottled gas.
	Limagás		Bottled gas.
	Energás		Bottled gas.
Venezuela	Repsol Venezuela		Oil extraction.

Source: El País Digital, No. 346, 14 April 1997, observed 14 April 1997; No. 393, 31 May 1997, observed 31 May 1997; and No. 400, 7 June 1997, observed 7 June 1997.

Natural gas was one of Repsol's main bets for the future, both in Spain and in Latin America. In Spain, Repsol's gas sales increased 28.3 percent between 1994 and 1996, even though in 1997 the gas division still generated only 22.3 percent of its total revenue. In 1997 Repsol had control over 95 percent of the Spanish market of bottled gas and 90 percent of the natural gas market (Repsol inaugurated an African-European gas pipeline between Algeria and Spain in late 1996).[91] For expansion in Latin America, Repsol created a joint-venture with two Spanish companies, Iberdrola and Gas Natural, called Gas Natural Latinoamericana, for distribution of natural gas. Gas Natural Latinoamericana bought 53 percent of Gas Natural ESP from Ecopetrol, the Colombian state-owned oil company, for $148 million, in June 1997. In February 1998 Repsol decided to sell its 50 percent share to Gas Natural.[92]

Endesa and Iberdrola also had a significant presence in Latin America. Endesa was the largest Spanish regional electricity distributor. The Spanish state was the major stockholder until June 1998, when it sold its 41.1 percent share in a public offering.[93] Endesa had a significant presence in Peru, where it bought two of Electroperú's eight power generating companies in 1995. It paid $120 million, along with Inversiones y Crédito and Cosapi of Peru, for 60 percent of Etevensa, and $60 million for 60 percent of Empresa Eléctrica de Piura (EEP), a gas-fired generating plant. Edelnor provided energy to the Lima region, whereas Etevensa and EEP served the northern part of the country. Endesa planned to supply electricity to the Central-North Interconnected System, which runs parallel to the coast. In 1996 Endesa acquired 60 percent of Edelnor for $170 million. Endesa led a consortium integrated by Enersis and Chilectra of Chile and Banco de Crédito and Cosapi of Peru. Edelnor was one of the two distribution enterprises that provided energy to Lima. In Argentina, Endesa was one of the stockholders of Edenor, a company that distributed electricity to two million people in Buenos Aires.[94]

Endesa's main acquisition in Latin America was 27.9 percent of Chile's Enersis in August 1997. In March 1998 both Endesa and Enersis reached an agreement to participate together in the privatization of several state-owned energy enterprises in Latin America between 1998 and 2003. In September 1997 Enersis was part of the consortium led by Endesa that presented the winning bid in the privatization of Colombia's energy producer Emgesa and distributor Codensa (the consortium was also integrated by Chile's Chilectra, Grupo Financiero Popular de Colombia and Fondelec, of the United States).[95] In April 1998 Endesa and Enersis presented the winning bid ($873.4 million) for the privatization of 51 percent of a Brazilian company, Coelce. This was the first time they operated together, after the creation of their alliance. Each company provided 41 percent of the funding (the remaining 18 percent was distributed among Chilectra and Electricidade de Portugal). Endesa extended its participation in Enersis up to 65 percent on 14 April 1999. This provoked serious debates in the Chilean Congress. On 29 April, Chile's Monopoly Commission blocked Endesa's move, but on 11 May it finally authorized the takeover.[96]

Endesa and Iberdrola (like the main banks allied with them, BCH and BBV) were engaged in open competition for the acquisition of a large number of electricity enterprises in Latin America. Endesa won Coelce over Iberdrola, which presented the second largest bid for the Brazilian company. Iberdrola, one of the largest regional electricity distributors in Spain (based in the Basque Country and allied with the main Basque bank, BBV) began operating in Latin America in 1992 and in 1998 it had operations in Argentina, Bolivia, Brazil and Chile. In its race against Endesa, Iberdrola paid $500 million for Companhia Energética de Rio Grande do Norte (Cosern), in northwestern Brazil in December 1997 and in July acquired 65.64 percent of another electricity company, Coelba, in the state of Bahia, also in northwestern Brazil.[97] In July 1998 Iberdrola participated in a consortium, along with Telefonica and BBV, which bought five of the twelve subsidiaries of Telebras privatized by the Brazilian government. Iberdrola was the main stockholder of one of them, Tele Leste Celular, a cellular telephone company that operates in the Bahia region.[98]

Table 6.13 Endesa's subsidiaries in Latin America in April 1998

Country	Subsidiary
Argentina	Dock Su, Easa, Edenor, Yacylec
Brazil	CERJ, Coelce
Chile	Enersis
Colombia	Capital Energía, Codensa, Emgesa, Luz de Bogotá
Dominican Republic	Cepm
Peru	Edelnor
Venezuela	Elecar

Source: Endesa, quoted in Santiago Carcar, "Endesa Adquiere la Compañía Brasileña Coelce en Pugna con Iberdrola", *El País Digital*, No. 699, 3 April 1998, "Economía" section (observed 3 April 1998); and *El Nuevo Herald*, 1998, "Pasa Firma Brasileña a Manos de Europeos", 3 April 1998, p. 6B.

Iberdrola participated in a consortium (made up by Iberdrola, Powerfin of Belgium and Enagas of Chile) that bought 51 percent of a thermal power station in Chile, Central Termoeléctrica Tocopilla, for $178 million in 1996.[99] Iberdrola and Gas Natural also invested in the gas sector in Argentina. Iberdrola operated through a subsidiary called Distribuidora Gas Litoral and Gas Natural under its own name.[100] Unión Fenosa and BCH bought 26 percent and 10 percent, respectively, of Bolivia's Transportadora de Electricidad, which provided energy to 20 distribution companies in that country.[101]

This acquisition shows the high degree of integration that exists within the alliance led by BCH, which participated directly with one of its allies in the electricity sector, Unión Fenosa, in the privatization of this Bolivian company. Unión Fenosa also purchased two of the three subsidiaries of Panama's Institute of Hydraulic Resources and Electrification, IRHE (Institutio de Recursos Hidráulicos y de Electrificación) on 11 September, 1998. Fenosa paid $301 million for Metro-Oeste S.A. and for Chiriquí S.A. A U.S. corporation, Constellation Power, acquired the third subsidiary, Noreste S.A., for $89.8 million.[102] The fourth Spanish electricity company with investments in Latin America, Hidroeléctrica del Cantábrico (HC), invested in Mexico in 1998. Its allied, Texas Utilities Corporation, won a concession to distribute gas in Mexico City in November 1998, and in December it invited HC to participate in this project through the acquisition of 15 percent of the venture. HC invested $100 million in these Mexican projects.[103]

The case of direct competition between Endesa and Iberdrola reflects Gomes-Casseres' theory that under collective competition, competition is fiercer. Each of these two enterprises, backed up by one of the main Spanish banks, BBV in the case of Iberdrola and BCH in the case of Endesa, engaged in fierce competition for markets in Latin America. However, this also shows that constellations do not always emerge among firms from the same sector. BCH participated in the privatization of Bolivia's Transportadora de Electricidad, along with Unión Fenosa, which led the consortium. BCH took a prominent role in a non-financial operation, to become one of the core stockholders of an electricity distributor. BBV and BCH bought significant stakes in non-banking businesses in Latin America. However, their executives emphasized that they were not interested in the management of these enterprises. They participated along with their allies because they saw that these investments could generate high returns. They gave the management of their subsidiaries to their allies in the energy sector, such as Unión Fenosa.

Gomes-Casseres did not analyze the high degree of cohesion that may emerge among firms from different sectors of activity. He restricted his analysis of alliances to firms within the same industry. The case of Spanish MNEs operating in Latin America shows that firms from several sectors came together and took the agreements reached for cooperation within Spain to foreign markets, in this case to Latin America. The main energy companies cooperated very closely with the bank within their constellation to expand their activities abroad, not only for logistic, but also for financial support.

Spanish direct investment in the energy sector began in 1992 and mounted after 1995. Several Spanish firms had clear plans to expand in that region to take advantage of the process of privatization of some state-owned energy companies. Repsol decided to invest $11.5 billion between 1997 and 2002. Gas Natural also planned to enter several Latin American markets. Iberdrola and Endesa were the first two Spanish regional energy distributors to initiate Latin American ventures and were followed by Unión Fenosa and HC, as part of a defensive strategy to prepare for liberalization in Spain.

Spanish firms in the energy sector had excess capital, ready to be invested where they saw opportunities for growth. In the 1980s and 1990s, they invested large amounts of capital in acquiring expensive equipment to upgrade their infrastructure. As a result, their production capacity became larger than demand in Spain. Given their monopolistic control over the Spanish market, their revenue in the early 1990s compensated for their investments. With no immediate equipment needs, large cash flows to come in the near future, and low interest rates below 4 percent in the late 1990s, Spanish firms accumulated excess capital, ready to be invested in growing markets, where they could exercise their competitive advantage.

The competitive advantage of Spanish firms in the energy sector (not Repsol) was their ability to develop new power-generating facilities and to upgrade existing stations, to improve distribution networks and infrastructure and to establish new ones. The economic boom of the 1980s and 1990s in Spain accelerated the energy needs of domestic firms and consumers. Spanish distributors had to seek new sources of energy for the growing Spanish demand, as well as to upgrade their distribution infrastructure, in order to transport energy from sources to clients. Economic liberalization and structural reforms in Latin America accelerated economic growth. A sufficient and continuous supply of energy was necessary. Spanish firms gained expertise over the 1980s and 1990s in Spain in developing the needed infrastructure and networks to overcome that problem and sought new markets to apply it. In Latin America they found a very familiar environment, not only in cultural terms, but also in terms of market structure and energy needs.

Notes

[1] The twelve members of the European Union reached an agreement to create a single European currency in the Dutch town of Maastricht in 1991 (Sweden, Finland and Austria joined the European Union in 1995). The agreement established the criteria (to be based on the macroeconomic figures of 1997) by which countries would be eligible to participate in the monetary union in 1999. Average inflation in 1997 should be equal to or lower than the average of the three countries with the lowest rate, plus 1.5 percent. Public deficit should be equal to or lower than 3 percent of GDP. Public debt should be equal to or lower than 60 percent of GDP. Interest rates should be 3 percent in December 1998. The national currency had to be part of the European Monetary System for a period of at least two years prior to the date of the monetary union and could not have appreciated or depreciated more than 15 percent with respect to the European average. Because only France, Ireland, Luxembourg and the United Kingdom met the debt criterion the European authorities decided to reinterpret this criteria, and accepted those countries whose public debt relative to GDP fell in 1997 with respect to the previous year. The president of the European Bank, Willem Duisenberg, announced on 25 March 1998 that Spain had met all the criteria, along with Austria, Belgium, Finland, France, Germany, Ireland, Italy, Luxembourg, The Netherlands, and Portugal. These eleven decided to adopt a common currency. Denmark, Greece, Sweden, and the United Kingdom did not.

[2] *El Mundo*, 30 June 1996. See also *ICE*, No. 2543, 12-18 May, 1997, pp. 41-53.

[3] Robert Grosse, "A Privatization Nightmare. Aerolíneas Argentinas", in Ravi Ramamurti (ed.), *Privatizing Monopolies. Lessons from the Telecommunications and Transport Sectors in Latin America*, Johns Hopkins University Press, Baltimore, 1996, pp. 203-220.

[4] Pablo Gerchunoff and Germán Coloma, "Privatization in Argentina", in Manuel Sánchez and Rossana Corona (eds.), *Privatization in Latin America*, IDB, Washington, D.C., 1993, pp. 251-299.

[5] Janet Kelly, "One Piece of a Larger Puzzle. The Privatization of Viasa", in Ravi Ramamurti (ed.), *Privatizing Monopolies*, pp. 241-277.

[6] *The Miami Herald*, 9 March 1997, Business section, pp. F1-F2.

[7] *ABC Electrónico*, 21 October 1996, "Economía" section, www.abc.es, observed 21 October 1996.

[8] *El Nuevo Herald*, 29 June 1997, "Moneda" section, p. 5B.

[9] Juan Jesús Aznárez, "Iberia Cierra la Venta del 10% de Aerolíneas a American Airlines y se Queda Con Otro 10%", *El País Digital*, No. 580, 4 December 1997, "Economía" section, www.elpais.es, observed 4 December 1997.

[10] Iberia. Quoted in *El País Digital*, No. 415, 23 June 1997, "Economía" section, observed 23 June 1997. The French Caribbean territories are excluded from these data.

[11] *The Miami Herald*, 20 October 1996, "Moneda" section, p. 7F.

[12] The Allende regime seized ITT's stake in CTC in 1971, but CTC was not fully nationalized until 1974, during the military period. See Adeoye A. Akinsanya, *The Expropriation of Multinational Property in the Third World*, Praeger Publishers, New York, 1980, pp. 138-139; and Paul E. Sigmund, 1980, *Multinationals in Latin America. The Politics of Nationalization*, The University of Wisconsin Press, Madison, 1980, pp. 148-149.

[13] Adeoye A. Akinsanya, *The Expropriation...*, pp. 115-146; and Paul E. Sigmund, *Multinationals in Latin America*, pp. 36-39.

14 Albert Carreras, Xavier Tafunell and Eugenio Torres, "Against Integration. The Rise and Decline of Spanish State-Owned Firms and the Decline and Rise of Multinationals, 1939-1990", in Ülf Olson (ed.), *Business and European Integration Since 1800. Regional, National and International Perspectives*, University of Göteborg, Göteborg, 1997, p. 32.

15 Ravi Ramamurti, "The New Frontier of Privatization", in Ravi Ramamurti (ed.), *Privatizing Monopolies...*, pp. 1-45.

16 Ibid., p. 11.

17 Juan José Durán Herrera and Fernando Gallardo Olmedo, "La Estrategia de Internacionalización de las Operadoras de Telecomunicaciones", *ICE*, No. 735, November 1994, p. 98.

18 John M. Kline, *Foreign Investment Strategies in Restructuring Economies. Learning From Corporate Experiences in Chile*, Quorum Books, Westport, 1992, p. 189.

19 Manuel Sánchez, Rossana Corona, Otoniel Ochoa, Luis Fernando Herrera, Arturo Olvera, and Ernesto Sepúlveda, "The Privatization Process in Mexico: Five Case Studies", in Manuel Sánchez and Rossana Corona (ed.), *Privatization in Latin America*, 1993, p. 162.

20 Ben Petrazzini, "Telephone Privatization in a Hurry. Argentina", in Ravi Ramamurti (ed.), *Privatizing Monopolies...*, p. 127.

21 Pablo Gerchunoff and Germán Coloma, "Privatization in Argentina...", p. 129.

22 Dominique Hachette, Rolf Lüders and Guillermo Tagle, "Five Cases of Privatization in Chile", in Manuel Sánchez and Rossana Corona (ed.), *Privatization in Latin America*, pp. 79-80. Also John M. Kline, *Foreign Investment Strategies...*, p. 190.

23 Thomas Kamm and Jonathan Friedland, "Looking for Gold Spanish Firms Discover Latin America. Business as New World of Profits", *The Wall Street Journal*, 23 May 1996, pp. A1, A9.

24 Carmen Jiménez, "Telefónica se Convierte en el Mayor Operador de Brasil", *El País*, 30 July 1998, p. 31.

25 Miguel Ángel Patiño, "El Único Operador Global en Latinoamérica", *Gazeta Mercantil Latinoamericana*, 10 August 1998, p. 6.

26 Miguel Ángel Patiño, "Telefónica y Sus Socios Invertirán Dos Billones en Brasil", *Expansión*, 30 July 1998, p. 3.

27 *El Nuevo Herald*, "El Salvador Subastará Acciones de Empresa de Telefonía Celular", 14 August 1998, "Moneda" section, p. 9B.

28 Telefonica, "Memoria Anual", http://www.telefonica.es/index/memoriaanual.html, 1999, and *The Miami Herald*, "Telefonica Enters Cell-Phone Field", 25 March 1999, p. 2C.

29 Telefonica: http://www.telefonica.com/dir1/index.htm.

30 Ravi Ramamurti, 1996, "The New Frontier of Privatization", p. 21.

31 Ignacio Santillana del Barrio, "Inversiones en Chile. La Perspectiva de Telefónica", *ICE*, No. 2372, 7-13 June 1993, pp. 1686-1689.

32 Thomas Kamm and Jonathan Friedland, "Looking for Gold...", pp. A1, A9.

33 Telefonica, "Memoria Anual".

34 *ABC Electrónico*, 1 March 1997, "Economía" section, observed 1 March 1997.

35 Gautam Naik and Carita Vitzthum, "BT, MCI Detail Pact with Telefonica. Agreement Creates a Force in Latin America, Marks a Blow to AT&T's Plans", *The Wall Street Journal*, 21 April 1997, p. A19.

36 *ABC Electrónico*, 17 April 1997, "Economía" section, observed 17 April 1997.

37 *El País Digital*, No. 347, 15 April 1997, "Economía" section, observed 15 April 1997.

[38] Javier del Pino, "Telefónica se Alía con WorldCom para Europa y con MCI para Abordar el Mercado de EEUU", *El País Digital*, No. 676, 10 March 1998, "Economía" section, observed 10 March 1998.

[39] *El Nuevo Herald*, "MCI y Worldcom Reciben Aprobación para Cerrrar Megafusión Millonaria", 16 September 1998, "Moneda" section, p. 4B.

[40] *El Nuevo Herald*, "Intereses Lusos en Pos de Telefónica", 28 March 1998, "Moneda" section, p. 4B.

[41] Juan Manuel Zafra, "Telefónica Fortalece su Alianza con Portugal Telecom, en Detrimento de su Nuevo Rival BT", *El País Digital*, No. 678, 12 March 1998, "Economía" section, observed 12 March 1998.

[42] *El País Digital*, No. 426, 3 July 1997, "Economía" section, observed 3 July 1998.

[43] *El Nuevo Herald*, 6 July 1997, "Moneda" section, p. 5B.

[44] *El País Digital*, No. 425, 2 July 1997, "Economía" section, observed 2 July 1997.

[45] *El País Digital*, No. 390, 28 May 1997, "Economía" section, observed 28 May 1997.

[46] David White, "In the Quest of Fabulous Wealth", *Financial Times*, special section III "Spanish Banking and Finance", 15 October 1996, p. IV.

[47] By the end of 1998 BBV increased its participation in Iberdrola from 7.7% to 11%. BBV, www.bbv.es, observed 21 December 1998.

[48] *ABC Electrónico*, 27 January 1997, "Economía" section, observed 2 January 1997.

[49] *ABC Electrónico*, 12 January 1997, "Economía" section, observed 12 January 1997.

[50] Not available.

[51] In January 1997. Source: *ABC Electrónico*, 27 January 1997, "Economía" section, observed 27 January 1997.

[52] Sebastian Edwards, *Crisis and Reform in Latin America. From Despair to Hope*, World Bank, Washington, D.C., 1995, pp. 204-207.

[53] Liliana Rojas-Suárez and Steven R. Weisbrod, *Financial Fragilities in Latin America. The 1980s and 1990s*, IMF, Washington, D.C., p. 10.

[54] Sebastian Edwards, *Crisis and Reform...*, pp. 207-208.

[55] Liliana Rojas-Suárez and Steven R. Weisbrod, *Financial Fragilities...*, p. 15.

[56] Sebastian Edwards, *Crisis and Reform...*, p. 208.

[57] David White, "In the Quest...", p. III.

[58] *El País Digital*, No. 431, 8 July 1997, "Economía" section, observed 8 July 1997.

[59] Banco de Santander. Quoted in *El País Digital*, "Los Beneficios del Santander Suben un 29.2% en 1997 y Superan los 110,000 Millones", 29 January 1998, "Economía" section, observed 29 January 1998.

[60] *El Nuevo Herald*, 8 March 1997, "Moneda" section, p. 5B.

[61] *El Nuevo Herald*, 23 March 1997, "Moneda" section, p. 6B.

[62] BBV. Quoted in *El País Digital*, 1 February 1998, "Economía" section, observed 1 February 1998.

[63] David White, "Old World Seeks Gold in the New", *The Financial Times*, special section "Latin American Finance: Banking and Investment", 14 March 1997, p. 4.

[64] The Brazilian Monetary Council authorized BBV to increase its control over equity in Banco Excel Económico up to 100 percent, on 30 July 1998. Source: BBV, www.bbv.es, observed 2 August 1998.

[65] Francisco Martín López Quesada, "La Inversión Extranjera y el Sector Financiero Chileno. La Experiencia del Banco Santander", *ICE*, No. 2372, 7-13 June 1993, p. 1695.

[66] Piedad Oregui, "Libretones y Supercuentas de Exportación. La Banca Española Hace Cultura Financiera en el Exterior con sus Productos Más Emblemáticos", *El País*

Digital, No. 570, 24 November 1997, "Economía" section, observed 24 November 1997.

[67] BBV. Quoted in Piedad Oregui, "Libretones y Supercuentas...".

[68] Ibid.

[69] Francisco Martín López Quesada, "La Inversión Extranjera...", p. 1695.

[70] Piedad Oregui, "Libretones y Supercuentas...".

[71] *El Nuevo Herald*, "Latinoamérica es Minita de Oro para Banca Hispana", 23 March 1997, "Moneda" section, p. 5B.

[72] BBV. Quoted in *El Nuevo Herald*, "Crecen Inversiones de Banco Español en Hispanoamérica", 18 March 1998, "Moneda" section, p. 4B.

[73] *Expansión*, "El BCH Ultima la Compra del Banco de Galicia de Argentina", 27 February 1998, observed 27 February 1998.

[74] David White, "Banco Bilbao Vizcaya to Merge with Argentaria", *The Financial Times*, 20 October 1999, p. 29.

[75] Jorge Rivera, "Botín Reclama del Gobierno Tensión y Rigor para Despejar las Dudas Sobre la Adhesión al Euro", *El País Digital*, No. 324, 23 March 1997, "Economía" section, observed 23 March 1997.

[76] *El Nuevo Herald*, "Enersis y Endesa Suscriben Alianza", 19 March 1998, "Moneda" section, p. 4B.

[77] Endesa and BCH. Quoted in R. Casado, "Endesa y el BCH Ratifican su Nueva Alianza y la Extienden a sus Negocios en Latinoamérica", *El País Digital*, 10 February 1998, "Economía" section, observed 10 February 1998.

[78] Saud Siddique, "Financing Private Power in Latin America and the Caribbean", *Finance and Development*, March 1995, Vol. 32, No. 1, pp. 18-21.

[79] Ibid.

[80] Ibid.

[81] Albert Carreras et al, p. 43.

[82] Luis Aparicio, "Repsol, en Manos Privadas", *El País Digital*, No. 346, 14 April 1997, "Economía" section, observed 14 April 1997.

[83] Ibid.

[84] Ibid.

[85] Ibid.

[86] Ludmila Vinogradoff, "Repsol Consigue Entrar en Venezuela Tras Ofrecer el Doble que sus Rivales", *El País Digital*, No. 398, 5 June 1997, "Economía" section, observed 5 June 1997.

[87] This was the highest amount paid for a Latin American company until then. The process of privatization of YPF occurred in two phases. The Argentinean government sold 14.99 percent of YPF's stokes to Repsol in January 1999 for $2.100 billion, and 85 percent in April, for $13.440 billion. In 1999, YPF had reserves of 3 billion barrels of oil and controlled 50 percent of Argentina's hydrocarbons market. Its privatization generated political discussions in the Argentinean Congress, where it was regarded as the key for foreign investors to access Argentina's natural resources, protected by previous democratic and military administrations. YPF's executives accepted Repsol's offer in May and, in June, Repsol gained control over 100 percent of YPF. Sources: Ken Warn, "The Winner Must Oil the Wheels", *The Financial Times*, special section III "Spanish Banking and Finance", 15 October 1999, p. 8; David White, "Repsol Eyes Front Runners with YPF Buy", *The Financial Times*, section "Companies and Finance: International", 22 January 1999, p. 24; Extel Financial Limited, "Repsol to Make 13.44 bln usd Bid for YPF", 30 April 1999; AFP-Extel News Limited, "YPF Board

Recommends Approval of Repsol Takeover Bid", 10 May 1999; AFP-Extel News Limited, "Outlook", 1 September 1999.

88 *El País Digital*, No. 344, 12 April 1997, "Economía" section, observed 12 April 1997.

89 Metrogas, Edenor and Pluspetrol were subsidiaries of the Astra group, before Repsol bought 47.5 percent of it in 1996. The Spanish oil company bought Grupo Comercial del Plata, JME Inversiones, Isaura, EG3, Refisan, Dapsa and Parafinas through Astra on 30 May 1997. Source: *El País Digital*, No. 346, 14 April 1997, observed 14 April 1997; No. 393, 31 May 1997, observed 31 May 1997; No. 400, 7 June 1997, observed 7 June 1997; and Repsol, www.repsol.es, observed 6 May 1997.

90 The companies marked with an asterisk are operated through Gas Natural Latinoamericana, a company created by Repsol and two Spanish companies, Iberdrola and Gas Natural to participate in gas extraction and distribution projects in Latin America, as well as to bid in the future privatization of gas fields and distributors in that region. Source: *El País Digital*, No. 346, 14 April 1997, observed 14 April 1997; No. 393, 31 May 1997, observed 31 May 1997; No. 400, 7 June 1997, observed 7 June 1997.

91 Luis Aparicio, "Repsol, en Manos Privadas...".

92 *Expansión*, "Repsol Abandona el Capital de Gas Natural Latinoamericana", 7 February 1998, observed 7 February 1998.

93 Santiago Carcar, "La Euforia Bursátil Anima al Gobierno a Vender su 41% de Endesa Para Ingresar 1,6 Billones", *El País Digital*, No. 701, 5 April 1998, observed 5 April 1998.

94 *Euromoney*, "The Rush to Finance Latin Energy", No. 326, June 1996, pp. 161-169; *Euromoney*, "In Search of Spanish Synergy", No. 309, January 1995, pp. 42-44; *The Oil and Gas Journal*, "Repsol, Pluspetrol Eye Latin America Accord", 3 February 1997, Vol. 95, No. 5, p. 35.

95 *El País Digital*, "Endesa se Adjudica Dos Eléctricas de Colombia por 337,000 Millones", No. 502, 17 September 1997, observed 17 September 1997.

96 *El País Digital*, No. 1075, 14 April 1999, "Economía" section, observed 14 April 1999; No. 1091, 29 April 1999, "Economía" section, observed 29 April 1999; and No. 1104, 12 May 1999, "Economía" section, observed 12 May 1999.

97 *El País Digital*, "Iberdrola Compra la Eléctrica Brasileña Cosern por 73800 Millones", No. 589, 13 December 1997, observed 13 December 1997.

98 Carmen Jiménez, "Telefónica Se Convierte...".

99 *Euromoney*, "The Rush to Finance...", pp. 167-168.

100 Ignacio Suárez-Zuloaga, "La Internacionalización Productiva de las Empresas Españolas, 1991-1994", *ICE*, No. 746, October 1995, pp. 102-103.

101 Unión Fenosa and BCH, quoted in *El País Digital*, No. 411, 19 June 1997, observed 19 June 1997.

102 *El Nuevo Herald*, "Pagan $301 Millones por Empresa Eléctrica Panameña", 12 September 1998, "Moneda" section, p. 6B.

103 AFP-Extel News Limited, "Hidrocantabrico to Invest 18 bln Pesetas in Mexico Under Eastern Group Accord", 14 December 1998.

7 Conclusion: The Competitive Advantage of Spanish MNEs

Spanish direct investment in Latin America became significant in the 1990s as a consequence of a conjunction of economic developments in Latin America and in Spain. On the one hand, Latin American governments implemented stabilization programs and structural reforms that made their markets more attractive to foreign investors. On the other, Spain's gradual integration into the European market since the early 1980s initiated a process of economic liberalization that allowed European firms to operate in Spain freely. Under competition, Spanish firms had to upgrade the quality of their goods and services not to lose ground to foreign enterprises. Spanish markets became more contestable and returns on investment began to shrink.

The debt crisis of the 1980s in Latin America marked the end of a period characterized by heavy state involvement in the economy. The inability of states to operate as efficient allocators of resources undermined the degree of competitiveness of Latin American economies. Investment was not made on the basis of market decisions, but on a series of constraints, such as ceilings on interest rates and the need to save credit for investment in some sectors deemed as socially important.

The heavy involvement of the state in resource-allocation mechanisms originated several market imperfections and made productivity fall. Investment in the less competitive enterprises undermined the overall rate of productivity of the economy. Public enterprises served social and political goals and did not follow a profit motive. The inability of the state to upgrade the technology made public firms lose productivity overtime and thus competitiveness. In the 1980s most state-owned enterprises were losing money. Private enterprises also failed to keep productivity rates up with overall world standards: tight barriers to entry into the market shielded domestic producers from foreign competition which granted a steady flow of revenue and, thus, eliminated their incentive to upgrade the products.

The policy shift occurred in the second half of the 1980s and in the early 1990s. With the rate of productivity at its lowest and an overall heavily-indebted economy, inflows of capital decreased between 1982 and 1984. The way out of the crisis came in the form of a radical policy shift, based on the belief that the traditional economic model based on heavy protection of local producers had failed. The new model emphasized economic liberalism and competition. A stable macroeconomic framework was necessary to create a favorable business climate. Macroeconomic stability was achieved by reducing the fiscal deficit of the state and the debt burden, decreasing government borrowing, in order not to crowd out private investment, and adopting realistic exchange rates.

Competition in the market was pursued through the elimination of restrictions on imports and on foreign direct investment, the elimination of legal restrictions on economic activities, and the privatization of state-owned enterprises. The availability of foreign goods in the market forced domestic firms to upgrade their technology in order to raise productivity rates and lower the cost of their goods. Privatization of state-owned firms provided revenue for the cash-starved state accounts and put inefficient public enterprises in the hands of private business people willing to turn them into profitable enterprises. The spirit behind these policies was the belief that the profit drive would encourage entrepreneurs to upgrade their technology and production techniques in order to increase productivity, reduce costs and increase the quality of the goods. All this, in turn, would raise living standards. According to Latin American policymakers, foreign firms would create jobs and accelerate economic growth because they would bring into the national economy more sophisticated technology and management techniques that would contribute to upgrade the overall productivity of the market and, in the long run, would be imitated by local firms.

The new business framework in Latin America was thus propitious for private foreign investors. The state backed out of the economy and called for foreign MNEs to play a leading role. How ready were Spanish firms to take advantage of this circumstance? After economic liberalization began in 1979, Spanish firms made a strong effort to raise their performance to European standards, in order to compete in the free market of the European Union. By being exposed to foreign competition, especially from European firms, Spanish companies upgraded their management and marketing techniques, their technology and their products, to please their demanding European customers.

Spain's integration into the European market generated a period of strong economic growth and development in Spain. In the early 1990s European authorities set the schedule for total liberalization of some key industries, such as telecommunications and energy. At the same time, they decided to adopt a single European currency in 1999, which threatened to allow a faster and easier movement of products and firms across Europe, thus increasing overall competition. The fear of stronger competition from European firms, and the fall of returns on investment within the Spanish market caused by slower economic growth moved Spanish firms to seek new markets.

Three theoretical frameworks illuminated this analysis of Spanish MNEs in Latin America in the 1990s: industrial organization approach, theory of the firm and alliance theory. Theory of the firm and industrial organization theory provided the point of departure. Both theory of the firm and industrial organization theory rest on the premise that firms make direct investments because they have some kind of competitive advantage over other firms in a particular activity and want to exploit it. A firm that estimates it has some type of advantage in its domestic market might want to keep exploiting that advantage abroad by establishing foreign operations.

This premise goes beyond the predictions of international economics theory and international trade theory. International economics takes MNEs as agents that engage in arbitrage and that export equity capital from countries where returns are low (low cost of capital) to countries where returns are high. This theory does not differentiate portfolio investment from direct investment and fails to explain why MNEs do not invest only in the economic sectors where returns are highest. In other words, it fails to account for the fact that MNEs invest in the business they do best, in which they have developed some kind of advantage. MNEs do not venture into new economic activities, even if the returns on investment for firms in that field are higher, because they lack the expertise.

The general theory of international trade rests on the belief that MNEs are a function of factor endowments, like trade flows. According to this theory, MNEs emerge when a firm finds the opportunity to link up its operations with an establishment in another country where the factors endowments are propitious for its activities. This perspective fails to predict the fact that Spanish MNEs took the lead over U.S. MNEs in some economic sectors in Latin America in the 1990s. U.S. firms were better endowed than Spanish MNEs in the banking, telecommunications and energy sectors, but did not invest large amounts of money in Latin America. Stephen Hymer's theory of industrial organization provides the explanation for this puzzle. The first factor to consider is "risk". U.S. companies and Spanish companies had a different evaluation of risk when they analyzed the Latin American market. U.S. firms tended to emphasize the risks over the opportunities the market offered, and Spanish MNEs saw that the possible gains of investing in fast-growing markets outweighed the political and economic risks in the long term. Spanish entrepreneurs, in fact, believed in the commitment of Latin American politicians to implement long-term structural reforms and in the sustainability of the policies implemented.

The second key notion provided by Hymer to understand the behavior of Spanish MNEs is "control". Direct investment by Spanish MNEs, as opposed to portfolio investment, took place in order to guarantee "control" over the operations. Control over what? Over their competitive advantage. Hymer's thesis rests on the premise that firms invest abroad in order to exploit their competitive advantage, something they do better than their competitors. The advantage of Spanish firms was their ability to adapt their products and services to the needs of developing and modernizing economies. Since the 1970s, Spain ceased to be a developing country and became a developed country. In this process, Spanish firms had to adapt to a long process of development, which shaped the nature of all economic activities. It was especially important in the development of business infrastructure, such as roads, buildings, financial markets, telecommunications and the banking and energy sectors.

The firms operating in those sectors had to upgrade their products to European standards in order to meet the growing demand coming from the European Union. In the process of transition from a relatively underdeveloped to a modern and developed economy, firms gained expertise. They learned how to adapt their products to the needs of the customers at every stage of development, the possibilities of expansion of each economic sector and the overall strategy of development to follow.

Telefonica learnt to satisfy the needs of the business community and, overall, those of the average customer. For example, Telefonica provided sophisticated telephone services to the business community while extending basic services to larger sectors of the population, especially in rural areas that lacked telephone access. Banks learnt to sell an array of new financial products to their customers, such as pension and investment funds, stocks and bonds, which not a long ago did not exist in the Spanish market. Energy firms had to increase their capacity to provide sufficient energy to meet the needs of an expanding economy.

Operation in a liberalizing market involves many uncertainties, such as the degree of success to which structural reforms will be accomplished, the rates of economic growth these reforms will generate, the degree of stability and smoothness of the whole process, and the degree of commitment of authorities with the reforms, among other things. Living through the process of liberalization of the Spanish economy allowed Spanish firms to make these uncertainties a little more predictable.

When the first reforms were implemented by the Latin American governments, North American and European firms were hesitant about the consistency of the reforms and the probability that they might be reversed.

Moreover, in the early 1990s Latin America was struggling to come out of a deep debt crisis. The income per capita of their citizens was low and many countries still had negative rates of growth, which made the economic outlook seem gloomy. With this perspective, investment in Latin America did not offer guarantees and was deemed highly risky.

The advantage of Spanish firms rested on their knowledge of and familiarity with the needs of economic liberalization, especially in the basic infrastructure sectors such as telephony, finance and banking and energy. They knew what products were needed in every economic activity and the tremendous possibilities for growth of sectors that had to be completely developed, in some cases almost from scratch. For this reason, Spanish firms moved to Latin America, sometimes through greenfield investment, most commonly through the acquisition of a domestic firm. In the processes of privatization of state-owned telephone companies, banks and energy enterprises, Spanish firms normally presented the largest bids. Their faith in the market was based on their assessment of the opportunity for business. As Telefonica's executive Ignacio Santillana put it, where others saw risk, the Spaniards saw potential.

Potential, "opportunity" for business, is one of Mira Wilkins' five parameters to explain foreign direct investment, within the framework provided by theory of the firm. Spanish firms saw a vast market in Latin America, needing several products they could provide. Some Spanish multinationals from the energy sector, such as Repsol, were seeking access to oil and natural gas, for both the Latin American and the Spanish market. Wilkins' second parameter, the "political climate", also favored Spanish FDI. Spanish MNEs saw in the liberalization measures implemented by Latin American governments a sufficient degree of commitment with the reforms and the assumption that these measures would not be reversed. The similarity of the Spanish and the Latin American processes of democratic transition, as well as the establishment of periodical Iberian-American summits served to reassure the Spanish business community that their investments would be legally protected and the market-oriented reforms respected.

Political, historical, linguistic and cultural similarities between Latin America and Spain made Latin America very familiar to Spaniards ("familiarity" parameter). The opportunity to interact in a familiar environment worked as an extra stimulus. Wilkins's "third country" parameter helps explain investment in two ways. On the one hand, the fear of losing ground to European competitors within their home market moved Spanish firms to seek new markets to expand. Secondly, the implementation of market-oriented reforms in most Latin American countries at the same time and the probability that economic integration processes be resuscitated, created the prospects of accessibility to a large Latin American market. Finally, the "corporate" parameter helps explain how Spanish firms developed their advantage. They grew in a liberalizing economy and their executives judged the possibilities for expansion in Latin America based on their own experience in the Spanish market.

A thorough analysis of the competitive advantage of Spanish MNEs *vis-à-vis* U.S. MNEs in Latin America in the 1990s requires a revision of the theoretical underpinnings of the main theories. The literature on MNEs relies heavily on the concept of "competitive advantage". A competitive advantage determines the degree of competitiveness of a firm in a particular industry (or in several industries), within a single market, or in many markets. The literature, however, does not provide a model to study the way in which a firm may develop a competitive advantage.

This book draws partially on rational choice methodology and reveals some of the shortcomings of it. Whereas rational choice is helpful in explaining when a firm may decide to make foreign direct investments, (therefore becoming a MNE,) it falls short of providing a helpful explanation of how a firm develops a competitive advantage. Gary Hamilton and Nicole Woolsey Biggart argue that:

> Market opportunities do indeed lead to innovations in organizational design but that these innovations are not simply a rational calculus of the most efficient way to organize. Organizational practices, instead, represent strategies of control that serve to legitimate structures of command and often employ cultural understandings in so doing. Such practices are not randomly developed but rather are fashioned out of preexisting interactional patterns, which in many cases date to preindustrial times. Hence, industrial enterprise is a complex modern adaptation of preexisting patterns of domination to economic situations in which profit, efficiency, and control usually form the very conditions of existence.[1]

A broader approach is needed that takes into consideration "environmental" factors, that is to say, the characteristics of the home markets of the firms and the conditions of the host markets in which they operate. The comparison of U.S. and Spanish MNEs will provide evidence to support this point.

This approach will show that a mere rational choice approach does not lead to predictions of how a competitive advantage emerges. The combination of rational choice with a transnational approach that situates the firm in a broader context is necessary to develop a better theory of multinational behavior. Risse-Kappen's "transnational relations" approach serves as a useful point of departure. The assumption that the firm is an egoist utility maximizing actor does not lead mechanically to the development of a competitive advantage. Rather, a competitive advantage is the result of the interaction of a series of factors, including the structures of both the international and the domestic market (both the home and the host markets) in which the MNEs are immersed; the firm's endowments (physical and non-physical); its interaction with the domestic governments (in the case of MNEs, of both the host and the home government); in a temporal context. A proper analysis of MNE competitive advantage needs to go beyond the analysis of the firm, and situate it in a broader historical, social, political, cultural, and economic context. Only by complementing rational choice methodology with an analysis of the structural constraints surrounding the firm can the student of international relations arrive at a better understanding of the workings of MNEs.

The prevalence of rational choice methodology in economics has facilitated important developments. Therefore, before dismissing rational choice in a facile way, it is necessary to review its foundations and recognize its contributions to the social sciences. William Riker argues that the physical sciences have achieved more success in developing valid theories because the events that they study are less ambiguous than those analyzed in the social sciences. That is to say, researchers are more certain about the content of the events they analyze.[2] The problem in the social sciences is how to slice up dynamic reality into static pieces that the scientist can observe. His solution is the insertion of boundaries into reality demarcating the limits when an event begins and ends. The unambiguous demarcation of an event allows the scientist to undertake an objective observation of it and eliminate the lack of definition of observable events:

> Observation requires us, however, to slice up this real-world continuity into pieces that we can observe. We do so by inserting static boundaries into dynamic reality. I call these boundaries *situations* –that is, the arrangement and interconnection among movers and actors just when an event begins or ends. At those points static situations are not to be thought of as real because they are instantaneous (i.e., without elapsed time, and hence also eternal). They have no significance other than to demarcate the portion of the continuous and real event we wish to discuss.[3]

Rational choice methodology demarcates the small events that it attempts to study very clearly: it concentrates on "individual choice", which consists of two elements: (1) Actors have a set of ordered preferences: they order alternative goals, values, tastes, and strategies on the basis of their preferences; (2) Actors choose from available alternatives so as to maximize their satisfaction, based on their preference ordering. The chooser assumes that the set of alternatives is finite and fixed in content and time of choice. Decisions made this way are assumed to be rational.[4]

The rational choice model allows scientists to generalize about small events (decisions), and it also allows them to generalize about intentions, therefore making it possible to extract empirical and deductive generalizations from observation, positive theories that illuminate prediction. Therefore, Riker concludes that the focus on individual choice solves the problem of objectivity of the social sciences. He argues that subjective science is based on subjective values, beliefs, or ideas. On the contrary, a science that relies on subjectively-demarcated events can reduce the degree of subjectivity introduced in the scientific process by concentrating on the study of small demarcated events (individual choice in the case of rational choice methodology).

Such a claim, when applied in the social sciences, assumes that societies (MNEs in this case of analysis) are just an aggregate of all the individuals that integrate them, and can therefore be defined as the result of the aggregation of individual decisions. Therefore, the validity of individual choice methodology to the study of MNEs is a function of its ability to capture the objective nature of firms, based on subjectively-demarcated events, or decisions. This approach assumes the apparent external independence of decisions, which seems to cast doubts on the validity of a mere "rational choice model" to analyze multinational behavior. If decisions are taken to be independent from external conditions, it follows that the only determinant of the decision of a firm to invest in a foreign country (and therefore become a MNE) is an assessment of the internal assets of the firm. This voluntaristic approach disregards the importance of environmental conditions (political and economic stability, size of the new market, trade and tax regulations, etc.) when making an investment decision.

Peter C. Ordeshook addresses this problem by opposing the concept of "strategic manipulability" to rational choice. "Strategic manipulability" refers to the strategic incentives of individuals (by extension firms) and their knowledge and beliefs about the preferences of others.[5] He argues that, when analyzing voting behavior, many "interdependent issues" must be analyzed together, such as what are the strategic incentives for voting on one issue rather than on another, who chooses the order in which issues are considered, what types of outcomes prevail if everyone is strategic, and what happens when new alternatives are introduced in the agenda. He concludes that these problems highlight the limitations of individual choice to fully comprehend the complexities of human nature, for taking decisions as independent acts.[6]

Ordeshook's concept of "interdependent choice" is crucial, because it helps situate the rational choice model in the agency/structure debate that characterizes the social sciences. "Interdependence" implies lack of independence or, in other words, a certain degree of dependence. The actions/choices of rational individuals (by extension firms) are constrained by their external (inter)dependence. A rational choice model theorist might argue that external interdependence (constraints) are internalized by rational individuals and incorporated into their rational processes when making choices. This argument, however, disregards the nature and characteristics of the external constraints. Since external constraints are multiple, their effects on individual choice are also multiple. Therefore, failure to analyze what those constraints are, leads necessarily to predictive failures.

A review of the theories of MNEs will show reliance on rational choice as their basic methodology. It will also show, however, that attempts have been made in recent years to overcome these limitations and to situate firms in a broader context (structures). None of these approaches provides an overarching framework that considers fully the implications of the domestic and the international markets in which firms operate. Mira Wilkins developed the most complete approach to MNEs by complementing the theory of the firm, inspired by rational choice methodology, with a series of structural constraints that limit and shape the choices of firms.

The concept of "interdependent choice" provides an adequate point to realize a quick review of the main frameworks that try to shed some light on the operations of MNEs. The first attempts to develop a theory of multinational enterprises took place in the 1950s when firms headquartered in the United States made considerable investments abroad. The initial frameworks were drawn from international economics and from international trade theory. The focus of international economics, however, was not on the firm per se, but on the export of equity capital that occurs when a firm starts a foreign subsidiary.

International economics regards MNEs as mere arbitragers of equity capital from countries where its return is low to countries where it is high. This approach subsumes the agent in an international structure. It assumes that MNEs should be based in the countries best endowed with capital where the domestic marginal productivity of capital is the lowest. Capital should thus move toward the countries least endowed with it, therefore with the highest marginal products of capital. Reality does not conform to this picture because the largest share of FDI takes place among developed countries, that is to say, among the countries best endowed with capital. The general equilibrium theory of international trade also provides a structural perspective that portrays MNEs as the result of a country's factor endowments (Ricardian perspective). The factor endowments of a country determine the nature of their MNEs. This approach disregards the firm-specific proprietary assets, as well as transaction-cost factors.[7]

A major revolution in the study of MNEs occurred in the 1960s, when Stephen Hymer rejected these prevailing structural approaches and argued that the object of analysis of MNEs should be the firm itself (the agent, instead of the structure.) He developed an approach called "industrial organization" that distinguished between "portfolio investment" and direct investment. Hymer concluded that the interest rate is the driving force behind portfolio investment, but that the keys to explain direct investment are the concepts of "control" and "competitive advantage" (know-how, technology, services, and more).[8]

On the one hand, "control" allows to conceive of direct investment abroad as an attempt to ensure the safety of an investment (the company that makes the direct investment seeks to control the operations of its subsidiary, instead of giving the control over its resources to another company), or as an attempt to remove competition of other companies from the market. On the other, "competitive advantage" explains why those firms that have advantages in a particular industry decide to exploit these advantages in new markets by establishing foreign operations. Hymer argued that competitive advantages are developed on the basis of the uneven distribution of skills across countries. FDI is chosen over licensing when the imperfections of the market (high transaction costs, imperfect information, etc) make it doubtful for a firm to capture through licensing all the profits it expects to accrue from its competitive advantage.[9]

Also in the 1960s, Raymond Vernon developed the "product cycle theory". He observed that the pattern of investment followed by U.S. MNEs was a function of the degree of development of the products they made. Drawing from trade theory, he claimed that the competitive advantage of U.S. MNEs was "knowledge", scientific knowledge, but also knowledge about the needs of the market. He argued that the high cost of labor in the United States created an incentive for firms to substitute capital for labor. Therefore, he described FDI as a process through which the production of a good shifted away from the United States to Europe and to other LDCs, after the products and production became standardized. In the early stage of development of a new product, the need to be close to the market concentrated the development and production activities in the United States. However, when the product became standardized, firms sought lower production costs. Eventually, the United States became a net importer of the goods.[10]

Raymond Vernon also developed the "location theory" of MNEs in the early 1970s, which bears great similarities with "product cycle theory". Location theory rests on two locational issues, the location of the processes of research and development themselves, and the location of production activities. At the early stages of development of a new product, a firm finds it efficient to internalize within its organizational structure and centralize the research and production in a single place close to the market: development engineering, cost analysts, production specialists, marketing, etc. Communication is quicker and the process of development of the goods is faster. As the product and production processes become standardized, production shifts to other locations where costs are lower.[11]

Out of the industrial organization approach, developed by Hymer, emerged the "theory of the firm" in the late 1970s. Like its predecessor, theory of the firm also made the firm its unit of analysis, and rejected industry-specific and broader approaches to FDI. The central concept of this framework was "internalization". Internalization is a response to imperfections in intermediate product markets that generate transaction costs. To minimize these costs, firms bring interdependent activities under common ownership and control. This explains why multiplant firms exist. A MNE is just a type of multiplant firm and FDI is a way of seeking product diversification and financial diversification.[12]

Mira Wilkins complemented this paradigm with a complete examination of five structural parameters that determine the decision of a firm to make foreign investments: the opportunity parameter (where there are opportunities to sell or to obtain), political (nature of the political situation), familiarity (geographic, cultural, political proximity), third country parameter (influence of neighboring countries), corporate parameter (the company's history, advantages, knowledge, experience, etc.).[13]

Finally, John Dunning developed the ownership-location-internalization model (OLI) in the 1980s. OLI was an eclectic model that integrated several theories, and emphasized the importance of structural location-specific advantages of countries and the ownership specific advantages of firms. Dunning argued that the ability of a firm to supply a market depends on its possessing certain assets not available to other enterprises. These assets must be capable of generating an income stream. They can be tangible assets such as natural resources, capital or manpower, or intangible assets, such as knowledge, organizational and entrepreneurial skills and access to intermediate and final goods markets.

Such assets can be location-specific in their origin and use (such as resource endowment or the legal, social and commercial environment), or firm-specific, but capable of being used with other resources, such as a legally protected right, or a commercial monopoly. Sometimes FDI emerges when the firm in the exporting country has a location-specific endowment advantage over the importing country. Ownership specific advantages are internal to particular enterprises and consist of tangible (such as resource capability and usage, technology, etc.) and intangible resources (like the ability to coordinate the interaction between separate but complementary activities better than other organizational mechanisms, and greater ability to operate in many diverse environments).[14] The propensity of a firm to engage in FDI is attributable not only to their possession of superior resources, including their ability to internalize markets, but also to their willingness to undertake further value-adding activities embodying these assets.

The concept of "competitive advantage" played a crucial role in the theories developed after the 1960s. However, none of them provided a model to explain how a firm develops a competitive advantage. Russell Wright believes that a competitive advantage no longer derives from the possession of physical resources, but from the possession of "difficult-to-imitate" resources (i.e., assets and skills). He argues that the competitive advantage of a firm is a function of the imitability of its resources, which in turn depends on three attributes: tacitness, tangibility, and firm-specificity. Intangible resources such as brand image, technological skill, management skill, and corporate culture are crucial. The firms that possess these types of intangible assets can penetrate a market fast and efficiently enough to make a profit. If these assets or skills are not subject to imitation, the firm may obtain a sustained competitive advantage that will allow it to exploit physical resources more completely than other firms, even if they possess the same type of physical resources, such as technology.[15]

Jeffrey Pfeffer contends that the source of competitive advantage has always shifted over time. In the past, firms have been able to develop a competitive advantage based on their access to technology, patents, or strategic position. He explains that these factors are becoming less and less relevant in developing a competitive advantage. Product life cycles are shortening and new-product introductions are coming much more rapidly. Therefore, relying on static product technology for success is becoming problematic. The increasing importance of free trade areas in the world is lowering the advantage that firms gained from access to protected markets and the globalization of financial markets has made credit more readily available, eliminating the advantage of having access to easier and safer credit. The tendency to specialize production to cater to the specialized tastes of particular segments of the population is also eliminating the advantages derived from economies of scale (product differentiation is becoming more important than low cost). His argument reinforces Wright's observation about the importance of developing competitive advantages based on resources that are intangible and difficult to replicate. However, he concludes that the main source of competitive advantage in the 1990s was the workforce itself and the organization and management of the workforce.[16]

David Collier agrees that intangible resources are key to having a competitive advantage. Nevertheless, he complements intangible assets with tangible assets. He affirms that a competitive advantage rests on the ability of a firm to provide the right combination of a series of tangible (goods) and intangible (service) attributes and is a function of the service/quality performance of a firm.[17] He believes that achieving a good quality product is easy and accessible to most firms, but service/quality performance is hard to attain because it involves management, which is the result of the application of ideals, principles, and a certain philosophy of management to a firm's operations. Since the managers of every firm have different ideals, principles, and philosophy, they are difficult to replicate. Consequently, excelling in service/quality is the toughest competitive strategy to implement, but also the most difficult to duplicate by competing firms. Therefore, it is the key to a competitive advantage.

The literature of competitive advantage emphasizes several aspects. First, the sources of competitive advantages shift over time. Second, intangible assets are more difficult to duplicate. Third, those assets that are based on human resources, such as ideas and organizational skills, are the most difficult to reproduce. I will evaluate these claims in my comparative analysis of U.S. and Spanish MNEs operating in Latin America in the 1990s. I agree with Wright and Pfeffer that intangible assets are fundamental to develop a competitive advantage, but I will draw on Collier's hypothesis, that a competitive advantage is the combination of both tangible and intangible assets.

The competitive advantage of U.S. MNEs is primarily technological. Douglass North argues that technology is one of the key aspects for the development of a country. Technology is in turn a function of the country's stock of knowledge (defined as the understanding of the natural environment) and the investment by the members of the society in inventions and innovations.[18] Institutions are fundamental to facilitate technological development. He defines institutions as sets of rules, compliance procedures, and moral and ethical behavioral norms designed to contain the behavior of individuals in the interests of maximizing the wealth of the group.[19] Property rights allocate the returns generated by innovations to the innovators, thereby creating an economic incentive to keep innovating. The United States has developed powerful property rights institutions that stimulate technological innovation and economic development. The role of the state is limited to the enforcement of property rights and institutional compliance.

Such favorable environment facilitated the technological leadership of U.S. firms. Nevertheless, the exploitation of technological advantages has not always been the motif of U.S. FDI. In the first half of the century, FDI was a natural prolongation of the domestic businesses. Agricultural companies occasionally invested in manufacturing abroad (in making boxes and in other activities related to their domestic operations). Mining companies manufactured brass and brass products outside the United States. Public utilities found in foreign manufacturing a way of diversifying domestic operations. Petroleum companies started large ventures in petrochemicals. Since the 1950s, however, foreign investment is no longer a function of the domestic activities. Rather, it is oriented to the host market, especially in transportation equipment (primarily automobiles), chemicals, machinery, food products, electrical machinery, and primary fabricated metals. Investors in these industries had an advantage in technology, which they had developed in the home market, and offered unique products abroad.[20]

To explain how U.S. MNEs achieved and sustained world technological leadership, it is necessary to put the U.S. MNEs in their politico-economic and historical context. Mira Wilkins argues that the growth of a firm's global operations is an aspect of the development of its businesses at home. After realizing a comprehensive study of the history of U.S. MNEs, she concludes that only the corporations that were technologically advanced, those that have distinctive products and advertising and marketing expertise in the U.S. market moved abroad, becoming prominent abroad and at home.[21]

The U.S. government did not play a direct role in pushing U.S. MNEs to invest abroad, but it passed several laws that eliminated the disincentives for U.S. firms to invest outside the United States. In the interwar period, the U.S. government encouraged only those investments that served (1) to increase U.S. exports, (2) to give Americans control over raw materials, (3) to break "foreign monopolies", and (4) to improve the strategic position of the United States abroad.[22] The dominant philosophy in Washington in this period was that foreign direct investment in manufacturing would involve an export of technology, skills, and management, thereby making them accessible to other countries. As a result, it had to be limited to those cases where the expected gains for the country outweighed the losses.

After W.W.II this philosophy changed dramatically. The Truman Administration believed that the U.S. economy would prosper in a prosperous world economy. Truman believed that U.S. FDI in other parts of the world would stimulate economic growth, and thus provide the foundation for a democratic world. In the first years after the war, the U.S. government promoted FDI in friendly countries, especially in Europe, and in the 1950s in LDCs.[23]

The creation of GATT in 1948 received a big boost from the United States. The U.S. government advocated a foreign policy that emphasized democratization and stability. The implementation of a free trade regime was the economic objective, and GATT was conducive to it. The government believed that foreign aid, and especially foreign direct investment, could serve these objectives. To encourage U.S. businesses to move abroad, it negotiated treaties to protect U.S. investors from double taxation and to prevent discrimination against U.S. capital. Congress introduced investment guaranties that covered convertibility or compensation resulting from the sale of foreign property in the Economic Cooperation Act of 1948, for the first time. The Economic Cooperation Administration was established in 1948 to provide financing for U.S. businesses willing to invest abroad. The Export-Import Bank (established in 1933) and the World Bank also made funds available for U.S. investors.[24]

Besides these policies, Mira Wilkins believes that the anti-trust policies of the United States may also have promoted FDI in a more indirect way. In the 1940s and 1950s, some U.S. companies that had created joint-ventures with foreign firms were accused by anti-trust authorities of pursuing monopolistic practices and forced to dissolve their overseas joint-ventures. Wilkins contends that, since U.S. firms could no longer rely on their international agreements (joint-ventures), they became more apt to consider exporting or enlarging exports from their foreign subsidiaries and affiliates. In other words, the door was open for a more complex multinational organization.[25]

This politico-economic context provided the structural constraints that influenced the behavior of U.S. firms when making their calculations. It is also necessary to consider the firm-specific characteristics that led businessmen to take the decision of investing abroad. The expansion of U.S. MNEs since the 1960s is also a consequence of their strength within their domestic market. As Vernon explained, the high income of the U.S. workers pushed firms to innovate and develop technologies that drove production costs down. The high labor costs were an incentive to develop technological innovations. The size of the domestic market provided sufficient revenue for firms to invest large amounts of money in their R&D departments, therefore increasing their technological lead. FDI abroad generated extra revenue, which could also be invested in further technological investigation.

The relative importance of investment in manufactures started to fall in the 1980s and 1990s, and investment in finance grew. According to the figures of the Trade Department, 36 percent of the stock of U.S. investment abroad in 1995 was in manufactures. Finance absorbed 30 percent.[26] In spite of this significant qualitative change, Magnus Blomstrom and Robert Lipsey contend that the competitive advantage of U.S. MNEs still rests on technology. To support this claim, they realize an analysis of the distribution of world exports of manufactured goods by technology class and a study of the shares of the United States in world exports of three technology classes of products, between 1966 and 1986. They consider high-technology goods, medium-technology goods, and low-technology goods. Their analysis shows that, out of the three categories, high technology is the sector in which the United States had its largest share over this period, and low technology is where it had the lowest shares.

The ratios of shares in each technology group to U. S. shares in total exports of manufactures increased in favor of the high technology goods. Between 1966 and 1986, the ratio for high technology goods grew from 1.40 in 1966 to 1.60 in 1986, the ratio for medium technology goods fell from 1.22 to 1.01, and the ratio for low technology goods also fell from 0.67 to 0.60.[27] Based on these data, Blomstrom and Lipsey conclude that, while technology is an element of U.S. competitiveness in general, it is even more important for the competitiveness of U.S. MNEs. Competitive advantage in technology rests on higher research and development (R&D) intensity. Therefore, they conclude that U.S. MNEs have a competitive advantage in those industries characterized by high investments in R&D at the world level.[28] In other words, technological competitive advantage applies also to the Latin American markets, but is not circumscribed to them. However, given the size and degree of development of the Latin American economies, demand for these kinds of goods is more limited there than in more developed countries. Therefore, U.S. MNEs investing in the manufacturing sector are not only producing for the local markets, but also for export.

John Cantwell argues that technological competitive advantage allows firms to achieve sustained growth, because of their technological capabilities. Technological competitiveness translates into lower unit costs and higher product quality, which is attributable to superior conditions of production and individual and organizational expertise, rather than to lower wage costs or better quality natural resource inputs and higher productivity rates.[29] This observation reinforces David Collier's claim that a competitive advantage rests so much on tangible assets (material technology) as on intangible assets (know-how derived from the application of technology in business).

Spanish MNEs gained salience for their participation in the liberalization and privatization processes undergone by Latin American countries in the 1990s. Between 1990 and 1994, Spanish MNEs invested in that region $2.654 billion. Only the figure of direct investment by U.S. MNEs surpassed that of Spanish MNEs in that period.[30] Spain surpassed the United States in 1998 as the leading single investor in the region, and in 1999 Spanish foreign direct investment (FDI) tripled U.S. FDI.[31] Ninety percent of Spanish FDI was concentrated in three sectors: telecommunications, banking and energy. In other words, as opposed to U.S. MNEs, which concentrate in manufacturing and finance, Spanish MNEs invested strongly in infrastructure: telecommunications, energy, and banking and finance.

The advantage of Spanish MNEs rested on their familiarity with and knowledge of the needs of the host Latin American markets: knowledge of and familiarity with the needs of economic liberalization, especially in the basic infrastructure sectors, such as telephony, finance, banking and energy. Their competitive advantage was the result of the experience that Spanish firms gained within Spain in the 1970s and 1980s, when Spain underwent a period of significant economic liberalization. The liberalization of Latin America in the 1990s gave them the opportunity to enter a new market where the environment was very similar to that of Spain in the previous decades, thereby reducing the transaction costs of operations and the need to adapt their goods and services to the peculiarities of the domestic market.

Some of the leading Spanish MNEs played a prominent role in the economic development that Spain experienced since World War II. The leading telecommunications company, Telefonica, was a state monopoly since 1944 when Spain's head of state Francisco Franco nationalized ITT's subsidiary in Spain.[32] The leading Spanish MNEs in the electricity sector, Endesa, Iberdrola, and Unión Fenosa had monopolistic power over the distribution of energy, each one in a different region within Spain. All of these companies, along with Repsol, the leading Spanish MNE in the petroleum and gasoline sector, were established with a varying degree of public capital. Strong companies with public capital and monopolistic power played a crucial role in the development strategy of the Franco regime and, after the transition to democracy in 1975, also in the early democratic government. The objective of this policy was to secure the provision of energy and good telecommunications to the business sector, at competitive prices, thereby increasing the overall competitiveness of Spanish firms.[33]

Political liberalization in Spain brought with it a process of economic liberalization. The state began to privatize some of the state monopolies (starting with Telefonica) in the 1970s. Privatization accelerated after 1982, when the Socialist Party won the elections and the new president Felipe González pushed for a liberal economic regime. The incorporation of Spain to the European Union in 1986 increased the demands of liberalization. The European Union set deadlines for the internal liberalization of the telecommunications sector in the year 1997, and for the energy sector in 2007. These conditions increased the incentive for European firms to become more efficient and productive, in order to withstand future competition. The challenge for Spanish firms was especially serious, given the fact that they were not as productive as their European rivals, and therefore they had to make a stronger effort to raise their productivity levels. The fact that many of them had just been totally privatized or were in the process of privatizing meant that they were still adjusting to a system of open market competition. Therefore, they had to improve their efficiency and productivity levels.

In 1987, when still under large government control, Telefonica made its first bid in the privatization of the Chilean telephone company.[34] The Spanish government pushed Telefonica to expand in Latin America. This strategy had both an offensive and a defensive goal. Telefonica tried to expand its business geographically to compensate for the losses it expected in Spain after liberalization, and at the same time it sought to increase its productivity rates before facing competition. The government also pushed the companies in the energy sector to invest in Latin America in the mid-1990s.

In Latin America, Spanish MNEs were facing conditions similar to those they had grown accustomed to in their home market: privatization of state-owned companies, transition from closed markets to open competition, high rates of economic growth, and great development needs. The economic environment in Latin America in the 1990s resembled that of Spain in the 1970s. The structural reforms applied by most Latin American governments, starting in the late 1980s, comprised a set of liberalizing policies, like the achievement of macroeconomic stability, trade liberalization, privatization of state-owned companies and deregulation of economic activities, including capital markets. Foreign capital played a fundamental role in the process of structural adjustment. It provided funding for the cash-starved governments (over 2,000 state-owned firms were privatized between 1985 and 1992), it substituted for domestic capital, and it brought into Latin America new techniques and management styles.[35]

Spanish MNEs were pushed for, not only by the Spanish government, but also by the Latin American governments that believed Spanish MNEs could bring with them the expertise developed in Spain over the years. The strong cultural and historical relationships between Spain and Latin America made the governments of these countries follow each other's societies very closely. Spain's transition served as a model to some Latin American leaders. Similarly, the success of Spain's economic transition inspired liberalization policies in Latin America. The role played by some state-owned companies in this process within Spain facilitated the entry of some of those Spanish firms in Latin America.

The similarity of the needs of the Latin American economy with those of Spain in the 1970s and 1980s gave Spanish firms a competitive advantage. They had the know-how and a type of technology and services that suited the needs of Latin America. They operated in a familiar environment, not only culturally, but also politically and economically. The development of basic infrastructure was crucial for the economies of Latin America to start growing: financial and banking infrastructure, energy, and telecommunications.

Moreover, Latin American governments saw in the inflow of investment from Spain a way of offsetting their historical dependence on U.S. capital. In 1988, the Spanish government negotiated directly with the Argentinean government to allow the Spanish telephone company, Telefonica, to buy 40 percent of the Argentinean telephone monopoly, Entel. The negotiations did not succeed because the deal faced political opposition in Argentina and the Legislature did not ratify it.[36]

The Argentinean government auctioned the Argentinean public airline carrier, Aerolíneas Argentinas, in 1990, but none of the major international companies submitted a bid. The government then opened negotiations with the Spanish government and with representatives of the Spanish public carrier, Iberia. As a result of the negotiations, Iberia decided to embark on a process of international expansion and acquired 30 percent of the shares of Aerolíneas Argentinas.[37] In 1997, the Ecuadorian government cancelled the privatization process of the country's pubic telephone company after Spain's Telefonica withdrew its bid. The executives of Telefonica argued that the conditions of the process were not appealing. Ecuadorian government officials said that they would be modified.[38]

Spanish firms had an advantage over local firms in the quality and variety of the goods and services they provided. They were technologically more sophisticated and more efficient. The Spanish telephone company had more sophisticated technology and was more productive than local operators. Spanish banks had more experience in the provision of a wide array of sophisticated financial services, some of which (pension funds, investment funds, a variety of saving schemes, etc.) were introduced in the Latin American markets in the 1990s. Spanish oil companies were more efficient than Latin American ones. When confronted with European and North American MNEs, Spanish firms were rarely more efficient and did not normally offer equally sophisticated products. Their advantage resided in their awareness of the markets, which allowed them to adapt their services to the needs of the economy at every stage of development: the transition from closed to open markets, the transition from state-owned to private-owned enterprises, and the need to improve the quality of infrastructure, in order to facilitate the pace of economic development.

This analysis of the competitive advantage of U.S. MNEs *vis-à-vis* Spanish MNEs in Latin America serves as an illustration of the limitations of theoretical models based on rational choice. The rational choice methodology provides useful assumptions that can be taken as points of departure for studies of MNEs. It takes individual choice to be the smallest objective indivisible unit of analysis, and assumes that the choices of individuals are determined by their nature as utility maximizers. However, these assumptions give rational choice methodology a deterministic character by arguing that actors only act in pursuit of their own interest, regardless of context.

The analysis of the competitive advantage of MNEs profits from this assumption. By equating MNEs with individuals, such analyses "personify" MNEs, and take them to be an aggregate of individual utility maximizers. However, these analyses cannot be complete if they fail to consider the social conditions around actors that constrain the number of possible choices available to them. In other words, it is necessary to study the choices of actors within the structures that constrain their behavior. This, applied to the study of competitive advantage, leads to the need to observe all the factors that shape MNEs, both domestic and international.

First, we must observe the operations of the firm in its domestic market: what its competitive advantage is and how it arises. A firm's products and managerial organization are the result of its operations in the domestic market where it interacts with its customers and with other firms competing to provide similar goods or services. They are a function of the ability of the firm to provide better products than its competitors to satisfy the demands of the market. Secondly, we need to know how the market operates and what its specific demands are. The domestic institutional framework is also very important. We need to consider what role the government plays in the economy and what its direct relation with the firms is (with the local MNEs in particular). Thirdly, international factors that impact the home country are also important when examining the domestic emergence of a competitive advantage, because domestic competition is to a large extent influenced by international factors, such as competition with foreign goods or foreign MNEs, international fluctuations (of trade, supply, demand, and more).

When a firm considers investment abroad, we need to look at the internal conditions that pull the firm from the outside, as well as the domestic conditions that push it to move overseas. The domestic characteristics of the host country are particularly important. First, because they shape the conditions under which the MNE will operate. Secondly, because they have an impact on the way the foreign company must operate (it will influence its strategic choices). It is therefore important to consider a fourth aspect, the domestic demand for the goods and services that the MNE offers. The institutional framework designed by the host government is the fifth factor. It forces the MNE to adjust in a certain way. The combination of all these factors determines the competitive advantage of a MNE. The advantage can be a tangible good or an intangible property, but it is normally a combination of both, a series of goods and services. Since the conditions of the market change over time, MNEs must work to conserve theirs or to develop new ones.

The combination of sophisticated products and services and familiarity with the market gave Spanish firms an advantage over their competitors. However, what made Spanish firms invest rather than license? Industrial organization theory analyzes the conditions under which the exploitation of a firm's advantage takes place better under licensing, as opposed to through direct investment. Licensing would be almost impossible for Spanish MNEs, because most of them are providers of services (as opposed to goods), and licensing would imply that the Spanish firm has to license its products to a local producer and, thereafter, monitor the way the licensee adapts those products to the needs of the market at every stage. In other words, the Spanish firm would have to create some type of a consulting division.

The ability to adapt those services to the needs of the market by the local franchisee, which was precisely the advantage of Spanish firms, would be left to the discretion of the franchisee. Spanish firms would give up their competitive advantage. For this reason, direct investment took place over licensing. The Spanish firms decided to exploit their advantage themselves. This proves Stephen Hymer's hypothesis that control over a firm's competitive advantage causes foreign direct investment. Theory of the firm also contributes to the analysis of Spanish FDI in Latin America with the idea of "internalization". In order to guarantee the final quality of the product or service, each firm internalized all processes of production and distribution, all transaction costs, to the retail level. In the case of the oil companies, such as Repsol, part of its investments in Argentina, Venezuela and Mexico were originated by the need to secure access to a sufficient amount of raw materials. Repsol pursued vertical internalization, from distribution upstream into refining first, and into extraction later. The lack of oil fields in Spain forced them to invest overseas, in this case in Latin America.

Stephen Hymer defined the firm as an organism that coordinates activities and reduces scale economies to a question of efficiency of information. Firms can coordinate their activities through the market or through internal management. If there were perfect information in the market, transaction costs would reflect substitution costs. Given the inability of the market to price intermediate goods and services correctly, the firm decides to internalize several activities. Hymer thus concludes that scale economies at the level of the firm result from internal organization. Oil distribution companies, such as Spain's Repsol, decided to integrate extraction into their organization to avoid the high price it paid in the early and mid-1990s for the oil that it had to buy from other producers. Telefonica decided to expand in several Latin American countries and install a fiber optic network linking all its subsidiaries in order not to have to rent other companies' network. Telefonica hoped it would be able to capture all the returns generated in the countries linked by its own infrastructure. BS, BBV and BCH tried to develop a Latin American network to internalize the financial services provided to their customers across the countries in which they operate.

Most Spanish MNEs that operated in Latin America in the 1990s were in an early stage of expansion. Mira Wilkins divides MNEs into three different categories, based on their stage of organization. In stage one, firms invest abroad to sell in that market or to gain access to resources. They do not get involved in complex activities and is managed from the parent. In stage two, the subsidiaries become more autonomous. They introduce new products, take larger functions and integrate their operations. In a third stage, the MNE has to accommodate the parent company's units as well as its new subsidiaries that provide the raw materials and products it needs, companies bought abroad with their subsidiaries, and subsidiaries and their affiliates, obtained as a result of mergers.

Most Spanish MNEs were in stage one in the 1990s. They expanded in Latin America to produce goods or services for the local market or to have access to resources. Some MNEs, however, diversified their operations, such as Telefonica, whose Argentine subsidiary inaugurated a cable television division in 1996. Telefonica did not have this service in Spain, but bought large shares in some Spanish communications companies, such as TV channels. BCH centralized all its Latin American businesses around its Chilean affiliate, O'Higgins-Santiago-BCH, and Repsol did the same with its Argentine branch Astra.

Product cycle theory and location theory provide some insights for the analysis of multinational behavior, and develop a comprehensive theory, like theory of the firm and industrial organization theory. The fact that Spanish firms brought to Latin America the products and services that they developed in their home market, seems to agree with the principles of product cycle theory. However, product cycle theory emphasizes that the products that are originally developed in the home country do not find a large demand in the host country, which serves as the locus of production for export back to the home country, in an early stage. The services developed by Spanish MNEs served the local market: telephone services, oil distribution, banking services. Even though not all social strata can afford their products, the share of the population that were potential customers in the early period after investment took place was much larger than that in Raymond Vernon's product cycle theory.

Similarly, location theory is effective at explaining the way Spanish MNEs developed their products. The interaction between the company and their customers, influenced by the needs of the market (development of rapid infrastructure such as financial services, telecommunications services, energy supply, etc.), determined the type of goods and services Spanish companies specialized in. However, location theory does not explain why Spanish companies decided to extend their operations to Latin America. It resembles product-cycle theory in its emphasis on product development.

The ownership-location-internalization model borrows from location theory, from theory of the firm, from industrial organization theory and from international trade theory. It provides an analysis of MNEs that emphasizes the importance of location as the starting point of multinational activity. The endowments of the country where a firm operates determines its comparative advantages (the natural endowments, the qualification of labor, which provides important ownership advantages, etc.) and its competitive advantages (which are ownership-specific, such as technology, access to markets, patents, organization, etc.). John Dunning concludes that the propensity of firms to make direct investment abroad depends on the willingness of the firms to engage in value-adding activities embodying those assets in foreign markets, and on the existence of market failure. Dunning borrows the idea of internalization from theory of the firm. Theory of the firm also captures the idea of competitive advantage and makes internalization the basis of its analysis in a simpler way. OLI is more complex than theory of the firm, which provides a more concise and precise framework to analyze the behavior of MNEs.

Alliance theory, as developed by Gomes-Casseres, also provides useful theoretical support to explain the expansion of Spanish MNEs in Latin America. Alliances generate a new type of "collective competition" which reduces the number of competitors in the market (firms that originally were competitors become allies in each constellation) but increases the number of competitors of similar capabilities, thereby making competition fiercer. In alliances, firms combine a series of capabilities that are difficult to coordinate through pure market transactions. In other words, they "internalize" a series of products and services without taking over the production of those products or services. Alliances give firms several static and dynamic advantages. They are better equipped than firms to combine inputs from a diverse set of capabilities (static) and to pursue changing opportunities by adjusting their sets of capabilities overtime (dynamic).

Most large Spanish MNEs operating in Latin America engaged in alliances with other firms, either Spanish, local, or from third countries. Telefonica understood the advantages of cooperating with other companies in order to be able to withstand competition from its most direct rivals. Since 1996, Telefonica tried to forge an alliance with major telephone operators to devise a comprehensive strategy of expansion in Latin America. When its first alliances with AT&T and with BT failed, in March 1998 Telefonica signed a third alliance with WorldCom, MCI, and Portugal Telecom to devise a common strategy of expansion in Latin America. Telefonica's goal was to submit a strong bid for the privatization of Brazil's largest telephone monopoly, Telebras, and integrate all its Latin American subsidiaries, develop a network of fiber optics linking them, and continue its expansion in Africa and Europe.

Similarly, the Spanish airline carrier, Iberia, was negotiating an alliance with AA and BA between 1998 and 2000. The motive behind Iberia's interest in creating an alliance also had to do with its financial problems. The Spanish government was preparing Iberia for privatization in 1998. Its deficits in the early 1990s and the poor economic performance of its investments in Latin America were a shadow over Iberia's privatization. The purpose of the Spanish government was that the alliance would include Iberia in a financially strong constellation, along with two powerful partners. Besides, Iberia would be able to retain part of its investments in Aerolíneas Argentinas. This would make the airline more appealing for prospective buyers.

The Spanish banks also sought to create alliances in Latin America. BCH centralized its Latin American ventures in its Chilean subsidiary, O'Higgins-Santiago-BCH. BCH allied with a local Chilean firm, Grupo Luksic, which helped coordinate BCH's strategy in Latin America and participated in some of its acquisitions. BBV did not have a single partner to work with in all of Latin America. Rather, BBV sought a local ally in each country. BS was the only bank that did not rely on a strong local partner. Instead, it hired a group of local executives to help manage its operations and develop in the new market. Finally, Argentaria created an alliance with Citibank in Colombia and Argentina. The Spanish company provided knowledge of the market and the U.S. bank contributed with its sophisticated financial services and larger financial resources. In the case of the other three Spanish banks, the Spanish party provided most of the bulk of the financial needs and the services and products to be marketed, whereas the local partner contributed with its expertise to inform the decision of the parent.

Gomes-Casseres did not analyze the importance of multi-sector alliances. BBV and BCH diversified their operations in Latin America by collaborating with some Spanish MNEs from the energy sector. BCH provided funding, contacts and logistics to its allies, Unión Fenosa and Endesa. BBV cooperated with Iberdrola and Telefónica. The reason for this behavior laid in their expectations of market growth in the telecommunications and energy sectors. In 1995, BCH and BBV estimated that the Spanish telecommunications market would grow, as liberalization proceeded in 1997. Economic growth, coupled with liberalization of the energy sector within Spain, opened the door for freer competition, and therefore the possibility for energy companies (whose operations were limited to a particular geographic area within Spain) to grow beyond their previous regional limitations. In 1995 BBV created an alliance with Iberdrola and Repsol. BBV bought part of the shares of these companies and committed to satisfy their financial needs. Similarly, BCH created an alliance with Endesa and Unión Fenosa, sealed by the acquisition of a significant share of stocks.

Liberalization in Latin America provided the opportunity for both banks and energy companies to extend their operations to the Western Hemisphere, where the alliances were maintained. The expansion of some of the Spanish energy companies in Latin America was motivated by the interest of their financial partners, who saw the opportunity for business in that sector. In spite of their influence in pushing energy companies to Latin America, bankers did not become engaged in the management of Latin American subsidiaries confined to the main technological partner: Endesa, Iberdrola, Repsol, Unión Fenosa, etc. Banks contributed resources for Spanish firms to participate in the privatization of state-owned enterprises in Latin America and, in exchange, gained part of the profits generated by the Spanish energy firms that were awarded the companies in the new markets. The role played by multi-sector alliances was vital in the expansion of Spanish MNEs to Latin America, but Gomes-Casseres did not study the gains that can be derived from this type of alliance, and focused on same-sector alliances instead.

Spanish FDI will continue to flow to Latin America after 2000. The positive experience of the early investors convinced other companies of the market possibilities existing in that region. Telecommunications and banking will still generate large amounts of investment. The Spanish telephone company is present in all the large countries in the region and in the Summer of 1998 it significantly increased its investments in Brazil. FDI will still continue to flow, while Telefonica invests in the development of new infrastructure and services and reorganizes its operations. Spanish banks also entered the largest markets and are not likely to keep buying new local financial entities. However, they will try to consolidate and expand the firms they acquired. This will require further investment flows.

The energy sector will produce the largest flows of FDI in the 2000s. The Spanish government designed a clear calendar for liberalization of this sector in Spain, which culminates in the year 2003 with the opening of the market to European competition. Spanish companies began to invest in Latin America in the early 1990s to gain economies of scale, as well as to learn to operate in a liberalized and highly competitive environment. Latin America served the purpose of providing resources for the Spanish market and as testing ground at the same time, as companies develop aggressive techniques to gain market share.

Spanish firms already played a key role in Latin America in 2000. In Argentina, Spanish MNEs generated almost 10 percent of GDP in 1997 and in Argentina, Brazil, Chile, and Peru, Spanish FDI already surpassed that coming from the United States. The successful performance of most Spanish companies was praised by local government officials, as well as by some leaders of multinational organizations. Enrique Iglesias, the chairperson of the Inter-American Development Bank, affirmed that Spanish banks were crucial in the development of financial markets in Latin America, contributing to increase the quality of banking in general, and the quality of credit and investment in particular. They also increased the confidence of citizens in their banks, thereby rising saving rates.

Latin American countries also increased their efforts to attract Spanish FDI at the state and business level (the government of Ecuador accused Telefonica of causing irreparable damage to that country when the Spanish company decided to withdraw its bid from the process for privatization of the national telephone company, which was postponed until 2003).[39] Some Latin American governments, along with the Spanish government, established periodical summits to promote Spanish FDI in the region. They facilitated contacts between Spanish firms looking for likely partners in the region and local candidates, seeking to create joint-ventures. Spanish politicians and business people were invited to participate in public debates, fora, conferences and broadcasts in Latin America to promote political and economic exchanges, thus reinforcing the Spanish presence in the area.

Spain used its economic presence in both the European Union and in Latin America as an instrument of foreign policy to increase its bargaining power with regard to both regions. The EU countries believed Spain could open the door to Latin America and the Latin governments saw Spain was the key to entrée into the European Union. Moreover, Spanish firms and political authorities saw Latin America as "Spain's natural market". There was a direct clash with U.S. interests over this point, because U.S. business people also saw Latin America as their "natural market". However, in spite of the rhetoric of the U.S. authorities about strengthening commercial and economic ties among the nations of the western hemisphere, the United

States did not work to crystallize those ideas and the European Union took the lead. In 1995, the European Union signed a trade and investment agreement with MERCOSUR and in the late 1990s it was preparing free trade agreements with Chile and Mexico. The free trade agreement with Mexico was finally signed in April 2000. It is anticipated that European-Latin America relations will be further strengthened after the institutionalization of the Euro-Latin American summits.

In terms of investment, Spanish firms took the lead, but firms from other EU countries followed suit. Even though EU direct investment in Latin America (including Spain's) was still $6 billion annually in the first half of the 1990s, compared to the $12 billion invested by U.S. firms, this figure tripled with regard to the 1980s. EU exports to Latin America grew in the 1990s by 136 percent to $42 billion (still a low figure compared to the exports of U.S. firms, worth $106 billion) and the European Union was the main extra-regional recipient of imports from nine Latin American countries, including Brazil and Argentina. The European Union was the main donor of foreign aid to Latin America ($2.2 billion annually, versus $736 million donated by the United States).

Latin American governments remain fearful of being too dependent on the United States on economic and trade issues. The European Union is willing to take advantage of this fear. On a trip to Latin America in 1997, France's president Jacques Chirac said that the "economic interests of Latin America are not with the United States, but with Europe". The European Institute for Relations with Latin America, IRELA, published a booklet emphasizing the resistance of both Latin Americans and Europeans to accept a post-cold war world dominated by the United States. The European Union estimated that Latin America can gain bargaining power *vis-à-vis* the United States if it strengthens relations with Europe, and encouraged Latin American governments to strengthen economic ties with the European Union.[40]

Attracted by the high returns on investment of Spanish MNEs, some U.S. firms put pressure on the U.S. government for it to play a stronger role in defending their interests against those of European investors. Some U.S. telephone companies requested the U.S. government to pressure the Latin American governments not to extend the monopoly concession to Telefonica, as it was expressed in the privatization rules. If the United States and the European Union renew their offensive to increase their economic presence in the region, Latin American governments will gain bargaining power.

Notes

[1] Gary G. Hamilton and Nicole Woolsey Biggart, "Market, Culture, and Authority: A Comparative Analysis of Management and Organization in the Far East", in Mark Granovetter and Richard Swedberg (eds.), *The Sociology of Economic Life*, Westview Press, Boulder, 1992, p. 182.

[2] William H. Riker, "Political Science and Rational Choice", in James E. Alt and Kenneth A. Shepsle (eds.), *Perspectives on Positive Political Economy*, Cambridge University Press, Cambridge, 1997, p. 168.

[3] Ibid., pp. 168-169.

[4] Ibid., p. 172.

[5] Peter C. Ordeshook, "The Emerging Discipline of Political Economy", in James E. Alt and Kenneth A. Shepsle (eds.), *Perspectives on Positive Political Economy*, p. 25.

[6] Ibid.

[7] Richard E. Caves, *Multinational Enterprise and Economic Analysis*, Cambridge University Press, New York, 1996, p. 24.

[8] Stephen Herbert Hymer, *The International Operations of National Firms: a Study of Direct Foreign Investment*, MIT Press, Cambridge (Massachusetts), 1976, p. 23.

[9] Ibid., p. 48.

[10] Raymond Vernon, "International Investment and International Trade in the Product Cycle", in John H. Dunning (ed.), *The Theory of Transnational Corporations* (Volume I), United Nations Library on Transnational Corporations, New York, 1993, p. 49.

[11] Ibid., p. 74.

[12] Peter J. Buckley and Mark Casson, *The Economic Theory of the Multinational Enterprise*, St. Martin's Press, New York, 1985, p. 11.

[13] Mira Wilkins, "The Evolution of Manufacturing Multinational Enterprise", in Tomás Szmrecsányi and Ricardo Maranhaõ (eds.), *História de Empresas e Desenvolvimento Econômico*, Editora Hucitec, São Paulo, 1996, pp. 71-104.

[14] John H. Dunning, "Trade, Location of Economic Activity and the Multinational Enterprise: a Search for an Eclectic Approach", in John H. Dunning (ed.), *The Theory of Transnational Corporations...*, p. 191.

[15] Russell W. Wright, *The Competitive Advantage of Knowledge-Based Resources in the Semiconductor Industry*, Garland Publishing, Inc., New York, 1997, pp. 3-4.

[16] Jeffrey Pfeffer, *Competitive Advantage Through People. Unleashing the Power of the Work Force*, Harvard Business School Press, Boston, 1994, p. 15.

[17] David A Collier, *The Service/Quality Solution. Using Service Management to Gain Competitive Advantage*, ASQC Quality Press, Wisconsin, 1994, p. 15.

[18] Douglass C. North, *Structure and Change in Economic History*, W.W. Norton & Company, New York, 1981, p. 4.

[19] Ibid., pp. 201-202.

[20] Mira Wilkins, *The Maturing of Multinational Enterprise: American Business Abroad from 1914 to 1970*, Harvard University Press, Cambridge (Massachusetts), 1974, p. 375.

[21] Ibid., p. 436.

[22] Ibid., p. 289.

[23] Ibid., p. 289.

[24] Ibid., p. 288.

[25]   Ibid., p. 300.
[26]   U.S. Trade Department, *Survey of Current Business*, Washington, D.C., July 1996, p. 47.
[27]   Magnus Blomstronm and Robert Lipsey, "The Competitiveness of Countries and Their Multinational Firms", in Lorraine Eden and Evan H. Potter (eds.), *Multinationals in the Global Political Economy*, St. Martin's Press, New York, 1993, p. 136.
[28]   Ibid., p. 139.
[29]   John Cantwell, "Innovation and Technological Competitiveness", in Peter J. Buckley and Mark Casson (eds.), *Multinational Enterprise in the World Economy. Essays in Honour of John Dunning*, Edward Elgar Publishing Limited, Aldershot, 1992, p. 21.
[30]   IRELA, *European Union-Latin American Economic Relations. Statistical Profile*, Madrid, 1996, p. 10.
[31]   KPMG, quoted in Claudia Mancini, "La Inversión Externa Marcó los Años 90", *Gazeta Mercantil Latinoamericana*, 7-13 February 2000, p. 22 N.
[32]   Albert Carreras, Xavier Tafunell and Eugenio Torres, "Against Integration. The Rise and Decline of Spanish State-Owned Firms and the Decline and Rise of Multinationals, 1939-1990", in Ülf Olson (ed.), *Business and European Integration Since 1800. Regional, National and International Perspectives*, University of Göteborg, Göteborg, 1997, p. 32.
[33]   Ibid., p. 37.
[34]   John M. Kline, *Foreign Investment Strategies in Restructuring Economies. Learning From Corporate Experiences in Chile*, Quorum Books, Westport, 1992, p. 189.
[35]   Sebastian Edwards, *Crisis and Reform in Latin America. From Despair to Hope*, World Bank, Washington, D.C., 1995, p. 170.
[36]   John M. Kline, *Foreign Investment Strategies...*, p. 187.
[37]   Robert Grosse, "A Privatization Nightmare: Aerolíneas Argentinas", in Ravi Ramamurti (ed.), *Privatizing Monopolies. Lessons from the Telecommunications and Transport Sector in Latin America*, The Johns Hopkins University Press, Baltimore, 1996, pp. 203-220.
[38]   *El País Digital*, "El Gobierno de Ecuador Acusa a Telefónica de 'Causar un Daño Irreparable al País'", No. 567, 20 November 1997, "Economía" section, www.elpais.es, observed 20 November 1997.
[39]   Ibid.
[40]   *El Nuevo Herald*, 30 June 1997, p. 5B.

Bibliography

ABC Electrónico (1996), 21 October, www.abc.es.

ABC Electrónico (1997), 12 January.

ABC Electrónico (1997), 27 January.

ABC Electrónico (1997), 1 March.

ABC Electrónico (1997), 19 March.

ABC Electrónico (1997), 17 April.

ABC Electrónico (1997), 19 April.

ABC Electrónico (1997), 20 April.

Aceña Moreno, Fernando (1994), "Instrumentos de financiación de Inversiones", *ICE*, No. 735 (November), pp. 63-74.

AFP-Extel News Limited (1998), "Hidrocantabrico to Invest 18 bln Pesetas in Mexico Under Eastern Group Accord", 14 December.

AFP-Extel News Limited (1999), "YPF Board Recommends Approval of Repsol Takeover Bid", 10 May.

AFP-Extel News Limited (1999), "Outlook", 1 September.

Agosin, Manuel R. (ed.) (1995), *Foreign Direct Investment in Latin America*, IDB, Washington, D.C.

Agosin, Manuel R. (1995), "Foreign Direct Investment in Latin America", in Manuel R. Agosin (ed.), *Foreign Direct Investment in Latin America*, IDB, Washington, D.C. pp. 1-38.

Agosin, Manuel R., J. Rodrigo Fuentes, and Leonardo Letelier (1994), "Chile: The Origins and Consequences of External Capital", in José Antonio Ocampo and Roberto Steiner (eds.), *Foreign Capital in Latin America*, IDB, Washington, D.C., pp. 103-142.

Akinsanya, Adeoye A. (1980), *The Expropriation of Multinational Property in the Third World*, Praeger Publishers, New York.

Alt, James E., and Kenneth A. Shepsle (eds.) (1997), *Perspectives on Positive Political Economy*, Cambridge University Press, Cambridge.

Anglade, Christian (1985), "The State and Capital Accumulation in Contemporary Brazil", in Christian Andrade and Carlos Fortin (eds.), *The State and Capital Accumulation in Latin America. Volume 1: Brazil, Chile, Mexico*, University of Pittsburgh Press, Pittsburgh, pp. 52-138.

Anglade, Christian, and Carlos Fortin (1985), *The State and Capital Accumulation in Latin America. Volume 1: Brazil, Chile, Mexico*, University of Pittsburgh Press, Pittsburgh.

Arregui Giménez, Andrés (1994), "Internacionalización de las Empresas de Servicios Públicos", *ICE*, No. 735, November, pp. 131-139.

Artana, Daniel, Óscar Libonatti, Cynthia Moskovits, and Mario Salinardi (1995), "Argentina", in Ricardo López Murphy (ed.), *Fiscal Decentralization in Latin America*, Inter-American Development Bank, Washington D.C., pp. 59-136.

Aznárez, Juan Jesús (1997), "Iberia Cierra la Venta del 10% de Aerolíneas a American Airlines y se Queda Otro 10%", *El País Digital*, No. 580, 4 December 1997, observed 4 December 1997.

Baer, W (1989), *The Brazilian Economy: Growth and Development*, Praeger Publishers, New York.

Basch, Miguel H. (1995) "Chile: Improving Market Mechanisms", in Miguel Basch, and Camilo Morales (eds.), *Expanding Access to Financial Services in Latin America*, IDB, Washington D.C., pp. 83-132.

Basch, Miguel, and Camilo Morales (eds.) (1995), *Expanding Access to Financial Services in Latin America*, IDB, Washington, D.C.

Beltrán i Fos, Eric, and Valentín Martínez Montero (1994), "Las Inversiones Exteriores de las Empresas Industriales Alimentarias", *ICE*, No. 735, November, pp. 119-130.

Bergad, Laird W. (1983), *Coffee and the Growth of Agrarian Capitalism in Nineteenth-Century Puerto Rico*, Princeton University Press, Princeton.

Bethell, Leslie (ed.) (1984), *The Cambridge History of Latin America. Volume I. Colonial Latin America*, Cambridge University Press, Cambridge.

Bird Rico, María (1992), "Telefónica Pursues Overseas Opportunities. Reconnecting with the Americas", *Telephony*, Vol. 223, No. 5, 3 August, pp. 6 and 16.

Blomstrom, Magnus, and Robert Lipsey (1993), "The Competitiveness of Countries and Their Multinational Firms", in Lorraine Eden and Evan H. Potter (eds.), *Multinationals in the Global Political Economy*, St. Martin's Press, New York, pp. 129-141.

Board of Governors of the Federal Reserve System (1982), *Federal Reserve Bulletin*, Washington, D.C., September.

Boeker, Paul H. (1993), *Latin America's Turnaround. Privatization, Foreign Investment, and Growth*, International Center for Economic Growth, Institute of the Americas, and ICS Press, San Francisco.

Brading, D.A. (1984), "Bourbon Spain and Its American Empire", in Leslie Bethell (ed.), *The Cambridge History of Latin America. Volume I. Colonial Latin America*, Cambridge University Press, Cambridge, pp. 389-440.

Braudel, Fernand (1972) *The Mediterranean and the Mediterranean World in the Age of Philip II*, Vol. I-II, Harper Torchbooks, New York.

Bresser Pereira, Luis Carlos (1992), "Economic Reforms and Economic Growth: Efficiency and Politics in Latin America", in Luis Carlos Bresser Pereira, José María Maravall, and Adam Przeworski, *Economic Reforms in New Democracies. A Social-Democratic Approach*, Cambridge University Press, Cambridge, pp. 15-76.

Bresser Pereira, Luis Carlos, José María Maravall, and Adam Przeworski (eds.) (1992), *Economic Reforms in New Democracies. A Social-Democratic Approach*, Cambridge University Press, Cambridge.

Buckley, Peter J. (1985), "A Critical View of Theories of the Multinational Enterprise", in Peter J. Buckley and Mark Casson (eds.), *The Economic Theory of the Multinational Enterprise*, St. Martin's Press, New York, pp. 1-19.

Buckley, Peter J., and Mark Casson (1985), *The Economic Theory of the Multinational Enterprise*, St. Martin's Press, New York.

Buckley, Peter J., and Mark Casson (eds.) (1992), *Multinational Enterprise in the World Economy. Essays in Honour of John Dunning*, Edward Elgar Publishing Limited, Aldershot.

Buettner, Michael (1997), "Foreign Firms Already Tapping Cuban Markets", *Jacksonville Business Journal*, 1 December, www.amcity.com/jacksonville/, observed 13 January 1998.

Buitrago Ortiz, Carlos (1982), *Haciendas Cafetaleras y Clases Terratenientes en el Puerto Rico Decimonónico*, Editorial de la Universidad de Puerto Rico, Río Piedras (Puerto Rico).

Bushnell, David, and Neill Macaulay (1994), *The Emergence of Latin America in the Nineteenth Century* (second edition), Oxford University Press, New York.

Cantwell, John (1992), "Innovation and Technological Competitiveness", in Peter J. Buckley, and Mark Casson (eds.), *Multinational Enterprise in the World Economy. Essays in Honour of John Dunning*, Edward Elgar Publishing Limited, Aldershot, pp. 20-40.

Carcar, Santiago (1998), "Endesa Adquiere la Compañía Brasileña Coelce en Pugna con Iberdrola", *El País Digital*, No. 699, 3 April, "Economía" section, observed 3 April 1998.

Carcar, Santiago (1998), "La Euforia Bursátil Anima al Gobierno a Vender su 41% de Endesa para Ingresar 1,6 Billones", *El País Digital*, No. 701, "Economía" section, 5 April, observed 5 April 1998.

Cárdenas S., Mauricio, and Felipe Barrera O. (1994), "The Macroeconomic Effects of External Capital: Colombia", in José Antonio Ocampo, and Roberto Steiner (eds.), *Foreign Capital in Latin America*, IDB, Washington, D.C., pp. 143-191.

Carreras, Albert, Xavier Tafunell, and Eugenio Torres (1997), "Against Integration. The Rise and Decline of Spanish State-Owned Firms and the Decline and Rise of Multinationals, 1939-1990", in Ülf Olsson (ed.), *Business and European Integration Since 1800. Regional, National and International Perspectives*, University of Göteborg, Göteborg, pp. 31-49.

Casado, R. (1998), "Endesa y el BCH Ratifican su Nueva Alianza y la Extienden a sus Negocios en Latinoamérica", *El País Digital*, No. 648, 10 February, "Economía" section, observed 10 February 1998.

Casamayor, Ramón (1997), "La Reconciliación de Endesa y BCH. La Eléctrica y el Banco Tratan de Recomponer su Alianza en el Sector Energético y de Telecomunicaciones", *El País Digital*, No. 570, 24 November, "Economía" section, observed 24 November 1997.

Casson, Mark (1985), "Entrepreneurship and the Dynamics of Foreign Direct Investment", in Peter J. Buckley and Mark Casson (eds.), *The Economic Theory of the Multinational Enterprise*, St. Martin's Press, New York, pp. 172-191.

Casson, Mark (1985), "Transaction Costs and the Theory of the Multinational Enterprise", in Peter J. Buckley and Mark Casson (eds.), *The Economic Theory of the Multinational Enterprise*, St. Martin's Press, New York, pp. 20-38.

Casson, Mark (1993), "Internationalization Theory and Beyond", in John H. Dunning (ed.) *The Theory of Transnational Corporations* (Volume I), United Nations Library on Transnational Corporations, New York, pp. 361-386.

Caves, Richard E. (1996), *Multinational Enterprise and Economic Analysis* (second edition), Cambridge University Press, New York.

Chaunu, Huguette, and Pièrre Chaunu (1955), *Séville et l'Atlantique (1504-1650)*, Librairie Armand Colin, Paris.

Chhibber, Ajay, Mansoor Dailami, and Nemat Shafik (eds.) (1992), *Reviving Private Investment in Developing Countries. Empirical Studies and Policy Lessons*, North-Holland, Amsterdam.

Chudnovsky, Daniel, Andrés López, and Fernando Porta (1995), "New Foreign Direct Investment in Argentina: Privatization, the Domestic Market, and Regional Integration", in Manuel Agosin, (ed.) *Foreign Direct Investment in Latin America*, IDB, Washington, D.C., pp. 39-104.

Collier, David A. (1994), *The Service/Quality Solution. Using Service Management to Gain Competitive Advantage*, ASQC Quality Press, Milwaukee.

Corona, Rossana (1996), "Impact of Privatization in Mexico on Economic Efficiency and Market Structure: Analysis of five Companies", in William Glade and Rossana Corona (eds.), *Bigger Economies, Smaller Governments. Privatization in Latin America*, Westview Press, Boulder, pp. 247-275.

Cristino Macho-Quevedo, Belén (1991), "Las Inversiones Españolas Directas e Inmobiliarias en el Exterior en 1990", *ICE*, 2-8 September, pp. 2677-2694.

Cueva, Ana de la (1994), "Las Inversiones Españolas en el Exterior Durante 1993", *ICE*, No. 2415, 6-12 June, pp. 1403-1409.

Darling, Juanita (1992), "Spain Rediscovers Latin America", *Los Angeles Times*, 19 July, pp. D1, D2.

Dietz, James L. (1986), *Economic History of Puerto Rico: Institutional Change and Capitalist Development*, Princeton University Press, Princeton.

Duce Hernando, Maitena (1996), "La Estimación de las Inversiones Directas en la Balanza de Pagos", *ICE*, No. 752, April, pp. 65-80.

Dunning, John H. (1974), *Economic Analysis and the Multinational Enterprise*, Praeger Publishers, New York.

Dunning, John H. (1993) "Trade, Location of Economic Activity and the Multinational Enterprise: a Search for an Eclectic Approach", in John H. Dunning (ed.), *The Theory of Transnational Corporations* (Volume I), United Nations Library on Transnational Corporations, New York, pp. 183-218.

Dunning, John H. (ed.) (1993) *The Theory of Transnational Corporations* (Volume I), United Nations Library on Transnational Corporations, New York.

Dunning, John H., and Rajneesh Narula (1994), "Transpacific Foreign Direct Investment and the Investment Development Path: The Record Assessed", *The Carolina Essays in International Business*, 10 May.

Durán Herrera, Juan José (1994) "Factores de Competitividad en los Procesos de Internacionalización de la Empresa", *ICE*, No. 735 November, pp. 21-42.

Durán Herrera, Juan José, and Fernando Gallardo Olmedo (1994), "La Estrategia de Internacionalización de las Operadoras de Telecomunicaciones", *ICE*, No. 735, November, pp. 89-103.

Eden, Lorraine, and Evan H. Potter (eds.) (1993), *Multinationals in the Global Political Economy*, St. Martin's Press, New York.

Edwards, Sebastian (1995), *Crisis and Reform in Latin America. From Despair to Hope*, World Bank, Washington, D.C.

El Mundo del Siglo XXI (1996), Madrid, 30 June.

El Nuevo Herald (1996), Miami, 20 December, p. 5B.

El Nuevo Herald (1997), 31 January, p. 4B.

El Nuevo Herald (1997), 9 February, p. 5B.

El Nuevo Herald (1997), 8 March, p. 5B.

El Nuevo Herald (1997), 9 March, p. 5B.

El Nuevo Herald (1997), 10 March, p. 4B.

El Nuevo Herald (1997), 11 March, p. 3B.

El Nuevo Herald (1997), 15 March, p. 4B.

El Nuevo Herald (1997), 23 March, p. 5B.

El Nuevo Herald (1997), 11 April, p. 5B.

El Nuevo Herald (1997), 17 April, p. 6B.

El Nuevo Herald (1997), 18 May, p. 4B.

El Nuevo Herald (1997), 1 June, p. 3B.

El Nuevo Herald (1997), 29 June, p. 5B.

El Nuevo Herald (1997), 30 June, p. 5B.

El Nuevo Herald (1997), 6 July, p. 5B.

El Nuevo Herald (1998), "Privatizarán el 25% del Capital de Endesa", 7 February, p. 6B.

El Nuevo Herald (1998), "Crecen Inversiones de Banco Español en Hispanoamérica", 18 March, p. 4B.

El Nuevo Herald (1998), "Enersis y Endesa Suscriben Alianza", 19 March, p. 4B.

El Nuevo Herald (1998), "Intereses Lusos en Pos de Telefónica", 28 March, p. 4B.

El Nuevo Herald (1998), "Pasa Firma Brasileña a Manos de Europeos", 3 April, p. 6B.

El Nuevo Herald (1998), "Pagan $301 Millones por Empresa Eléctrica Panameña", 12 September, p. 6B.

El Nuevo Herald (1998), "MCI y Worldcom Reciben Aprobación para Cerrrar Megafusión Millonaria", 16 September, p. 4B.

El País (1984), *Anuario*, Madrid.

El País (1985), *Anuario*, Madrid.

El País (1986), *Anuario*, Madrid.

El País (1987), *Anuario*, Madrid.

El País (1988), *Anuario*, Madrid.

El País (1989), *Anuario*, Madrid.

El País (1990), *Anuario*, Madrid.

El País (1991), *Anuario*, Madrid.

El País (1992), *Anuario*, Madrid.

El País (1993), *Anuario*, Madrid.

El País (1994), *Anuario*, Madrid.

El País (1995), *Anuario*, Madrid.

El País (1996), *Anuario*, Madrid.

El País (1997), *Anuario*, Madrid.

El País Digital (1997), no. 318, www.elpais.es, 17 March, "Economía" section, observed 17 March 1997.

El País Digital (1997), No. 320, 19 March, "Economía" section, observed 19 March 1997.

El País Digital (1997), No. 322, 21 March, "Economía" section, observed 21 March 1997.

El País Digital (1997), No. 324, 23 March, "Economía" section, observed 23 March 1997.

El País Digital (1997), No. 344, 12 April, "Economía" section, observed 12 April 1997.

El País Digital (1997), No. 346, 14 April, "Economía" section, observed 14 April 1997.

El País Digital (1997), No. 347, 15 April, "Economía" section, observed 15 April 1997.

El País Digital (1997), No. 349, 17 April, "Economía" section, observed 17 April 1997.

El País Digital (1997), No. 373, 11 May, "Economía" section, observed 11 May 1997.

El País Digital (1997), No. 374, 12 May, "Economía" section, observed 12 May 1997.

El País Digital (1997), No. 378, 16 May, "Economía" section, observed 16 May 1997.

El País Digital (1997), No. 382, 21 May, "Economía" section, observed 21 May 1997.

El País Digital (1997), No. 388, 26 May, "Economía" section, observed 26 May 1997.

El País Digital (1997), No. 389, 27 May, "Economía" section, observed 27 May 1997.

El País Digital (1997), No. 390, 28 May, "Economía" section, observed 28 May 1997.

El País Digital (1997), No. 392, 30 May, "Economía" section, observed 30 May 1997.

El País Digital (1997), No. 393, 31 May, "Economía" section, observed 31 May 1997.

El País Digital (1997), No. 395, 2 June, "Economía" section, observed 2 June 1997.

El País Digital (1997), No. 398, 5 June, "Economía" section, observed 5 June 1997.

El País Digital (1997), No. 400, 7 June, "Economía" section, observed 7 June 1997.

El País Digital (1997), No. 412, 19 June, "Economía" section, observed 19 June 1997.

El País Digital (1997), No. 416, 23 June, "Economía" section, observed 23 June 1997.

El País Digital (1997), No. 425, 2 July, "Economía" section, observed 2 July 1997.

El País Digital (1997), No. 426, 3 July, "Economía" section, observed 3 July 1997.

El País Digital (1997), No. 431, 8 July, "Economía" section, observed 8 July 1997.

El País Digital (1997), "Endesa se Adjudica Dos Eléctricas de Colombia por 337.000 Millones", No. 533, 17 September, "Economía" section, observed 17 September 1997.

El País Digital (1997), "El Gobierno de Ecuador Acusa a Telefónica de 'Causar un Daño Irreparable al País'", No. 567, 20 November, "Economía" section, observed 20 November 1997.

El País Digital (1997), "Iberdrola Compra la Eléctrica Brasileña Cosern por 73.800 Millones", No. 589, 13 December, "Economía" section, observed 13 December 1997.

El País Digital (1998), "Aspectos Principales del Acuerdo", No. 676, 10 March, "Economía" section, observed 10 March 1998.

El País Digital (1998), No. 852, 2 September, "Economía" section, observed 2 September 1998.

El País Internacional (1996), Madrid, 2 September, p. 21.

El País Internacional (1996), 23 December, p. 21.

Euromoney (1995), "In Search of Spanish Synergy", No. 309, January, pp. 42-44.

Euromoney (1996), "The Rush to Finance Latin Energy", No. 326, June, pp. 161-169.

Expansión (1998), "El BCH Ultima la Compra del Banco de Galicia de Argentina", www.expansion.es, 27 February, observed 27 February 1998.

Expansión (1998), "Repsol Abandona el Capital de Gas Natural Latinoamericana", 27 February, observed 27 February 1998.

Extel Financial Limited (1999), "Repsol to Make 13.44 bln usd Bid for YPF", 30 April.

Evans, Peter, and Gary Gereffi (1982), "Foreign Investment and Dependent Development: Comparing Brazil and Mexico", in Sylvia Ann Hewlett and Richard S. Weinert (eds.), *Brazil and Mexico. Patterns in Late Development*, Institute for the Study of Human Issues (ISHI), Philadelphia, pp. 111-168.

Fanelli, José María, and Mario Damill (1994), "External Capital Flows to Argentina", in José Antonio Ocampo, and Roberto Steiner (eds.), *Foreign Capital in Latin America*, IDB, Washington D.C., pp. 35-101.

Financial Times (1996), "Infrastructure in Latin America", special report, 13 September, pp. 1-4.

Fisher, John (1985), *Commercial Relations Between Spain and Spanish America in the Era of Free Trade, 1778-1796*, Centre for Latin American Studies, Liverpool.

Fortin, Carlos (1985), "The Political Economy of Repressive Monetarism: the State and Capital Accumulation in Post-1973 Chile", in Christian Anglade and Carlos Fortin (eds.), *The State and Capital Accumulation in Latin America. Volume 1: Brazil, Chile, Mexico*, University of Pittsburgh Press, Pittsburgh, pp. 139-209.

Francés, Antonio (1996), "A Planned Approach to Telephone Privatization: Venezuela", in Ravi Ramamurti (ed.), *Privatizing Monopolies. Lessons From the Telecommunications and Transport Sectors in Latin America*, The Johns Hopkins University Press, Baltimore, pp. 147-173.

Fritsch, Winston, and Gustavo Franco (1991) *Foreign Direct Investment in Brazil: Its Impact on Industrial Restructuring*, Development Centre Studies, OECD, Paris.

Gamarra, Eduardo A. (1994),"Crafting Political Support for Stabilization: Political Pacts and the New Economic Policy in Bolivia", in Smith, William C., Carlos H. Acuña, and Eduardo A. Gamarra (eds.), *Democracy, Markets, and Structural Reform in Latin America: Argentina, Bolivia, Brazil, Chile, and Mexico*, Transaction Publishers, New Brunswick, pp. 105-128.

García de Quevedo, José Carlos, and Rosa Hontecilla (1994), "Los Acuerdos Bilaterales de Promoción y Protección Recíproca de Inversiones", *ICE*, No. 735, November, pp. 75-80.

Gerchunoff, Pablo, and Germán Coloma (1993), "Privatization in Argentina", in Manuel Sánchez, and Rossana Corona (eds.), *Privatization in Latin America*, IDB, Washington D.C., pp. 251-300.

Gerchunoff, Pablo, and Guillermo Cánovas (1996), "Privatization: the Argentine Experience", in William Glade and Rossana Corona (eds.), *Bigger Economies, Smaller Governments. Privatization in Latin America*, Westview Press, Boulder, pp. 191-218.

Glade, William, and Rossana Corona (eds.) (1996), *Bigger Economies, Smaller Governments. Privatization in Latin America*, Westview Press, Boulder.

Gomes-Casseres, Benjamin (1996), *The Alliance Revolution. The New Shape of Business Rivalry*, Harvard University Press, Cambridge.

Góngora, Mario (1975), *Studies in the Colonial History of Spanish America*, Cambridge University Press, Cambridge.

Gonzales de Olarte, Efraín, Teobaldo Pinzás García, and Carolina Trivelli Ávila (1995), "Peru", in Ricardo López Murphy (ed.), *Fiscal Decentralization in Latin America*, IDB, Washington, D.C., pp. 243-290.

González Iban, Roberto (1989), "Inversiones Directas en el Exterior y Exportaciones", *ICE*, 3-9 April, pp. 1353-1357.

Goodman, Al (1999), "Top Spanish Bank to Buy a Rival for Billions in Stock", *The New York Times*, section C "Business/ Financial Desk", 16 February, p. 2.

Gootenberg, Paul (1989) *Between Silver and Guano. Commercial Policy and The State in Postindependence Peru*, Princeton University Press, Princeton.

Graham, Edward M. (1996) *Global Corporations and National Governments*, Institute for International Economics, Washington, D.C.

Granovetter, Mark, and Richard Swedberg (eds.) (1992), *The Sociology of Economic Life*, Westview Press, Boulder.

Grosse, Robert (1996), "A Privatization Nightmare: Aerolíneas Argentinas", in Ravi Ramamurti (ed.), *Privatizing Monopolies. Lessons From the Telecommunications and Transport Sectors in Latin America*, The Johns Hopkins University Press, Baltimore, pp. 41-100.

Gutiérrez Lousa, Manuel (1996), "Movimientos de Capitales y Fiscalidad. El Caso de España", *ICE*, No. 753, May, pp. 81-96.

Hachette, Dominique (1996), "Fiscal Aspects of Privatization", in William Glade and Rossana Corona (eds.), *Bigger Economies, Smaller Governments. Privatization in Latin America*, Westview Press, Boulder.

Hachette, Dominique, Rolf Lüders, and Guillermo Tagle (1993), "Five Cases of Privatization in Chile", in Manuel Sánchez, and Rossana Corona (eds.), *Privatization in Latin America*, IDB, Washington, D.C., pp. 41-100.

Hamilton, Gary G., and Nicole Woolsey Biggart (1992), "Market, Culture, and Authority: A Comparative Analysis of Management and Organization in the Far East", in Mark Granovetter and Richard Swedberg (eds.), *The Sociology of Economic Life*, Westview Press, Boulder, 181-221.

Haring, Clarence Henry (1964), *Trade and Navigation Between Spain and the Indies in the Time of the Hapsburgs*, Peter Smith, Gloucester (Massachusetts).

Hewlett, Sylvia Ann, and Richard S. Winert (eds.) (1982), *Brazil and Mexico. Patterns in Late Development*, Institute for the Study of Human Issues (ISHI), Philadelphia.

Hymer, Stephen Herbert (1976), *The International Operations of National Firms: A Study of Direct Foreign Investment*, MIT Press, Cambridge.

Hymer, Stephen Herbert (1993), "On Multinational Corporations and Foreign Direct Investment", in John H. Dunning (ed.), *The Theory of Transnational Corporations* (Volume I), United Nations Library on Transnational Corporations, New York, pp. 23-43.

ICE (1978), "Inversiones Directas de Capital Español en el Extranjero en 1977", Spanish Ministry of Commerce, Madrid, No. 1611, 16 February, pp. 537-541.

ICE (1979), "Inversiones Directas de Capital Español en el Extranjero en 1978", No. 1661, 1 February, pp. 349-354.

ICE (1980), "Inversiones Directas de Capital Español en Empresas Extranjeras", No. 1712, 24 January, pp. 289-291.

ICE (1981), "Las Inversiones Españolas en el Exterior en 1980", No. 1765, 29 January, pp. 383- 389.

ICE (1982), "Inversiones Directas de Capital Español en el Extranjero en 1981", No. 1817, 28 January, pp. 293-297.

ICE (1983), "Inversiones Españolas Directas en el Exterior en 1982", No. 1871, 10 February, pp. 389-393.

ICE (1984), "Inversiones Españolas Directas en el Exterior en 1983", No. 1922, 2 February, pp. 295-299.

ICE (1985), "Las Inversiones Directas Españolas en el Exterior Durante 1984", No. 1972, 17 January, pp. 169-174.

ICE (1986), "Las Inversiones Directas Españolas en el Exterior Durante 1985", No. 2026, 10-16 March, pp. 851-858.

ICE (1988), "Las Inversiones Españolas Directas e Inmobiliarias en el Exterior Durante 1987", No. 2123, 29 February-6 March, pp. 739-748.

ICE (1989), "Las Inversiones Españolas Directas e Inmobiliarias en el Exterior Durante 1988", 27 February-5 March, pp. 869-879.

ICE (1990), "Las Inversiones Españolas Directas e Inmobiliarias en el Exterior Durante 1989", 12-15 March, pp. 997-1008.

ICE (1990), "Cooperación Económica Comercial Entre México y España", 8-14 October, pp. 3697-3700.

ICE (1992), "Las Inversiones Españolas Directas e Inmobiliarias en el Exterior Durante 1991", No. 2315, 27 February-7 March, pp. 718-733.

ICE (1993), "Inversiones Españolas Directas en el Exterior", No. 2359, 1-7 March, pp. 489-509.

ICE (1995), "Inversiones Españolas Directas en Empresas Extranjeras", No. 2448, 20-26 March, pp. 43-55.

ICE (1996), "Inversiones Españolas Directas en Empresas Extranjeras", No. 2491, 26 February-3 March, pp. 51-65.

Investors Chronicle (1996), 27 September, p. 102.

Investors Chronicle (1996), 4 October, p. 96.

IRELA (1996), *Annual Report, 1995*, Madrid.

IRELA (1996), *The European Union and Mercosur: Towards a New Economic Relationship? Base Document*, Madrid, June.

IRELA (1996), *European Union-Latin American Economic Relations. Statistical Profile*, Madrid, 15 November.

Jaspersen, Frederick Z. (1996), "Capital Flows to Latin America 1982-1992: Trends and Prospects", in William Glade and Rossana Corona (eds.), *Bigger Economies, Smaller Governments. Privatization in Latin America*, Westview Press, Boulder, pp. 27-58.

Jiménez, Carmen (1998), "Telefónica se Convierte en el Mayor Operador de Brasil", *El País*, 30 July, p. 30.

Jiménez Aguirre, Carlos (1994), "La Protección de las Inversiones en el Exterior. Instrumentos Existentes", *ICE*, No. 735, November, pp. 81-88.

Johnson, H.B. (1984), "The Portuguese Settlement of Brazil, 1500-1580", in Leslie Bethell (ed.), *The Cambridge History of Latin America. Volume I. Colonial Latin America*, Cambridge University Press, Cambridge, pp. 249-286.

Juan y Peñalosa, Rafael de (1993), "Relaciones de la Comunidad Europea con Paraguay", *ICE*, No. 2378, 19-25 July, pp. 2169-2175.

Kamm, Thomas, and Jonathan Friedland (1996), "Looking for Gold Spanish Firms Discover Latin America. Business as New World of Profits", *The Wall Street Journal*, 23 May, pp. A1-A9.

Kelly, Janet, (1996), "One Piece of a Larger Puzzle: The Privatization of VIASA", in Ravi Ramamurti (ed.), *Privatizing Monopolies. Lessons From the Telecommunications and Transport Sectors in Latin America*, The Johns Hopkins University Press, Baltimore, pp. 241-277.

Klein, Herbert S. (1973), "Structure and Profitability of Royal Finance in the Viceroyalty of the Río de la Plata in 1790", *Hispanic American Historical Review*, Vol. 53, No. 3, August 1973, pp. 440-469.

Kline, John M. (1992), *Foreign Investment Strategies in Restructuring Economies. Learning From Corporate Experiences in Chile*, Quorum Books, Westport.

Lasso de la Vega y Pedroso, Alfonso (1993), "Las Inversiones Directas de España en Chile", *ICE*, No. 2372, 7-13 June, pp. 1677-1683.

Lau, Stephen F. (1996), *The Chilean Response to Foreign Investment*, Praeger Publishers, New York.

Leon, Craig (1996), "Expanding Range of Opportunities", *Institutional Investor*, December, Vol. 30, No. 12, pp. 8-12.

Lockhart, James and Stuart B. Schwartz (1983), *Early Latin America. A History of Colonial Spanish America and Brazil*, Cambridge University Press, Cambridge.

López Murphy, Ricardo (ed.) (1995), *Fiscal Decentralization in Latin America*, IDB, Washington, D.C.

López Murphy, Ricardo, Óscar Libonatti, and Mario Salinardi (1995), "Overview and Comparison of Fiscal Decentralization Experiences", in Ricardo López Murphy (ed.), *Fiscal Decentralization in Latin America*, IDB, Washington, D.C., pp. 1-58.

López Segrera, Francisco (1973), *Cuba: Capitalismo Dependiente y Subdesarrollo (1510-1959)*, Editorial Diógenes, S.A., Mexico City.

Lüders, Rolf J. (1996), "Did Privatization Raise Enterprise Efficiency in Chile?", in William Glade and Rossana Corona (eds.), *Bigger Economies, Smaller Governments. Privatization in Latin America*, Westview Press, Boulder, pp. 219-246.

Maclead, Murdo J. (1984), "Spain and America: the Atlantic Trade, 1492-1720", in Leslie Bethell (ed.), *The Cambridge History of Latin America. Volume I. Colonial Latin America*, Cambridge University Press, Cambridge, pp. 341-388.

Mancini, Claudia (2000), "La Inversión Externa Marcó los Años 90", *Gazeta Mercantil Latinoamericana*, 7-13 February, p. 22 N.

Mansuy-Diniz Silva, André (1984), "Portugal and Brazil: Imperial Re-Organization", in Leslie Bethell (ed.), *The Cambridge History of Latin America. Volume I. Colonial Latin America*, Cambridge University Press, Cambridge, pp. 469-510.

Marcos, Ángel (2000), "HC Vende a Gas Natural Sus Activos de Gas en México y Recupera 12.000 Millones", *La Nueva España*, www.lanuevaespana.es, 28 July, "Economía" section, observed 28 July 2000.

Marín, Manuel (1995), "La Política Comercial Común y las Nuevas Zonas Emergentes: América Latina y Asia", *ICE*, No. 744-745, August-September, pp. 99-107.

Martín López-Quesada, Francisco (1993), "La Inversión Extranjera y el Sector Financiero Chileno", *ICE*, No. 2372, 7-13 June, pp. 1693-1697.

Martínez Burgos, Félix (1994), "El Apoyo Institucional a la Internacionalización de la Empresa", *ICE*, No. 735, November, pp. 43-52.

Maza Arroyo, Sofía de la (1994), "Internacionalización de la Banca Española. Alianzas y Acuerdos de Colaboración", *ICE*, No. 735, November, pp. 104-118.

Meier, Barry (1996), "Banco Santander of Spain Completing Chile Bank Bid", *The New York Times*, 11 April, p. D 19.

Mesa, Roberto (1969), *El Colonialismo en la Crisis del XIX Español*, Editorial Ciencia Nueva, Madrid.

Mesa-Lago, Carmelo (1996), "Pension Reform in Latin America: Importance and Evaluation of Privatization Approaches", in William Glade and Rossana Corona (eds.), *Bigger Economies, Smaller Governments. Privatization in Latin America*, Westview Press, Boulder, pp. 89-134.

Morales, Camilo (1995), "Expanding Access to Financial Services and Support for Small Enterprise", in Miguel Basch, and Camilo Morales (eds.), *Expanding Access to Financial Services in Latin America*, IDB, Washington, D.C., pp. 1-34.

Morán Reyero, Pilar (1994), "La Inversión Directa Española en el Exterior en 1992", *ICE*, No. 2366, 26 April-2 May, p. 1115.

Morán Reyero, Pilar (1994), "La Inversión Directa Española en el Exterior: Evolución Reciente", *ICE*, No. 735, November, pp. 3-19.

Mota Gómez-Acebo, Juan de la (1990), "COFIDES. Inversiones en el Exterior, Desarrollo y Exportación", *ICE*, 26 November-2 December, pp. 4334-4341.

Naik, Gautam, and Carita Vitzhum (1997), "BT, MCI, Detail Pact with Telefonica", *The Wall Street Journal*, 21 April, p. A 19.

Nieto, Rosario (1990), "Un Análisis de la Exportación Española a Latinoamérica", *ICE*, 26 November-2 December, pp. 4362-4367.

North, Douglass C. (1981), *Structure and Change in Economic History*, W.W. Norton & Company, New York.

Noya, Nelson (1995), "Uruguay: Credit Promotion and Market Efficiency", in Miguel Basch, and Camilo Morales (eds.), *Expanding Access to Financial Services in Latin America*, IDB, Washington, D.C., pp. 223-276.

Ocampo, José Antonio, and Roberto Steiner (1994), "Foreign Capital in Latin America: An Overview", in José Antonio Ocampo, and Roberto Steiner (eds.), *Foreign Capital in Latin America*, IDB, Washington D.C., pp. 1-34.

Ocampo, José Antonio, and Roberto Steiner (eds.) (1994), *Foreign Capital in Latin America*, IDB, Washington, D.C.

OECD (1989), *International Investment and Multinational Enterprises. Investment Incentives and Disincentives: Effects on International Direct Investment*, Paris.

OECD (1993), *National Treatment for Foreign-Controlled Enterprises*, Paris.

OECD (1993), *Promoting Foreign Direct Investment in Developing Countries*, Paris.

OECD (1995), *Foreign Direct Investment. OECD Countries and Dynamic Economies of Asia and Latin America*, Paris.

Olsson, Ülf (ed.) (1997), *Business and European Integration Since 1800. Regional, National and International Perspectives*, University of Göteborg, Göteborg.

Ordeshook, Peter C. (1997), "The Emerging Discipline of Political Economy", in James E. Alt and Kenneth A. Shepsle (eds.), *Perspectives on Positive Political Economy*, Cambridge University Press, Cambridge, pp. 9-30.

Oregui, Piedad (1997), "Libretones y Supercuentas de Exportación. La Banca Española Hace Cultura Financiera en el Exterior con sus Productos Más Emblemáticos", *El País Digital*, No. 570, 24 November, "Economía" section, observed 24 November 1997.

Palacios Pérez, José (1994), "Análisis Comparativo del Tratamiento Fiscal de las Inversiones en el Exterior", *ICE*, No. 735, November, pp. 53-62.

Paredes-Molina, Ricardo, and Ravi Ramamurti (1996), "Ownership and Competition in Chile's Airline Industry", in Ravi Ramamurti (ed.), *Privatizing Monopolies. Lessons From the Telecommunications and Transport Sectors in Latin America*, The Johns Hopkins University Press, Baltimore, pp. 177-202.

Patiño, Miguel Ángel (1998), "Telefónica y Sus Socios Invertirán Dos Billones en Brasil", *Expansión*, 30 July, p. 3.

Patiño, Miguel Ángel (1998), "El Único Operador Global en Latinoamérica", *Gazeta Mercantil Latinoamericana*, 10 August, pp. 6-7.

Perera Gómez, Eduardo (1995), "Presencia de España en Cuba", *ICE*, No. 2471, 25 September-1 October, pp. 29-37.

Petrazzini, Ben (1996), "Telephone Privatization in a Hurry: Argentina", in Ravi Ramamurti (ed.), *Privatizing Monopolies. Lessons From the Telecommunications and Transport Sectors in Latin America*, The Johns Hopkins University Press, Baltimore, pp. 108-146.

Pfeffer, Jeffrey (1994), *Competitive Advantage Through People. Unleashing the Power of the Work Force*, Harvard Business School Press, Boston.

Pino, Javier del (1998), "Telefónica se Alía con WorldCom para Europa y con MCI para Abordar el Mercado de EEUU", *El País Digital*, No. 676, 10 March 1998, "Economía" section, observed 10 March 1998.

Price Waterhouse (1996), *Corporate Taxes. A Worldwide Summary*, Price Waterhouse, London.

Ramamurti, Ravi (ed.) (1996), *Privatizing Monopolies. Lessons From the Telecommunications and Transport Sectors in Latin America*, The Johns Hopkins University Press, Baltimore.

Ramamurti, Ravi (1996), "Telephone Privatization in a Large Country: Mexico", in Ravi Ramamurti (ed.), *Privatizing Monopolies. Lessons From the Telecommunications and Transport Sectors in Latin America*, The Johns Hopkins University Press, Baltimore, pp. 108-146.

Ramamurti, Ravi (1996), "The New Frontier of Privatization", in Ravi Ramamurti (ed.), *Privatizing Monopolies. Lessons From the Telecommunications and Transport Sectors in Latin America*, The Johns Hopkins University Press, Baltimore, pp. 1-45.

Riker, William H. (1997), "Political Science and Rational Choice", in James E. Alt and Kenneth A. Shepsle (eds.), *Perspectives on Positive Political Economy*, Cambridge University Press, Cambridge, pp. 161-181.

Rippy, J. Fred (1977), *British Investment in Latin America, 1822-1949*, Arno Press, New York.

Riverend, Julio Le (1985), *Historia Económica de Cuba*, Editorial de Ciencias Sociales, Havana.

Riveros, Luis, Jaime Vatter, and Mauel R. Agosin (1995), "Foreign Direct Investment in Chile, 1987-1993: Utilization of Comparative Advantages and Debt Conversion", in Manuel Agosin (ed.), *Foreign Direct Investment in Latin America*, IDB, Washington, D.C., pp. 105-136.

Rojas-Suárez, Liliana, and Steven R. Weisbrod (1995), *Financial Fragilities in Latin America. The 1980s and 1990s*, IMF, Washington, D.C.

Román, Manuel (1997), *Growth and Stagnation of the Spanish Economy. The Long Wave: 1954-1993*, Avebury, Aldershot.

Ros, Jaime (1994), "Financial Markets and Capital Flows in Mexico", in José Antonio Ocampo, and Roberto Steiner (eds.), *Foreign Capital in Latin America*, IDB, Washington D.C.

Ros, Jaime (1994), "On the Political Economy of Market and State Reforms in Mexico", in Smith, William C., Carlos H. Acuña, and Eduardo A. Gamarra (eds.), *Democracy, Markets, and Structural Reform in Latin America: Argentina, Bolivia, Brazil, Chile, and Mexico*, Transaction Publishers, New Brunswick, pp. 297-324.

Rozenwurcel, Guillermo, and Raúl Fernández (1995), "Argentina: Overcoming Perceptions of Credit Risk", in Miguel Basch, and Camilo Morales (eds.), *Expanding Access to Financial Services in Latin America*, IDB, Washington, D.C., pp. 35-82.

Sánchez T., Fabio, and Catalina Gutiérrez (1995), "Colombia", in Ricardo López Murphy (ed.), *Fiscal Decentralization in Latin America*, IDB, Washington, D.C., pp. 189-242.

Sánchez, Manuel, and Rossana Corona (eds.) (1993), *Privatization in Latin America*, IDB, Washington, D.C.

Sánchez, Manuel, Rossana Corona, Luis Fernando Herrera, and Otoniel Ochoa (1993), "A Comparison of Privatization Experiences: Chile, Mexico, Colombia and Argentina", in Manuel Sánchez, and Rossana Corona (eds.), *Privatization in Latin America*, IDB, Washington, D.C., pp. 1-40.

Sánchez, Manuel, Rossana Corona, Otoniel Ochoa, Luis Fernando Herrera, Arturo Olvera, and Ernesto Sepúlveda (1993), "The Privatization Process in Mexico: Five Case Studies", in Manuel Sánchez, and Rossana Corona (eds.), *Privatization in Latin America*, IDB, Washington, D.C., pp. 101-200.

Sánchez González, Manuel (1996), "Fiscal Aspect of Privatization in Mexico", in William Glade and Rossana Corona (eds.), *Bigger Economies, Smaller Governments. Privatization in Latin America*, Westview Press, Boulder, pp. 163-188.

Sánchez-Robles, Blanca (1995), "Iberoamérica en la Segunda Mitad del S. XX: Tres Enfoques Alternativos de Política Económica", *ICE*, No. 741, May, pp. 111-129.

Santillana del Barrio, Ignacio (1993), "Inversiones en Chile. La Perspectiva de Telefónica", *ICE*, No. 2372, 7-13 June, pp. 1685-1691.

Secretaría General Técnica (1995), "La Economía Mexicana y España", *ICE*, No. 2443, 13-19 February, pp. 3855-3861.

Siddique, Saud (1995), "Financing Private Power in Latin America and the Caribbean", *Finance and Development*, March, Vol. 32, No. 1, pp. 18-21.

Sigmund, Paul E. (1980), *Multinationals in Latin America. The Politics of Nationalization*, The University of Wisconsin Press, Madison.

Skaggs, Jimmy M. (1995), *The Great Guano Rush. Entrepreneurs and American Overseas Expansion*, St. Martin's Griffin, New York.

Skidmore, Thomas E., and Peter H. Smith (1997), *Modern Latin America*, Oxford University Press, New York.

Smith, William C., and Carlos H. Acuña (1994), "Future Politico-Economic Scenarios for Latin America", in Smith, William C., Carlos H. Acuña, and Eduardo A. Gamarra (eds.), *Democracy, Markets, and Structural Reform in Latin America: Argentina, Bolivia, Brazil, Chile, and Mexico*, Transaction Publishers, New Brunswick, pp. 1-28.

Smith, William C., Carlos H. Acuña, and Eduardo A. Gamarra (eds.) (1994), *Democracy, Markets, and Structural Reform in Latin America: Argentina, Bolivia, Brazil, Chile, and Mexico*, Transaction Publishers, New Brunswick.

Sola, Lourdes (1994), "The State, Structural Reform, and Democratization in Brazil", in Smith, William C., Carlos H. Acuña, and Eduardo A. Gamarra (eds.), *Democracy, Markets, and Structural Reform in Latin America: Argentina, Bolivia, Brazil, Chile, and Mexico*, Transaction Publishers, New Brunswick, pp. 151-182.

Sosa López, Lizardo (1995), "Guatemala: Liberalizing the Formal Financial System", in Miguel Basch, and Camilo Morales (eds.), *Expanding Access to Financial Services in Latin America*, IDB, Washington, D.C., pp. 133-174.

Stein J. Stanley, and Barbara H. Stein (1970), *The Colonial Heritage of Latin America. Essays on Economic Dependence in Perspective*, Oxford University Press, New York.

Steiner, Roberto, and Úrsula Giedion (1995), "Characteristics, Determinants and Effects of Foreign Direct Investment in Colombia", in Manuel Agosin (ed.), *Foreign Direct Investment in Latin America*, IDB, Washington, D.C., pp. 137-178.

Stone, Irving (1987), *The Composition and Distribution of British Investment in Latin America, 1865 to 1913*, Garland Publishing, Inc., New York.

Suárez-Zuloaga, Ignacio (1995), "La Internacionalización Productiva de las Empresas Españolas, 1991-1994", *ICE*, No. 746, October, pp. 89-103.

Telefonica (2000) "Memoria Annual", http://www.telefonica.es/index/memoriaanual.html, observed 21 June 2000.

Telefonica (2000), "Valor para el Accionista a Través de un Enfoque Global. Aviso Legal", http://www.telefonica.com/dir1/index.html, observed 23 June 2000.

The Miami Herald (1996), *Hemisphere 1996*, 1 April.

The Miami Herald (1996), 20 October, p. 7F.

The Miami Herald (1997), 9 March, pp. F1-F2.

The Miami Herald (1997), 30 May, p. 1C.

The Miami Herald (1997), 15 June, pp. 1F-2F.

The Miami Herald (1999), "Telefonica Enter Cell-Phone Field", 25 March, p. 2C.

The Oil and Gas Journal (1997), "Repsol, Pluspetrol Eye Latin America Accord", Vol. 95, No. 5, 3 February, p. 35.

Torres, Miguel A. (1993), "El Sector Vitivinícola en Chile", *ICE*, No. 2372, 7-13 June, pp. 1699-1700.

Trueba, Eduardo (1989), *Sevilla Marítima (Siglo XVI)*, Gráficas del Sur, Seville.

UNECLAC (1996), *Economic Panorama of Latin America 1996*, Santiago.

UNECLAC (1996), *1980-1995. The Economic Experience of the Last 15 Years*, Santiago.

United Nations (1996), *World Investment Report, 1996. Investment, Trade and International Policy Arrangements*, New York.

US Trade Department (1996), *Survey of Current Business*, July, Washington D.C.

Velarde, Julio, and Martha Rodríguez (1995), "Peru: Consolidating Financial Reforms", in Miguel Basch, and Camilo Morales (eds.), *Expanding Access to Financial Services in Latin America*, IDB, Washington, D.C., pp. 175-222.

Vernon, Raymond (1974), "The Location of Economic Activity", in John H. Dunning (ed.), *Economic Analysis and the Multinational Enterprise*, Praeger Publishers, New York, pp. 89-114.

Vernon, Raymond (1993), "International Investment and International Trade in the Product Cycle", in John H. Dunning (ed.), *The Theory of Transnational Corporations* (Volume I), United Nations Library on Transnational Corporations, New York, pp. 44-60.

Vicens Vives, J. (1971), *Historia de España y América*, Vol. V, Editorial Vicens Vives, Barcelona.

Warn, Ken (1999), "The Winner Must Oil the Wheels", *The Financial Times*, section "Survey-Mergers and Acquisitions", 22 September, p. 8.

Welch, John H. 1996. "Capital Flows and Economic Growth: Reflections on Latin America in the 1990s", *The Quarterly Review of Economics and Finance*, Vol. 36, Special Issue: pp. 101-114.

Wheatley, Jonathan (1996), "Joining the Carnival?", *Accountancy: The Journal of Incorporated Accountants*, November, pp. 32-34.

White, David (1996), "In the Quest of Fabulous Wealth", *The Financial Times*, special section (III) "Spanish Banking and Finance", 15 October, p. IV.

White, David (1997), "Old World Seeks Gold in the New", *The Financial Times*, special section "Latin American Finance: Banking and Investment", 14 March, p. 4.

White, David (1999), Banco Bilbao Vizcaya to Merge with Argentaria", *The Financial Times*, 20 October, p. 29.

White, David (1999), "Repsol Eyes Front Runners with YPF Buy", *The Financial Times*, section "Companies and Finance: International", 22 January, p. 24.

Wilkins, Mira (1974), *The Maturing of Multinational Enterprise: American Business Abroad from 1914 to 1970*, Harvard University Press, Cambridge.

Wilkins, Mira (1988), "The Free-Standing Company, 1870-1914: an Important Type of British Foreign direct Investment", *Economic History Review*, 2nd series, XLI, pp. 259-282.

Wilkins, Mira (1991), *The Growth of Multinationals*, Edward Elgar Publishing Limited, Aldershot.

Wilkins, Mira (1994), "Hosts to Transnational Investments - A Comparative Analysis", in Hans Pohl (ed.), *Transnational Investment from the 19th Century to the Present*, Franz Steiner Verlag, Stuttgart, pp. 25-69.

Wilkins, Mira (1994), "Comparative Hosts", *Business History*, No. 36, January, pp. 18-50.

Wilkins, Mira (1996), "The Evolution of Manufacturing Multinational Enterprise", in Tomás Szmrecsányi, and Ricardo Maranhaõ (eds.), *História de Empresas e Desenvolvimento Econômico*, Editora Hucitec, São Paulo, pp. 71-104.

Wolf, Eric R. (1990), *Europe and the People Without History*, University of California Press, Berkeley.

Wright, Russell W. (1997), *The Competitive Advantage of Knowledge-Based Resources in the Semiconductor Industry*, Garland Publishing Inc., New York.

Wu, Kang (1995), *Energy in Latin America. Production, Consumption, and Future Growth*, Praeger Publishers, Westport.

Yáñez, José H., and Leonardo Letelier S. (1995), "Chile", in Ricardo López Murphy (ed.), *Fiscal Decentralization in Latin America*, IDB, Washington, D.C., pp. 137-188.

Zafra, Juan Manuel (1998), "Telefónica Culmina la Alianza con WorldComy MCI Tras Dos Años de Incertidumbres y Cambios", *El País Digital*, No. 675, 9 March 1998, "Economía" section, observed 9 March 1998.

Zafra, Juan Manuel (1998), "Telefónica Fortalece su Alianza con Portugal Telecom, en Detrimento de su Nuevo Rival BT", *El País Digital*, No. 678, 12 March, "Economía" section, observed 12 March 1998.

Zuleta, Luis Alberto J., Lino Jaramillo G., Carlos Eduardo Ballén, and Ana María Gómez (1993), "Privatization in Colombia: Experiences and Prospects", in Manuel Sánchez, and Rossana Corona (eds.), *Privatization in Latin America*, IDB, Washington, D.C., pp. 201-250.

Index

References from Notes are indicated by 'n' after page. In the case of '*' after category see the List of Abbreviations (pp. x-xv)

For Product Safety Concerns and Information please contact our EU
representative GPSR@taylorandfrancis.com
Taylor & Francis Verlag GmbH, Kaufingerstraße 24, 80331 München, Germany